$12.95

Day Hikes and Trail Rides

In and Around Phoenix

by

Roger and Ethel Freeman

Gem Guides Book Co.

315 Cloverleaf Drive, Suite F · Baldwin Park, CA 91706

1991

Printing history: First printing October 1988.   Revised edition January 1991.

Library of Congress Cataloging-in-Publication Data

Freeman, Roger D., 1933-
Day hikes and trail rides in and around Phoenix

Bibliography: p.
1. Hiking--Arizona--Phoenix Region--Guide-books.
2. Trails--Arizona--Phoenix Region--Guide-books.
3. Phoenix (Ariz)--Description and travel--Guide-books.
4. Christiansen, Charles Milo, d. 1985.   I. Freeman, Ethel, 1936-
II. Title.
GV199.42.A72P484   1991   917.91'73   90-084971
ISBN 0-935182-50-0

Published in the United States of America by Gem Guides Book Company, 315 Cloverleaf Drive, Suite F, Baldwin Park, California 91706

Cover design (Camelback Mountain): Al Ferros (Emphasis! Printing Ltd.)
Photo credits: Dedication picture courtesy Claudia Christiansen; Perl Charles photographed by Dorothy V. Gilbert (March 1970), republished with permission of the <u>Phoenix Gazette</u>
Cartography: Weller Cartographic Services Limited
Printed and bound in the United State of America by Walsworth Publishing Co., Marceline, MO

LIABILITY WAIVER

Table of Contents

Dedication

This book is dedicated to the memory of Charles Milo Christiansen, in honor of his role in the successful effort to preserve the mountain wilderness within the Phoenix area and thus create the Phoenix Mountains Preserve. Christiansen served Phoenix in the role of Parks and Recreation Director from 1969 to 1978 and as General Services Manager from 1978 until his death in 1985.

Chris Christiansen was one of the earliest and most active leaders in the fight to protect a wilderness area in the Phoenix Mountains. When the mountains were threatened by developers in the early 1970s, he spearheaded the drive to bring public attention to the impending plight of this beautiful region. This led to the passage of local bond issues and acquisition of federal grants to acquire the land for the Phoenix Mountains Preserve. The fact that this Preserve exists today - to be enjoyed by thousands of residents and visitors alike - is due in no small part to Christiansen's leadership and vision. In recognition of his role in saving the Phoenix Mountains, the Charles M. Christiansen Trail was established in the Preserve in 1986.

On the national level Christiansen's abilities in the field of parks and recreation were also recognized and valued. He served as president both of the National Recreation and Park Association and of the American Park and Recreation Society. An active proponent of outdoor recreation and conservation, he was the recipient of many professional honors, including the Distinguished Fellow Award, the highest honor bestowed on parks and recreation professionals.

Christiansen's knowledge and appreciation of the Phoenix Mountains was not gained sitting behind a desk. He was an avid hiker and backpacker who knew the dusty trails of the region as well as anyone. His favorite city mountain was probably Squaw Peak, which he climbed several times each week. He also could frequently be found atop Camelback or other mountains in the area; sometimes getting in shape for a backpacking trip and at other times sharing a Phoenix sunset with his family or with a friend.

Primarily Christiansen came to the mountains because they made him feel free. Those people who knew him well maintain that he was never more himself than when he was out walking the hills. There he found challenge and contentment, beauty and exercise. If he gave a large part of himself to the mountains it is because they gave so very much to him.

Many people in the Phoenix area have walked a mile - or ten - in the desert with Chris. He introduced many people to Arizona's unique wilderness, some of whom had never imagined that they would ever be more than a hundred yards from a car. On those days when he climbed Squaw Peak alone he would often come down with several new friends.

Chris Christiansen is remembered fondly by those whose lives he touched. If mountains have memories, then no doubt the Phoenix Mountains retain within their keeping a part of his spirit and love for life.

Foreword

Roger and Ethel Freeman have compiled this guidebook with much care. The story of the effort to provide the City of Phoenix with a unique open space preserve within a rapidly developing urban area, in which I had the honor to play a part, will help you to appreciate the Freemans' book almost as much as your personal participation in the hikes and trail rides recommended herein.

In April of 1971, when I was Mayor, the Arizona State Horsemen's Association and the Western Saddle Club invited my family and me on a trail ride to show us how land development was beginning to encroach on a wilderness area located within our growing metropolis. It became apparent that unless action was taken immediately the natural beauty in our midst would be lost forever.

The subsequent events can only be touched upon here. Voters passed a bond issue for the open space program in 1973. Many groups and individuals deserve credit for this accomplishment. The youth of Phoenix sponsored two rock concerts to help finance publicity for the bond program; Western Savings printed and distributed 30,000 color posters of a mountain scene; and our political leaders solidly supported the bond issue.

The critical element of our mountain park system was the development of Echo Canyon Park on Camelback in the early 70s. A condition of the Bureau of Outdoor Recreation grant that enabled the City to establish this park was the guarantee of access from Echo Canyon to the summit of Camelback Mountain. It ultimately became necessary to purchase residential property in the adjacent town of Paradise Valley in order to gain the necessary access.

In the past our pioneers went to town for relaxation and recreation. Today our patterns have reversed. The stressed urbanite seeks refuge in the out-of-doors. Camping, hiking, trail rides and picnics replenish mind, body and spirit. With a 9,000 acre Mountains Preserve virtually in our midst and the largest municipal park in the country, South Mountain Park, our citizens have unmatched open space. This book will help provide a very special motivation for them and our visitors to enjoy a unique mountain experience just minutes away.

John D. Driggs, Mayor of Phoenix (1971-1974)

Foreword

As one of the great desert cities of the world, Phoenix has an invaluable asset in the Mountains Preserve. America's largest municipal park is South Mountain Park; Camelback Mountain is a landmark that denotes Phoenix the world over.

The citizens of Phoenix had the vision to keep a part of the Sonoran desert wilderness right in the City with the Mountains Preserve system. The community established the Phoenix Mountains Preserve starting in the 1960s, but the magnitude of the job meant that the acquisition of land continued until the final bond program authorization of 1988. Finally we are going to be able to complete the Mountains Preserve! Over the years, the cost of acquiring Preserve land has escalated, and it is a tribute to the citizens of Phoenix and their love for the mountains that the goal has not eluded us.

The remarkable popular support of citizens for the Mountains Preserve comes from the fact that almost anyone can reach the Preserve in just minutes from any part of our City and thousands use the Preserve every day of the year.

Until now, there has been no commonly available guidebook and maps to introduce the uninitiated to one of America's great urban resources. Many thousands have gone into the Preserve on foot or horseback and have delighted in the trails and discoveries. But even the more experienced miss some splendid vistas, some points of historic interest and some great trails because we did not know where to find them.

This book, *Day Hikes and Trail Rides In and Around Phoenix*, will open the door for many and invite them into the Phoenix Mountains Preserve and the other mountain parks in Maricopa County. On behalf of the citizens of Phoenix, I applaud Roger and Ethel Freeman for their hard work and diligence in bringing us closer to the natural wonder that surrounds us.

Terry Goddard, Mayor of Phoenix (1984 - 1990)

Preface

It may seem strange that outsiders, and Canadians at that, have completed this project. We became enthusiastic about the Phoenix area mountains almost by chance when passing through on our way to and from the Grand Canyon. Having discovered that there was no hiking guide to the area and that detailed information was not easy to obtain, we contacted Jim Colley of the Phoenix Parks, Recreation and Library Department. From there, everything else followed: a warm welcome for our efforts and interest from his staff and then the same from Bill Richwine and the Maricopa County Parks Department. The City of Glendale, Arizona State Parks, and the Tonto National Forest staff also welcomed us. This book is a testament to our belief (and theirs) that this project could and should be done because of the fine hiking and riding opportunities available within a 40-mile radius of downtown Phoenix.

The project has taken more than four years of field work, many meetings, an extensive correspondence, plus considerable consultation with maps, airphotos, and reviewing of multiple drafts. We are indebted to the many who helped us.

The roughly 40-mile radius of downtown was chosen because it delineates an area generally within an hour's drive, convenient for day trips. (One large and important area just a bit beyond our limit is the Superstition Wilderness in the Tonto National Forest, already covered in another guide.) Several land management agencies are responsible for the area we have covered. Each has a somewhat different policy with regard to trail designations and we have adhered to their wishes in this regard. Within the City of Phoenix we have included all recreationally important trails on public land (whether or not they are officially designated or maintained) in the Phoenix Mountains Preserve, Camelback Mountain, Papago Park, and South Mountain. In Maricopa County parks, on the other hand, only designated trails have been included.

Many of the trails were developed for use by horses, or simply by horse usage. Most are still so used, and there is no reason why horsemen and hikers cannot happily co-exist. It therefore seemed appropriate to address this guide to both user groups. Generally we have not attempted to specify the appropriateness of a particular trail's usage by horses except insofar as "hiker-only" trails have been designated by a land management agency, or indirectly by means of descriptions of trail conditions and steepness.

Heavily used desert trails are subject to braiding and new trails are often easily established by casual use. Many trails consequently have many junctions, usually unsigned, that can be confusing. We have dealt with this problem by giving a general description followed in most cases by a very detailed, almost encyclopedic tabular description, meant only for actual use on the trail.

Because the format of this guide requires coordination of general (narrative) descriptions, tabular (detailed) descriptions, and maps, it is important to read the section *"How to Use This Guide."* The *"Suggestions for Hikers"* and *"On Horseback in the Phoenix Area"* sections also have some essential pointers.

A few words must be said about responsibility. *While we have taken every precaution of which we are aware to obtain and publish accurate information and to have it reviewed by staff of the relevant land management agency, there are some limitations of which the reader should be aware:*

(1) There is no implied guarantee of complete accuracy. In particular, there is much more detail available for Phoenix than for the Maricopa County Parks and the Tonto National Forest because of the availability of recent airphotos.

(2) Although each agency has reviewed the text, no official endorsement is implied or should be assumed.

(3) Trails may change due to erosion and other weather-related influences, usage patterns, and agency policy. Most are not regularly maintained or patrolled on the ground, and few are signed or otherwise marked; many are rough and steep. It is not difficult to become lost or to twist an ankle. The whole point of hiking or riding in the mountains is to get away from a city-like atmosphere that includes where and when you may park or cross the street. So enjoy your excursion, *but realize that you are accepting the risks entailed.*

Note: This is a revised edition. It includes corrections and many additions to the text (especially Camelback, North Mountain/Shaw Butte, Squaw, South Mountain, Estrella, McDowell, Usery and Lost Dutchman) and to the maps. We wish to thank those who helped bring these changes to our attention.

We need your help!!!

You can help maintain the accuracy and usefulness of this guide in future editions. If you become aware of errors or changes or have suggestions, let us know at the address below. The responsible agency should also be informed. You will find their addresses and phone numbers in the *"Resources"* appendix, and the trail descriptions are already organized according to the responsible agency.

Roger and Ethel Freeman, Box 2033, Point Roberts, WA 98281
Phone: (604) 263-3900

Acknowledgements

So many people and organizations have contributed to this book that it is likely some will be missed in this extensive list. Such omissions are unintentional and should be brought to our attention.

First we would like to thank our publisher, Al Mayerski of Gem Guides, and our cartographer, Angus Weller. Our special thanks go to our contributors, former Mayor Terry Goddard, former Mayor John Driggs, Margaret Bohannan, L.V. Yates, Jim Colley, Bill Richwine, Ken Mahoney, and "Pete" Weinel. Claudia Christiansen and her son John played a special role by preparing the dedication.

As for the many others, we find it easiest to list them according to their agency or group.

City of Phoenix

Main Office, Parks, Recreation & Library Department: In addition to Jim Colley, Del Seppanen (now retired) and Bernie Freese were our major collaborators for the first 18 months of this project. Subsequently Jim Coffman took over this role. Additional assistance was rendered by the following: Bill Peifer, Jim Burke, Diana Decker, Yvonne Garrett (resigned), and Steve Turner.

Northeast District: Sarah Hall-Jara, Jeff Spellman, Barb Hart (resigned), Laurie Kennedy (resigned), Stan McDonald, Don Slater, Bill Murray, Mark Wisehart.

East District: Seth Monoson (resigned), Randy Singh, Ted Koester, Don Wildermuth (resigned).

Northwest District: Bruce Swanson, Vera Perkins, Karen Mischlispy (transferred), Lois Kloosterman (resigned).

South District: Tod Johnson (resigned), Ted Shobe (retired), Darion Gilbert, Frank Scherer, Steve Kandybowicz, Bob Perling.

Former Mayor Goddard's office: Bonnie Bartak, assistant to Mayor Goddard.

We also were fortunate to have the support of the Parks and Recreation Board.

Maricopa County

Central Office: Robert Hogg (who played a major coordinating role), Howard Gillmore, and Bob Herring.

Estrella Mountain Regional Park: Mark Lansing, Keith Alexander (resigned), Gary Hyduke (now at Lake Pleasant), Jerry Waehner.

McDowell Mountain Regional Park: Ken Taylor, John De Young.

Usery Mountain Recreation Area: Jim Reichwein (now at White Tank), Jerry Waehner (now at Estrella), Bob Ingram, Doug Prince.

White Tank Mountain Regional Park: Robert Herring (now in Central Office), Jim Reichwein, Leo Drumm.

We also had helpful collaboration with the Maricopa County Hiking and Equestrian Trails Committee.

Arizona State Parks

Central Office: Don Myers was kind enough, without warning, to take the time to introduce us to their work. Larry Mutter hiked with us and gave counsel on many occasions before Ken Mahoney arrived. Their support has been unflagging and is much appreciated.
Lost Dutchman State Park: Bob Sherman, Steve Jakubowski.
We also met with the Arizona Hiking and Equestrian Trails Committee.

City of Glendale

Lee Stanley and Lee Waldron have both provided us with much useful information.

Tonto National Forest

Our first contact was with Dick Spray in the Albuquerque office (now retired). He named Lee Redding and W.G. ("Pete") Weinel as contacts and Pete and Russ Orr (ranger) have served as our major collaborators.

Bureau of Land Management

Although no areas under the BLM are currently included in this book, that is likely to change in the future. We had helpful talks with Rich Hanson and correspondence with Jim May.

Phoenix Mountains Preservation Council

Dottie and 'Gil' Gilbert, Dave Gironda, Jane Hudson, Chuck and Maxine Lakin, Charles (Chuck) Monroe, Anna Marsolo, and Paul Diefenderfer all showed interest in the project and were helpful in various ways.

Mountaineers, Inc.

Dave Gironda, Craig Lindsay, and Carol Ann Muller shared their local knowledge with us.

Others

Arizona Highways: Wesley Holden, Vicky Hay, Carol Allen, Colleen Hornung
Arizona State Horseman's Association: Bob Bentley
Desert Botanical Garden: Robert Breunig, Director
Cooper, Kenney, and Landis Aerial Survey companies
Cornerstone Inn: our regular hostelry: pleasant, quiet, and friendly
Gem Guides: Al Mayerski, George Wilson
Michael Baker, Jr., Inc., Consulting Engineers: John Rorquist
The Pointe: Pete Cervantes
Recreational Equipment, Inc.: Jerry Chevassus, Jack Mehegan
Sierra Club: Sue Thomas

How to Use This Book

General Advice

Since the tabular descriptions are very detailed, *it is very important to read the following section* to understand how these relate to the maps. Although we have provided maps and access diagrams, there is no substitute for a city road map and we advise that you obtain one.

Trail Areas, Indicators, and Features

There is a special organization in this Guide of some of the trail areas in the Phoenix Mountains Preserve. Lookout and Shadow Mountains have their own sections because they are geographically isolated. In the extensive contiguous area from Shaw Butte to Squaw Peak, the arbitrary divisions are shown on the index map on the back cover. (For other areas, the situation is self-explanatory. The index map shows the geographic trail areas and therefore their corresponding book sections.) Note that summits of interest that are unnamed may be referred to by their elevation, thus **"Peak 1781."**

Each major trail has a text (and map) indicator. This is either: (a) the official number or letter and name (if any), or (b) our own arbitrary letter (in Phoenix) or number (in Glendale), so that these are not confused with official numbers or letters of designated trails. All text numbers or letters are shown in brackets (such as [B]), and in boxes on the maps.

Matching Book Descriptions and the Maps

Maps are in a separate section at the back of the book. Each has its number outside the map border in the upper right-hand corner.

Each trail section indicates the *map number* (which may be on more than one map). *NOTE:* if a trail is shown on the map in red but not numbered this is an indication that it has no independent description, but can be found under the numbered (or lettered) trail or road from which it diverges. There are many very short trail segments to which this applies. In some cases where the trail is short and without many notable features there is a short narrative description without tabular detail. *Trails indicated in black* are either partly on private land or for other reasons regarded as closed, undesirable, or of no significance. They are shown only to eliminate confusion at trail junctions and for safety reasons; please do *NOT* regard their inclusion as a recommendation for use.

The direction of description chosen is usually from a lower elevation to a higher (if definitely an ascent), or from a road or trail access point to a point of interest. The Charles M. Christiansen Trail has its description divided into several segments; there is a separate summary tabulation for its entire length.

Abbreviations Used in Tabular Descriptions

L = left   N = north   NE = northeast   mi = mile
R = right   S = south   NW = northwest   VP = viewpoint
elev. = elevation   SE = southeast   4WD = 4 wheel drive
PC = Perl Charles Trail   SW = southwest
CMC = Charles M. Christiansen Trail

Similarly, "half-L" and "W-bound" should be self-explanatory.

Using the Detailed Tabular Descriptions

The reverse or "Read Up" column on the right of the tabular descriptions serves as a useful source of information when travelling in the direction of the description: it indicates how far you still have to go. The descriptions themselves have to be reversed mentally for travel in the opposite direction.

For example:

[A]

General Description.   This is a short side-trail with a good view of the summit ridge of Camelback. It crosses the Camel's Neck and follows the cliffs to a subsidiary ridge.

Access. From 0.55 mile on the Camelback Mountain Trail [141].

Read Down	Detailed Trail Description	Read Up
0.00	From Camelback Mountain Trail [141], turn sharp R, ascending toward ridge-top.	0.16
0.04	Ridge (Camel's Neck) with good views. Descend toward cliffs ahead.	0.12
0.08	Reach foot of cliffs of Camel's Head. (On return, be sure to follow along below cliffs, not trail of use that descends.) Turn L and follow rocks at foot of cliffs.	0.08
0.10	Reach bottom of descent (small wash); ascend, keeping along foot of cliffs.	0.06
0.12	Pass small glen to R, in cliff wall.	0.04
0.16	Reach top of ridge (1,950'). Good VP. Trails of use continue to SW.	0.00

Note that in reading up, "L" becomes "R" and vice versa, and "ascend" becomes "descend."

Suggestions for Hikers

With the Assistance of L. V. Yates

The following hints are not meant to be exhaustive or definitive. (Detailed information is available in sources listed in the Bibliography, Appendix C).

Everyone has different views on what is important in hiking. The season of the year, age, experience and size of party, elevation and length of trip all can create highly variable circumstances for which it is difficult to make general pronouncements. Seasoned hikers tend to be highly individualistic and therefore the ideas expressed here are mostly intended for the novice.

Safety

(1) Be sure to leave word about your start, destination, and estimated time of return with someone reliable. *If rescue is required, contact the Maricopa County Sherriff's office, whose job it is to call out the rescue team.*

(2) Large groups tend to separate into slow and fast hikers. Periodically check on your party, and have an experienced person bring up the rear. *Do not travel alone, especially in back-country.*

(3) *Be prepared for changes in the weather.* The return route and familiar landmarks may become obscure or confusing when weather conditions change. Take extra clothing on moderate to long hikes.

(4) *Be prepared for injury* (bring first-aid material) *and for getting lost* (bring some food and ample water). Pack a flashlight and extra batteries.

(5) Don't roll rocks down steep slopes or cliffs. Someone may be below.

(6) In summer, flash floods are possible in normally dry washes, so use care. If there are thunderstorms in the area, descend from elevated areas to avoid lightning.

(7) Prospect holes or pits left by miners can be dangerous. Stay out of them!

(8) Poisonous reptiles and insects live in the desert. You are very unlikely to have trouble if you only put your hands and feet in places you can see.

(9) The spines of some types of cactus, especially the "jumping" cholla, are very easy to collect in your skin, even through your shoes. Carry a comb and strong tweezers or long-nosed pliers to remove them.

Comfort

(1) *Rule #1 is: bring sufficient water. This cannot be overemphasized.*

(2) Wear comfortable clothing; use a hat, sunscreen and sunglasses.

(3) If you are not experienced and fit, take short hikes before long ones. This will give you a chance to assess your fitness and break in hiking boots. Bring an extra pair of socks. Treat potential blisters before they become major problems (carry moleskin, readjust socks when you rest).

(4) Insects are not generally a major problem, but at certain times (especially near dusk) there may be mosquitoes, large and small flies, spiders, and bees. Bring repellent, and of course your medicine if you are subject to severe reactions from specific stinging insects.

(5) Leave valuables at home. The next best place is in the trunk of your car.

(6) Take a spare car key and remember to turn off your headlights!

(7) Experienced hikers keep a master check-list so they are not likely to forget an item of importance.

Mountain Ethics

Most of us enjoy hiking not only for exercise, but for the closer contact we feel with nature. *A respectful attitude to man and nature* makes many of these recommendations redundant: the ideas are then mostly "common sense."

(1) Flowers, rocks, and other "specimens" should be left in place. The best guide is "take nothing but pictures, leave nothing but footprints." An exception is garbage thoughtlessly left by others. This you *can* take out!

(2) Keep to the trails -- *please do not cut across switchbacks* -- it will contribute to the trail's eventual destruction through erosion.

(3) Do not remove markers, signs, or cairns -- they are not souvenirs. Someone's safety or life could depend upon them.

(4) Please do not deface the desert with graffiti. It is especially important to respect Indian petroglyphs if you come across them.

(5) *"Pack it in -- pack it out" applies to everything.* Orange peels, candy wrappers, pop bottles or cans are unsightly and non-biodegradable. Bury no refuse -- animals will dig it up.

(6) If you must smoke on the trail, be especially careful in disposing of cigarettes and matches.

(7) Respect private property.

(8) Other users of the mountains will be grateful if you avoid creating unnecessarily loud noises (for example, with ghetto-blasters) .

(9) Use of trail-bikes or other all-terrain vehicles off designated roads is prohibited in all park areas. Report problems to the responsible managing agency.

On Horseback in the Phoenix Area

For me, there is no greater pleasure than riding in harmony with a good horse, enjoying the beauty and wildlife of the Arizona desert.

To make the equestrian's trip more enjoyable and safe, here are a few tips that will be of help.

Water. For the rider, a canteen of water is a necessity. For the horse, there will be little or no water along the trails in this guide. You may want to check with the appropriate managing agency. Be sure not to over-water a hot horse.

Clothing. Long, sturdy trousers, or chaps, are essential because of catclaw and cactus in some areas. Wear a hat with a brim for protection against the sun and a long-sleeved shirt. Shoes or boots with a heel are a must so that your foot will not hang up in the stirrup should you be thrown.

Equipment. A well-shod, good-conditioned, trail-savvy mount is advisable, because many of the trails are steep, narrow and rocky. The usual first-aid kit is good, plus a comb and pliers to extract cactus spines from you or your horse. Beware particularly of cholla. Horses encountering it for the first time can panic when, by brushing past it, it sticks to them.

Hikers and Bicyclists. A horse and rider can be intimidating to hikers, so act accordingly, with consideration and courtesy, when you meet them on the trail.

Because of their unpredictability, horses do have the right-of-way over all other trail users. Upon seeing or hearing a horse approach, a hiker should step off on the downhill side of the trail, stand quietly without moving or making any fast movements, and speak in a calm and friendly voice. The horse may perceive a human, especially with a backpack, as some sort of monster coming down the trail and "spook," endangering both the rider and the hiker.

Similarly, the sight of a human astride a bicycle, silently moving towards them, or coming from behind, can frighten horses. The bicyclist should stop, announce his presence, and allow the horse to pass. Alternatively, when overtaking, give the rider time to move off the trail, then pass slowly with caution.

Rental Stables. Both the Phoenix and Maricopa County Parks and Recreation Departments have a list of reliable rental stables. You may also consult the Yellow Pages of the phone directory. Most stables can arrange guided rides.

Happy trails!

> *Margaret Bohannan, Former Chairman*
> *Arizona Hiking and Equestrian Trails Committee*

Weather

With an annual rainfall of only 7.5 inches, Phoenix is usually sunny, especially in the months of October through June. Snow in the valley is rare. During the summer months of July and August, however, the daily high temperature may be 105° or even as high as 115°. Afternoon and evening thundershowers are common, and moist air may be sucked up from the Gulfs of Mexico or California. Below are the average daily maximums for each month:

Month	Average Daily Maximum	Month	Average Daily Maximum
January	66°	July	105°
February	70°	August	103°
March	75°	September	98°
April	83°	October	88°
May	93°	November	75°
June	102°	December	67°

The best season is generally from late October through early May. But despite the high temperatures, one can usually hike and ride in the Valley's mountains during the summer if precautions are taken:

(1) On days expected to be very hot, go very early in the morning, wear protective clothing (a hat, sunscreen, and light clothing), and bring plenty of water (at least a gallon if you will be out all day).

(2) If you are new to the area or have any health problems, start out with very short trips and build up slowly.

Because of the warmth, there is a temptation to hike or ride in shorts and a short-sleeved shirt and not to bring clothing to cover arms and legs -- this is a mistake. Severe sunburn occurs easily during the summer months, but may occur at any time of the year, especially in those with light complexions. Heat exhaustion may be prevented by taking enough fluid and resting periodically in the shade.

Cool weather in combination with fatigue and wet, windy conditions may lead to *hypothermia* (dangerous lowering of the body's central core temperature). Due to impaired judgment, the impending hazard may not be perceived.

Although you are not likely to see one, the area is subject to duststorms known as *haboobs* (miniature sandstorms), which are usually over quickly. Smaller disturbances known as *dust devils* can often be seen in the valleys.

Life in the Desert

No matter how arid the subtropical Sonoran desert looks, it abounds in beautiful and interesting animal and plant life. You will realize this if you enter the mountains after a rain and smell the creosote bush or see the blooming of the ocotillo. Did you know that the brittlebush can produce two different types of leaves, depending upon whether the season is moist or dry?

The easiest way to learn about plant life is to visit the Desert Botanical Garden adjacent to Papago Park at 1201 N. Galvin Parkway.[1] The Garden also offers guided Garden and wildflower tours, bird walks, classes and workshops (including special children's programs) and more. There is a Wildflower Hotline from March through the end of April with taped current reports.

There are many books on the subject. Most bookstores carry a few, but the gift shop at the Desert Botanical Garden has an excellent selection so you can choose the ones that suit you. Our favorite is the *Deserts* book of the Audubon Society (McMahon, 1985), because it includes wildflowers, trees, shrubs, cacti, birds, reptiles, mammals, and insects. Others books are listed in Appendix C.

You are likely to see the following in the area covered by this book: *trees:* palo verde, mesquite, and ironwood; *shrubs:* creosote bush, white bursage, brittlebush, ocotillo, fairy duster, jojoba, ratany, desert hackberry, desert broom, chuparosa; *cacti:* saguaro, cholla, barrel cactus, fishhook, prickly pear, hedgehog; *desert agave* and *yuccas*; lizards, rattlesnakes, desert cottontails and black-tailed jackrabbits; coyotes; and groundsquirrels. Among the insects there are spiders, ants and bees.

Geology

The mountains in the Phoenix area reveal their structure much more readily than in other parts of the country where the rocks are covered with thick layers of soil, or with forest. Your enjoyment of the desert will be enhanced if you take the opportunity to learn about the land in the areas you visit.

This can be done through taking courses and on field trips with clubs or schools, but reading and observing are also sufficient to acquire more knowledge. We have supplied some information in certain sections of this guidebook, but not the complete explanation of all of the terms used. A geology book on Arizona will be very helpful. We recommend the books by Nations and Stump (1981) and Chronic (1983).

---

[1]Garden hours are 9:00 a.m. till sunset from September through June, and 7:00 a.m. till sunset in July and August. There is an admission fee for non-members. Call 941-1225.

Phoenix Parks

An Introduction

Phoenix citizens are gifted with breathtaking scenery, vast wide open spaces and steep rugged mountains, all components of a casual and relaxed southwestern lifestyle. From the beginning, citizens have been an integral part of the Parks, Recreation and Library Department's efforts to protect our natural resources. As a result of this harmonious relationship, the Preserves in Phoenix comprise almost 24,000 acres, an extraordinary feat for a major metropolis.

As early as 1920, citizens organized a drive to preserve South Mountain Park, which borders Phoenix on the south side. Through a continuing, concerted effort of City staff and citizens, the desert mountain park now boasts over 16,000 acres and holds the distinguished title of being the largest municipal park in the world.

The Charter of the Parks, Playgrounds and Recreational Board was approved by voters in 1933. In the '60s continued growth and development threatened to deplete our most treasured assets. Bulldozers began gouging roads and peaks were torn apart by dynamite. The City of Phoenix began to seek ways to protect our slopes and, in 1972, a master plan for the Phoenix Mountains Preserve was instituted. Following that successful precedent, a committee is currently working to develop a master plan specifically for South Mountain. Together, staff and citizens will maintain the integrity of the area.

Phoenix has more than 130 community, neighborhood, district and desert mountain parks. The successful 1988 bond election in Phoenix allocated an additional $139.2 million for parks, recreation and libraries. This will allow us to acquire new parkland, complete the mountain preserves, enhance existing parks, renovate old parks and construct a 29-acre park over a downtown freeway which will serve as a showcase for downtown festivities.

None of this would have been possible without community participation. The Adopt-A-Trail Program is just one of a multitude of opportunities available for volunteer service. Organizations can adopt an entire trail or a segment. In return, they provide labor and sometimes material to maintain the trail, as well as sponsor fundraising activities for the trail's benefit. An entire trail in Squaw Peak Park, which is near the center of the city, was once threatened with the possibility of destruction. But after it was adopted by a local hiking club and restored, the trail continued to provide public access to this wilderness area.

Phoenix citizens and park staff will continue to fill their new and demanding role as residents of a rapidly growing, vibrant outdoor city.

James A. Colley, Director
Parks, Recreation and Library Department

City of Phoenix

Camelback/Echo Canyon Park

Introduction. At 2,704', Camelback Mountain is the highest peak in the Phoenix Mountains and a prominent landmark. In addition to the very popular summit trail, there are unusual rock formations, cliffs, caves, spires, and gendarmes like the Praying Monk. The Camel's Head and Bobby's Rock area are used for rock-climbing instruction and practice. The mountain is bounded by private property; please avoid trespassing.

History. The interesting story of how part of Camelback Mountain and its access were preserved for the public is briefly outlined here:

The federal government reserved Camelback Mountain for an Indian reservation in 1879, then later changed its mind and issued deeds to private individuals from 1888-1900. Thus all of the mountain, except for State-owned portions reserved for schools, fell into private hands. During the 1920s to 1940s even these lands were sold.

Interest in preserving the mountain started in earnest with the Camelback Improvement Association in 1954 at a time when the mountain was not yet part of the City. Petitions were filed with Maricopa County against planned encroachments, though these had no legal status. The Maricopa County Planning and Zoning Commission decided on a maximum building elevation of 1,600' in approving subdivision or construction plans -- but this had no legal force and people continued to build above that level.

Community groups that were formed in the late 1950s explored various possibilities, including the establishment of a state or county park, land trades, and purchases. Efforts to persuade landowners to deed land over to Maricopa County failed.

In November of 1960 the Arizona Conservation Council and Arizona Conservation Foundation were formed. The Council started a drive to protect land above 1,600' and started land acquisition proceedings. The federal government declined to declare Camelback a national monument. Congress also took no action on two bills introduced in 1962 (by John Rhodes) and in 1963 (by Barry Goldwater) to enable land exchanges.

In 1963-64 bills were introduced into the state legislature to enable state land exchanges, but these failed in spite of Governor Fannin's support. In 1965 the Preservation of Camelback Mountain Foundation, under the chairmanship of Barry Goldwater, was formed under the auspices of the Valley Beautiful Citizens Council. This represented a community-wide effort to acquire as much of the summit as possible, and culminated in success. In May of 1968 Mrs. Lyndon Johnson presided over a ceremony to conclude the acquisition process, along with Secretary of the Interior Stewart Udall, who presented a check for matching funds to Mayor Graham.

Saving of the mountaintop, however, was not the end of the story. Access to the mountain was problematic and was contested by local landowners. The fence above the homes on the Camelback Mountain Trail represents an easement obtained only with great difficulty (the opening of Echo Canyon Park in November of 1973 is mentioned by John Driggs in his Foreword).

Today the old trail to the summit from the east still crosses private land. A new right-of-way, parking area, and connecting trail must be secured before legal access will be available. This process is now under way.

Geology. Camelback is of unusual geological interest. The Camel's Head consists of inclined, layered rock sediments (sandstones) of Tertiary age [70-100 million years ago], carved in places into alcoves and recesses by the wind. The Camel's hump, however, is composed of massive, ancient granite [Pre-cambrian -- 1.5 billion years ago], originally formed from a cooling molten mass that was buried and later [60 million years ago] uplifted and weathered by wind and water. The expected sequence of Paleozoic and Mesozoic rocks between the Head and Back are missing (an "unconformity" in geological terms). The granite is about the same age as the lowest rocks in the Grand Canyon, whereas the sediments are younger than the Canyon's rim.[1]

Maps. *Our Map 1.* The USGS Paradise Valley 1:24,000 topo (1973) shows the area and part of the main trail, but detail is lacking.

Access. The park's entrance is off McDonald Drive just east of Tatum Boulevard, where Echo Canyon Place leads south 0.2 mile to the road end.

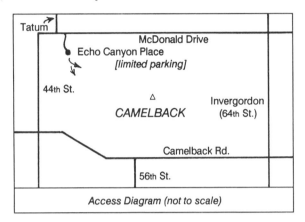

Access Diagram (not to scale)

Facilities. This is a "totally natural" park with two ramadas, a parking lot, a drinking fountain at the trail-head, but no other facilities.

Recommended Hikes. Trail numbers used are the official numbers for designated trails, or in one case our own letter designation [A]. The Camelback Mountain Trail itself is steep and much more difficult than its length would indicate. The Echo Canyon Trail is much easier, but has few distant views.

Cautions. *Parking is difficult on weekends: come early.* There have been many accidents on Camelback. Unless you are experienced and properly equipped, avoid the temptation to climb on the cliffs and rock formations. Stay on the trails!

[141] Camelback Mountain Trail

General Description. This is an unusual and popular trail. There are several spectacular sandstone rock formations along the way. Use great care: there are segments over steep, open rock or slippery dirt and gravel; part of the trail is braided and there are some steep drop-offs.

---

[1]Adapted from: "Geology of Camelback Mountain" by J.D. Forrester (Dean, College of Mines, University of Arizona, Tucson)(1959), and H. Chronic (1983) *Roadside Geology of Arizona,* Missoula, Montana: Mountain Press Publishing Co.

From the trail-head cross a wash, then start a steady ascent past rock formations and trail junctions to a minor ridge-top at 0.30 mile. A fence is followed along the base of a huge cliff (part of which overhangs -- see book cover) with sections requiring a hand-rail. At the top of a rise the railing ends and fine views start near the Camel's Neck. The trail crosses and recrosses the crest, then follows several gullies to the summit at 1.16 miles. Total ascent is 1,300'. For greatest enjoyment, allow at least a half-day for this trip.

At the summit there is a panoramic view, especially noteworthy toward Camelback's lower rock formations and across to Squaw Peak.

Access. From the road end (Echo Canyon Place) and ramada, go straight ahead, descending into a wash.

Read Down	Detailed Trail Description	Read Up
0.00	From parking lot (1,440'), pass ramada and descend.	1.16
0.01	**Junction:** trail R leads S for 0.11 mi, then ascends E to junction on [241] at 0.17 mi, just 100' S of ramada. Cross wash and ascend.	1.15
0.10	Pass huge rock on L (used for rock-climbing practice). On R is **junction** with [241], also leading 205' to ramada.	1.05
0.13	**Junction:** trail on R to ramada and [241], where this trail bears L.	1.04
0.15	Trail diverges and rejoins twice.	1.01
0.20	**Junction:** good VP 75' to L.	0.96
0.25	**Junction:** trails of use on R, then on L.	0.91
0.30	Top of rise (elevation 1,700'). Turn R. Fence line ahead. Trail levels briefly.	0.86
0.31	Parallel fence. Cliff above on R.	0.85
0.33	Ascend; start steep ascent in 150'.	0.82
0.38	Top of rise (elevation 1,740'). Descend; start steep ascent in 50'.	0.76
0.41	Hand-rail starts. Use caution.	0.74
0.43	Top of rise; drop briefly. Hand-rail ends.	0.72
0.45	Turn L, follow fence line at easier grade.	0.71
0.48	Hand-rail starts again.	0.68
0.50	Ascend steeply, with hand-rail.	0.66
0.52	Top of rise (1,940'), end of hand-rail. Excellent VP off trail to L.	0.63
0.55	**Junction:** trail [A] sharp R leads onto neck of Camel, with fine views, to cliffs.	0.60
0.57	Descend.	0.59
0.59	Ascend, then level off briefly.	0.57
0.61	Start steep rocky ascent up gully.	0.54
0.65	Top of rise (2,060'). Cross to S side of ridge.	0.50
0.67	Ascend to S of crest.	0.48
0.70	Top of rise (2,080'). Rocky knob on R.	0.45
0.72	Edge of crest line; trail meanders back and forth.	0.44
0.74	Go L, up over rocks at head of ravine, then cross it.	0.42
0.75	Cross over crest. Two routes diverge; take either. Canyon on L with rock formations. (Looking back, one can see a hole in the rock.)	0.41
0.81	Bear R, ascend up gully to SE. Above, there is a formation looking like a bird's head. Trail is braided; use care ascending up shallow valley.	0.35
1.04	Start ascent around S side of small ridge.	0.11

[for continuation, see page 25 following color pictures]

2. North Mountain from Peak 1700
   [Previous page: 1. "The Cave" on Camelback]   *3. Squaw: Perl Charles Trail*

4. From Shadow Mountain, toward Lookout Mountain

5. Stony Mountain

7. Shaw Butte from the south
    [Previous page: 6. Squaw Peak Summit Trail]   *8. Camelback rock formations*

9. Squaw: Circumference Trail

10. South Mountain: on the Alta Trail

11. Lookout Mountain

12. South Mountain: on the National Trail

14. South Mountain: National Trail
    [Previous page: 13. "Fat Man's Pass"]

15. Sierra Estrella from South Mountain

16. Sierra Estrella from park

17. Estrella: Rainbow Valley Trail

18. McDowell: standing stone

19. McDowell: lush vegetation

20. *McDowell: cholla abound on Lousley Hill*

21. *Usery: Pass Mountain*

22. Usery: Pass Mountain Trail

23. White Tank: Willow Springs Trail

24. White Tank: rugged terrain

25. Lost Dutchman: edge of Superstitions

26. Lower Salt River Nature Trail
  [Following page: 28. Squaw Peak]   *27. Coon Bluff: Lower Salt River*

Read Down	Detailed Trail Description, continued	Read Up
1.06	Turn L and up rocks.	0.10
1.11	Bear L (NE); bear L in 200'.	0.04
1.16	*Summit (2,704')*. Walk 225' to W along ridge for good view of Camel's Neck and Head area. Use care on NE side above steep cliffs.	0.00

[241] Echo Canyon Trail

General Description. This trail, less well known than the summit trail, leads into a rocky bowl with unusual opportunities for exploration. The rock formations offer varied photographic possibilities under different light and weather conditions. The trail is less well defined than the summit trail, and there are many trails of use that may be confusing. Total ascent is about 75'.

Access. From Camelback Mountain Trail [141] at 0.12 mile.

Read Down	Detailed Trail Description	Read Up
0.00	Leave Camelback Mountain Trail [141] at 0.12 mi, heading S toward a ramada in view ahead (elevation 1,530').	0.48
0.03	**Junction:** [To R, side-trail leads W, to R of a sharp rock formation, reaching narrow gully in 385' and start of steep route in 435'. Gully leads to top of ridge with good views.] Turn L here and ascend.	0.44
0.04	Ramada atop minor ridge (1,535') and **junction:** to L, trail leads back to Camelback Mountain Trail [141] in 60'. Main trail descends gradually SW.	0.42
0.06	**Junction:** wide track. Turn L, up-hill here. (R is new trail descending 0.17 mi to Camelback Mountain Trail 65' from trail-head.)	0.40
0.08	**Junction:** turn R, drop over rock into minor wash on narrow trail, heading straight toward cliff face.	0.38
0.09	**Junction:** turn R at base of cliff (to L, trail of use heads back to ramada by different route in 290').	0.37
0.14	"Cave" in cliff on L (overhang) with fine view from it. Descend past it.	0.32
0.19	**Junction (4-way):** trail of use crosses [descends on R; ascends L to hollow rock]. 25' further on, another branch of this trail of use crosses.	0.29
0.20	**Junction:** trail of use ascends L into bowl beneath cliffs.	0.28
0.24	**Junction:** trail of use descends R to private property.	0.24
0.30	Height-of-land (1,540'). Good VP just 50' to R. Descend 60' with Bobby's Rock on R, cliffs of Camel's Head on L. Pass ahead where trail ends is visible.	0.18
0.33	Switchback to R on descent. There are many confusing trails of use. Bear L.	0.15
0.36	Cross wash, then ascend.	0.12
0.38	**Junction:** cross trail of use; contour along hillside.	0.10
0.43	Two small wind-carved alcoves in rocks on L. Pass one last trail of use.	0.05
0.48	*Pass* (1,485'), end of official trail. (Ahead, poor trail descends under and around huge boulders for 0.2 mile into private housing development - no trespassing.) On L at pass is spectacular cliff wall with overhang. On R is large rock, easily climbed for good views into rocky bowl that trail has crossed.	0.00

[A]

General Description.   This is a short side-trail with a good view of the summit ridge of Camelback. It crosses the Camel's Neck and follows the cliffs to a subsidiary ridge.

Access. From 0.55 mile on Camelback Mountain Trail [141].

Read Down	Detailed Trail Description	Read Up
0.00	From Camelback Mountain Trail [141], turn sharp R, ascending toward ridge-top.	0.16
0.04	Ridge (Camel's Neck) with good views. Descend toward cliffs ahead.	0.12
0.08	Reach foot of cliffs of Camel's Head. (On return, be sure to follow along below cliffs, not trail of use that descends.) Turn L and follow rocks at foot of cliffs.	0.08
0.10	Reach bottom of descent (small wash); ascend, keeping along foot of cliffs.	0.06
0.12	Pass small glen to R, in cliff wall.	0.04
0.16	Reach top of ridge (1,950'). Good VP. Trails of use continue to SW.	0.00

The eastern ridge of Camelback, from the summit

City of Phoenix

Papago Park

Looking southwest from the Hole-in-the-Rock

Introduction. Papago Park contains 888 acres and is literally in the midst of the city. In addition to its better-known facilities it has hiking, jogging, riding, orienteering and bicycling trails. Elevations range from 1,200' to almost 1,700'.

History.[1] Originally an Indian townsite ("Papago" is a Pima name), it was a homesteading area (1889) and then was established as Papago Saguaro National Monument by Congress in 1914. This designation was abolished in 1930. The land was granted to the State of Arizona except for parcels transferred to the National Guard, sold to the City of Tempe, or purchased by the Salt River Valley Water Users Association. In 1932 some of the land was allotted to the Military District, Cactus Gardens, the Arizona Game and Fish Department, and the Salt River Agricultural Improvement and Power District. It finally became a City of Phoenix park (originally "Cactus Park") in 1959. In its early days it was too rugged for easy approaches because of the difficult desert brush and plants. The first road into the park area was built in 1916 with volunteer labor.

The pyramidal Hunt's Tomb (on top of one of the buttes just north of the Zoo) is that of George Wiley Paul Hunt (1859-1934), Arizona's seven-term governor, his wife, her parents, and three of her relatives. An Act of Congress was required to authorize the structure, a gift of school children and friends. The Hunt Bass Hatchery is at the foot of the knoll.

Geology. The Salt River Valley was formed some 29-30 million years ago, with extensive faulting events. More recent vulcanism (6-15 million years ago) helped form the up-thrown red rock (iron oxide-hematite) as part of what geologists call the "Basin and Range Province." Included within the park boundary are three buttes of a sedimentary formation that is directly related to Camelback Mountain's "Head" and therefore called the "Camel's Head Formation." The holes in the rocks are called *tafoni* and are characteristic of arid regions. They were not caused by wind, but by water that remained in holes and cracks, slowly soaking up and breaking down the minerals in the rocks. Overlying the bedrock landform known as a *pediment* is a thin veneer of sand and rock which has worn away in several spots to reveal bedrock outcrops. These made the land unsuitable for farming.

Maps. *Our map 2.* The 1:24,000 USGS Tempe topo (1952, photorevised 1982) shows the physical features but not the trails. Extensive reconstruction of Galvin Parkway, park access roads and parking areas in 1988 has made previous maps obsolete.

Access. The park's entrances are reached from Galvin Parkway between E. Van Buren and McDowell Road. (The access roads were rebuilt in 1988.)

---

[1]Information in this section and on Geology was adapted from R. M. Hochhaus' "Papago Park: An Informational Background Report" (June 1, 1983), kindly provided by the Parks, Recreation & Library Department.

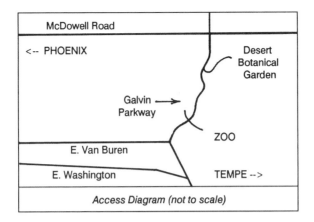

Access Diagram (not to scale)

Facilities. Open from 6:00 a.m. to midnight, the park provides an 18-hole golf course and facilities for softball, archery, fishing in several small lakes, and picnicking in addition to the adjacent Phoenix Zoo and Desert Botanical Garden. There are picnic ramadas with drinking water and firepits, Hunt's Tomb and the Eliot Memorial. Equestrian use is popular from nearby stables, with several riding trails (not described here) adjacent to the golf course. An orienteering course has been provided through cooperation with Recreational Equipment, Inc [REI] in Tempe; a map is available from them or from the East District Office [see Appendix B].

Recommended Hikes. There are a number of isolated rock outcrops. Hunt's Tomb is at the top of one of these in the southeastern section of the park, reached by a short trail from the parking area. A landmark known as the "Hole-in-the-Rock" adjacent to the Desert Botanical Garden is popular for climbing. There is also good walking or jogging along the bikeway: along the Arizona Cross Cut Canal from McDowell Road on the north into the Desert Botanical Garden, then from the Hunt's Tomb area almost to the Alegre Drive crossing of the Canal where the bikeway leads into Canal Park (contiguous on the park's eastern side), to the College Avenue/McKellips Road area. (The map also shows several other outcrops that are off-limits to the general public, one adjacent to the Arizona National Guard Military Reservation, one on the Municipal Golf Course, and another between the Park and the Water Treatment Plant.) The trail indicators used here are our own arbitrary letters (e.g., [B]), since no trail has been officially designated.

Cautions. Climbing on the steep sandstone rocks is for experts only and is not recommended for the ordinary hiker. Beware of road traffic through the park. Several areas have been heavily scarred by all-terrain vehicles and the maze of tracks can be confusing.

NOTE: The three short circuit trails described here are *hiker-only*. (There are separate riding trails along the golf course to the west.)

[A] (Park High Point)

General Description. A circuit trip of 0.8 mile provides variety, with a short climb to a saddle between the two parts of the butte at 0.16 mile and a steep descent to the amphitheater at 0.24 mile. The trail then circles around the east side of the butte to return to its starting point. Ascent is 250'.

Access. From Galvin Parkway opposite the Zoo and Park entrance, take the road on the opposite (west) side, then head north. Just after the road turns sharp left near a butte, you will see the Eliot Ramada on your left. Park there. Walk back east along the road for 250' or along a path just north of the road to the junction at the road.

Read Down	Detailed Trail Description	Read Up
0.00	From junction at road 250' E of Eliot Ramada parking lot, head N up track.	0.80
0.01	**Junction:** cross track and continue up toward gully.	0.78
0.08	Enter gully, continue ascent (avoid trail of use on L).	0.71
0.16	Top of rise (about 1,500'). VP to N. Descend to L. *Use care,* trail is steeper than on other side.	0.64
0.22	**Junction:** avoid trail to R; keep L, continue descent.	0.57
0.24	Top of amphitheater. Go to R along edge of it.	0.56
0.27	SE corner of amphitheater. Continue E.	0.52
0.32	**Junction:** where track crosses, go straight.	0.48
0.33	**Junction:** pass another track coming up from L.	0.46
0.37	With bluff ahead, keep to L of it where trail of use goes R and ascends.	0.43
0.39	Top of rise. Bear R away from track descending on L; descend gradually.	0.41
0.48	**Junction:** track descends L. Continue around flank of butte to S, then SW.	0.31
0.62	**Junction:** track descends on L.	0.18
0.68	**Junction:** tracks descend L & continue to R. Continue straight, descend slightly (upper route bearing R also leads back, parallelling road).	0.12
0.70	**Junction:** lower track. Go R, generally parallelling road.	0.09
0.80	**Junction:** *you are now back at start* (upper route enters here from R).	0.00

[B] Central Butte

General Description. There are two circuit trips here (0.63 mile and 0.73 mile), as well as the short spur that leads to the high point on the butte at 0.22 mile. Ascent is about 150', depending upon which circuit trip is chosen.

Access. From the Eliot Ramada parking area, reached as described under trail [A]. (The Memorial, dedicated in 1964, is in recognition of William C. Eliot's contribution to the development of parks in the City of Phoenix, and Papago Park in particular.)

Read Down	Detailed Trail Description	Read Up
0.00	From Eliot Ramada parking lot's W end, take path heading SW.	0.27
0.01	Turnstile entrance into enclosure.	0.26
0.02	Eliot Memorial Ramada. Continue SW toward gate.	0.25
0.04	Leave enclosure thru gate, taking track SW toward butte.	0.23
0.14	**Junction:** to R is circuit trip returning. Go straight, ascending.	0.13
0.16	**Junction:** ahead trail ascends 130' (past another junction) to high point on butte (trail can then be followed 150' E to return to this circuit. Go L here to take either circuit.	0.11
0.19	**Junction (4-way):** trail sharp R ascends back toward top of butte trail (track also descends half-L). Continue.	0.08
0.27	**Junction:** wide track crosses. Here you can go R for the shorter circuit, or continue ahead for longer one.	0.00

Longer Circuit

0.00	Leave junction, continue around flank. Cross tracks in 60', 135', 225'.	0.32
0.07	**Junction:** 2 tracks descend to L in open area. Continue slightly R, around flank of butte.	0.25
0.10	**Junction:** track sharp L.	0.22
0.13	**Junction (4-way):** tracks L & R. Ascend.	0.29
0.16	**Junction (4-way):** tracks descend L & R.	0.16
0.21	**Junction (4-way):** eroded track ascends on R, descends on L.	0.11
0.25	**Junction:** *sharp R is shorter circuit.* Go slightly R.	0.07
0.28	**Junction:** cross track, continue around flank.	0.04
0.32	**Junction:** *you are now back at junction 0.14 mi from road,* 0.59 mi from start.	0.00

Shorter Circuit

0.00	Leave junction, ascend steadily up broad track.	0.22
0.02	**Junction:** trail of use enters from L. Continue ascent.	0.19
0.08	**Junction:** at top of rise, trail sharp L is eroded, ascends 135' toward side of subsidiary butte. Continue, descending.	0.13
0.11	**Junction:** where eroded track continues, descending, bear R on trail.	0.11
0.12	**Junction:** trail of use descends on L. Continue slightly R.	0.10
0.14	**Junction:** take wide track descending to L.	0.07
0.15	**Junction:** *longer circuit* enters from L. Track continues descending toward golf course. *Turn sharp R here* to return.	0.07
0.18	**Junction:** cross track, continue around flank of butte.	0.04
0.22	**Junction:** *you are now back at junction 0.14 mi from road,* 0.49 mi from start.	0.00

[C] Hole-in-the-Rock

General Description. This is a popular area for unusual views toward the south and southwest, and an easy short hike of only 0.14 mile. The hike can be extended around the north side of the butte for a total of 0.22 mile. Ascent is about 120'. *Use care on rock!*

Access. Drive to the Zoo entrance off Galvin Parkway, but take a left turn. Pass a side-road and then a parking area on the right, then turn left, passing the ranger station on the right. At a 5-way junction, head straight across and into the parking area. Take the trail at the east side of the parking area.

Read Down	*Detailed Trail Description*	*Read Up*
0.00	From parking area, head E around the butte.	0.14
0.08	**Junction:** 125' to R is spur trail to another parking area and road loop. Turn L (N) and ascend steps, then turn L.	0.06
0.14	Reach Hole-in-the-Rock (just before final ascent, minor trail continues ahead, turning left around butte to return to road in 400', just N of where you started).	0.00

Looking north from the Eliot Ramada

City of Phoenix

Lookout Mountain Area

Introduction. Lookout Mountain, the northernmost part of the Phoenix Mountains Preserve, is a visually striking feature lying between Bell Road on the north, 7th Street on the west, Cave Creek Road on the east, and Thunderbird Road on the south. It consists of a prominent summit butte (2,054') and a sharp, steep knob that is 1,964' high, separated by a col at 1,883'. To the west of these summits (separated by a 1,690' pass) is a lower north-south ridge with three summits increasing in height from north to south: 1,704', 1,724', and 1,843'.[1] *(NOTE:* In 1991 this area was being connected to the other parts of the Preserve by a corridor through the Pointe golf course north of Thunderbird, and new trails were being developed, so major changes are under way.)

Maps. *Our map 3.* USGS Union Hills (1964, photorevised 1981) and Sunnyslope (1965, photorevised 1982) 1:24,000 topos.

Access. There are two major access points: (1) the best is to drive 0.9 mile south of Bell Road to the end of pavement on 16th Street, just before a water tank. There is ample parking here, but no signs. (2) The other, with limited parking, is at the eastern end of Coral Gables Drive, east of 7th Street, where it turns south to become 12th Street. Here there is a widening of the pavement. (There are 3 minor accesses: at the end of 19th Street; at the east end of Tierra Buena off of 11th Street; and off Tierra Buena at 13th Street.)

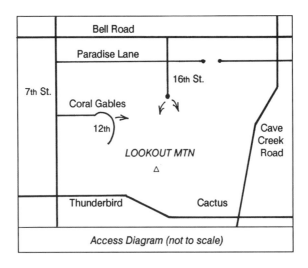

Access Diagram (not to scale)

Facilities. New trail developments are under way (see map 3 for concept).

[Previous page: Lookout's summit from the Knob]

---

[1]Note that some of the elevations used here differ slightly from those on the USGS topo map because more recent work has been done by Landis Aerial Survey.

Terminology. *The trail system described here will make little sense to the reader without looking at the map at the same time.* Unnamed summits and some passes are referred to by their elevations.

Recommended Hikes and Trail Rides. Since there are no official trails at this time, trail letters indicators used are our own, for purposes of identification only, e.g., [C]. The best approaches to Lookout Mountain are [A] and [B]. The "Ridge Trail" [E] is also attractive and can be combined in various ways with other trips. Most of the summits are too steep for horses.

Cautions. *Note that none of these approaches is maintained, signed, or otherwise dependable.* There are many other approaches from private land. Access through those areas to Preserve land is illegal for non-residents; they are not described here except to identify junctions. New trails are expected soon, including a circumference trail, and an access from the City's new Lookout Mountain Park near 18th Street & Winchcomb. Many trails of use without recreational significance are not included here.

[A] Summit Trail (West)

General Description. This is the most direct approach to both the Summit and the Knob. From the parking area just below the water tower, a combination of tracks ascends 200' with increasing steepness to become a trail. This heads into the col at 0.31 mile. From there a rough trail and scramble up open rock to the west ends at the Knob in 290'. The main trail continues east to the Summit at 0.48 mile. Total ascent to the Summit is 540'; to the Knob it is 490'. Both high points have fine views.

Access. Take 16th Street and park just below the water tower on the right. A track ascends southwest but is not very distinct, partly because of the barriers that have been erected. At the top of a rise, however, the main track will easily be seen heading directly toward the Knob.

Read Down	Detailed Trail Description	Read Up
0.00	Leave parking area (1,550') on poorly defined track heading SW.	0.48
0.06	**Junction:** join main track by bearing L and ascending. (There are two alternates here that soon rejoin.)	0.42
0.09	Open area. Bear slightly L toward a steep track visible on slope ahead.	0.39
0.11	**Junction:** road R [K], across dirt barrier, leads to W. Ascend steeply.	0.37
0.23	**Junction:** at end of track where poor trail continues ahead, turn R, and cross slope on trail (elevation 1,760').	0.25
0.24	**Junction:** steep narrow trail to L ascends to join [B] in 110'.	0.24
0.27	**Major Junction:** [B] goes L here, returns to l6th Street. Head SW toward col.	0.21
0.30	**Junction:** ignore faint trail ascending L.	0.17

0.31	**Junction:** col (1,883'). Ahead [C] descends to S. [On R, two trails lead onto the Knob: (1) R leads to an outcrop (not the top) in 210', ascending 100'. (2) L keeps to S side of ridge, ascending steeply for 220'; there it turns R, scrambling up rocks to 290' or 0.05 mi to top of the Knob at 1,964' and very fine views.] For main trail continuation, turn L at col: easier way is L of a large rock (another goes to R of it).	0.16
0.34	Switchback R and up (many minor trails of use here).	0.13
0.36	**Junction:** join other trail from col; head E briefly, on crest, then keep N of crest line.	0.12
0.45	Reach crest again.	0.03
0.48	*Summit of Lookout Mountain (2,054').* Fine VP. (Poor route leads off steep rocks at E end of ridge, doubles back to NW, then descends to a trail leading back to E side of 16th Street (not recommended.)	0.00

[B] Summit Trail (East)

General Description. From the 16th Street access point this trail skirts the water tower fence and joins a wide track that ascends to a level, confusing area at 0.21 mile. Here it turns right and contours along the north-facing slope of Lookout Mountain to join [A] at 0.36 mile. Total ascent is 325' to the junction. The summit is at 0.57 mile via [A].

Access. Just south of the parking area for [A] and north of the water tower fence line a trail will be seen heading east.

Read Down	*Detailed Trail Description*	*Read Up*
0.00	Head E, just to the L (N) of fence line.	0.36
0.04	**Junction:** where track continues ahead (E), turn R and ascend past corner of fence.	0.32
0.14	**Junction:** on L is [L]. Bear slightly R, continuing steep ascent on wide track.	0.22
0.21	**Junction:** reach edge of flat, open area. Trail to L leads onto small hump on ridge in 110'. Keep R across flat area. [Trails of use lead up very steep summit ridge for 0.28 mi -- not recommended.]	0.16
0.24	**Junction:** trail sharp L leads back to hump in 235'. Ascend to SW.	0.12
0.32	**Junction:** faint trail joins from R, ascending. 25' beyond, steep track ascends on L toward summit (not recommended approach). Trail route ahead leads into and out of a small draw.	0.04
0.33	**Junction:** trail on R descends to [A] in 110'. Continue, ignoring trails of use.	0.03
0.36	**Junction:** this trail ends at [A]. Sharp R leads back to 16th Street in 0.27 mile. For Summit, take [A] for 0.21 mile further.	0.00

[C]

General Description. This trail and wide track ascends from the pass between the Knob and Peak 1843 to the col between the Summit and the Knob at 0.28 mile. It can thus be used in combination with other trail segments to reach Lookout Mountain from the west. Ascent is 200'.

Access. Reach the pass where this trail starts by taking [A] or [B].

Read Down	Detailed Trail Description	Read Up
0.00	From pass, elevation 1,690', head E along bumpy ridge on narrow trail.	0.28
0.02	**Junction:** steeper trail ascending L leads to col ahead. Head SE.	0.26
0.06	Cross wash, then two more at 0.11 and 0.13 mi.	0.22
0.16	**Junction:** track on R leads to private land. Go L up this track, ascending more steeply. *Note for descent:* where trail departs from track, it is not well defined.	0.12
0.18	**Junction:** faint trail on R.	0.10
0.22	Bear slightly L and ascend much more steeply.	0.06
0.28	**Junction:** col between Knob and Summit (1,883'). *NOTE:* just before col, steeper trail departs on L across a rocky area to return to 0.02 mile on this trail. To L and R in col are trails to Knob (0.05 mi) and Summit (0.16 mi) described under [A].	0.00

Lookout and the Knob from Peak 1843

[D] Peak 1704

General Description. This trail is a wide track as far as the pass at 0.14 mile; there are several junctions. The top is reached at 0.21 mile. Views are good, but are blocked by peaks to the south and east. Ascent is 200'.

Access. From the east end of Coral Gables Drive, east of 7th Street, where there is a widening as Coral Gables becomes 12th Street. There is limited parking here. A Preserve sign may be seen and a trail ascends north a short distance to reach the wide track heading east.

Read Down	Detailed Trail Description	Read Up
0.00	From road, ascend to E (1,500').	0.21
0.10	**Junction:** old road [F] heads S (access to Peak 1843). Continue ascent.	0.11
0.14	**Junction in pass:** Ridge Trail [E] on R (S) leads to Peaks 1724 and 1843; ahead trail [K] descends into valley and leads to 16th Street access. Turn L and ascend broad ridge.	0.07
0.15	**Junction:** take R fork where trail splits (L leads onto end of ridge ahead).	0.06
0.18	Ridge crest; grade eases.	0.03
0.21	**Junction:** on summit, short (25') spur L leads to actual high point (1,704'); trail ahead continues onto flat end of ridge and descends 0.27 mi to a narrow concrete ditch which it follows W to E end of Tierra Buena off 11th St.	0.00

[E] "Ridge Trail"

General Description. This is a pleasant trail from the pass on [D] near Peak 1704, leading up and over Peak 1724 and then via a longer ascent to Peak 1843, which has good views, especially of Lookout Mountain itself. Along the way there are several complicated junctions. Total ascent is 270'.

Access. From the pass on [D], 0.14 mile east of Coral Gables access point, via [F] to summit of Peak 1843, or other trail segments ([G], [H], [J]) from the northeast (see map).

Read Down	Detailed Trail Description	Read Up
0.00	From pass between Peaks 1704 and 1724 on [D], ascend trail to S (1,630').	0.30
0.07	**Junction:** straight ahead leads to old mine site in 90', reaches crest as very faint, poor trail in 325'; go sharp L here, switchbacking up onto ridge crest.	0.23
0.12	**Junction** at summit of Peak 1724. (Just beyond, faint trail from mine site rejoins ridge beyond a large saguaro cactus.) Descend.	0.18
0.17	**Junction** at pass (1,690'): track to R drops to meet [F] in 0.11 mi; to L, track drops only 255' (80' in elevation) to join [G]. Ascend to S.	0.13
0.18	**Junction:** way diverges -- take either.	0.12
0.20	**Junction:** trails rejoin.	0.10
0.24	**Junction:** ignore faint trail to R; continue ascent.	0.06

0.25	**Junction:** to L, wide trail [H] descends to pass 1690; turn R.	0.05
0.26	Cross a flat area, then turn L and then R (use care in locating route).	0.04
0.28	Reach crest of ridge; grade eases.	0.02
0.30	**Junction** at *Summit of Peak 1843*. Fine Views. [F] enters from W here, over steep rocks. To S is a steep drop-off (use care).	0.00

[F] Peak 1843

General Description.   This trail starts as a wide track (old road) leading at an easy grade along the western flank of the ridge for 0.25 mile. It then joins a steep trail to the summit, which is reached at 0.41 mile. This is steeper than an ordinary hike and has some tricky spots, especially in wet or windy weather. It is definitely preferred for the ascent, not a descent. Total ascent is 350'.

Access. Take [D] for 0.10 mile to where this rough old road heads south.

Read Down	Detailed Trail Description	Read Up
0.00	From junction with [D], head S on old road.	0.41
0.11	**Junction:** track ascends E to intersect Ridge Trail [E] in pass at 0.11 mile. Continue, crossing two small washes.	0.30
0.22	**Junction:** where sign ahead indicates private land (just before height of land and private home) leave track, taking trail to L on level. [One can also continue on track to junction and turn L. At junction, track continues S and then E to Pass 1690, 0.44 mi.]	0.19
0.25	**Junction:** wide track intersects trail. Go L on it, ascending more and more steeply.	0.16
0.34	Way eases on crest, becomes pleasant.	0.07
0.37	**Junction:** faint trail to L ends. Go straight up open rock, using care.	0.04
0.40	**Junction:** trail L leads past overhang in rock (shelter), joining [E] later on, avoiding summit itself. Go straight up steep rock.	0.01
0.41	*Summit* (1,843'). Very steep drop-offs to N and S. Trail [E] continues along crest, then descends to N along ridge; or [H] can be taken to Pass 1690.	0.00

[G]

General Description. A wide track on the eastern slope of the ridge leads up from the [K] junction in the valley to a pass between Peak 1843 and the Knob at 1,690'. Ascent is 160'.

Access. Reach the junction with [K] via [D], a total of 0.22 mile east of Coral Gables access point, or 0.39 mile from 16th Street via [A] and [K]. The upper end (Pass 1690) is reached via [C] or [H].

Read Down	Detailed Trail Description	Read Up
0.00	From junction with [K], ascend side of ridge on wide track.	0.26
0.09	**Junction:** ignore trail joining on L.	0.17
0.11	**Junction:** wide trail R ascends to pass on [E] in 255'.	0.15
0.20	**Junction:** faint trail ascending sharp R from crossing of wash leads to [J] in 90'. Just beyond, this track diverges. Go either way.	0.06
0.23	**Junction:** alternate rejoins. Ascend.	0.03
0.26	**Junction:** this trail ends at Pass 1690 where trails [C] (L to Lookout Mountain) and [H] (R to Peak 1843) diverge. Track ahead leads S & W 0.44 mi to [F].	0.00

[H]

General Description. Peak 1843 can be reached from Pass 1690 on [G] and [C] by this short segment leading to [E]. The ascent is about 60'.

Access. From Pass 1690. Among others, it is reached by [G].

Read Down	Detailed Trail Description	Read Up
0.00	From Pass 1690, and junction with [G] and [C], go directly W up the ridge.	0.10
0.04	**Junction:** faint trail joining from R is [J]. Continue up on distinct trail, just N of, and below, crest line.	0.06
0.10	**Junction:** trail descending ridge to N is Ridge Trail [E]. This trail ends. Continuing on [E] leads to Summit in 0.05 mi.	0.00

[J]

General Description. This is an alternate approach to the top of Peak 1843 from the Ridge Trail [E] to [H].

Access. From the pass on the Ridge Trail [E] at 0.17 mile, a wide un-numbered track descends northeast toward the valley. Just below the summit of the pass, this fainter trail heads southeast. At the trail's other end, on [H], its start may be difficult to locate.

Read Down	Detailed Trail Description	Read Up
0.00	Trail leaves track just below pass on [E].	0.12
0.07	**Junction:** narrow trail descends L for 90' to join [G] where it crosses a wash. Continue S on level trail, then ascend gradually.	0.05
0.09	**Junction:** to L, spur reaches [G] in 50'. Keep to R and ascend.	0.03
0.12	**Junction:** this trail ends at [H]. To reach summit, turn R and take [H] and then [E] for 0.11 mi.	0.00

[K]

General Description. A wide track, descending from the ridge into the valley, then crossing it to join [A] at 0.36 mile. By combination of [D] from Coral Gables and part of [A], it is a total of 0.61 mile between the two major access points. Ascent is 120', descent is 140'.

Access. For the western end, take [D] to the pass in the ridge at 0.14 mile. For the eastern end, take [A] for 0.11 mile, where the two tracks rejoin.

Read Down	Detailed Trail Description	Read Up
0.00	From [D] at 0.14 mi (in pass), descend wide track.	0.36
0.08	**Junction:** track sharp R is [G] ascending to Pass 1690.	0.28
0.09	**Junction:** ahead is track leading to Tierra Buena Lane in 0.25 mi. Bear R, descending gradually to NE.	0.27
0.13	**Junction:** old road on R.	0.23
0.15	Descend to cross wash; ascend out of it to cross wide, open area, passing a cairn. There are several dirt and rock barriers.	0.21
0.36	**Junction:** this trail ends at [A], 0.11 mi above its start at 16th Street, where alternate routes rejoin. Turning to R here will take you to the col on Lookout Mountain in 0.20 mi.	0.00

[L]

General Description. From a minor access point this trail ascends steadily for 0.19 mile to join [B].

Access. From the cul-de-sac at the end of 19th Street, south of Monte Cristo. There is very limited parking.

Read Down	Detailed Trail Description	Read Up
0.00	From end of 19th Street, head SW.	0.19
0.02	**Junction:** poor trail on L to Karen Drive.	0.17
0.03	**Junction:** ignore trail to R.	0.16
0.08	**Junction:** on L, 2 other tracks (steep, with loose rock) ascend; sharp R track descends. Go straight up steep rocky track, then level off at 0.15 mi.	0.11
0.18	**Junction:** track descends on R.	0.01
0.19	**Junction:** this trail ends at [B]. (From here it is 0.43 mi to Summit via [A] & [B], and 0.14 mi back to 16th St. trail-head via [B].)	0.00

City of Phoenix

North Mountain/Shaw Butte

North Mountain Park and Squaw Peak

Introduction. At 2,104' North Mountain is a major landmark. Although somewhat lower than Squaw Peak and Camelback, its summit provides a wide panorama. A paved road, gated near where it leaves 7th Street, rises almost to the fenced transmission towers at the summit. The area contains several subsidiary ridges and dozens of trails, most of them short and unmaintained, as well as a section of the Charles M. Christiansen Trail. To the northwest, Shaw Butte (2,149') has two summits. There are three approaches, two on service roads and one via trail. The tops of the two summits are private land (Arizona Public Service Company) but are open to the public at this time.

History. Around the turn of the century, the North Mountain area served as a campground for the Phoenix Indian School's pupils and their families. There are a number of closed mining shafts and pits, evidencing earlier interest in copper mining.

Maps. *Our map 5.* The USGS Sunnyslope 1:24,000 topo (1965, photorevised 1982) shows a few trails, the North Mountain road and the roads up Shaw Butte (with a few inaccuracies).

Access. North Mountain Recreation Area is served by a paved loop road reached from Peoria at 7th Street. The Christiansen Trail is best reached from Mountain View Park (6th Drive between Mountain View and Cinnabar). An access point on the west side of 7th Street has been acquired but the trailhead was not in place in 1990. Shaw Butte can be reached from the south end of Central Avenue or the north end of 15th Avenue north of Shangri-La Road.

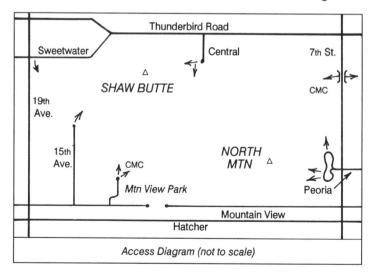

Access Diagram (not to scale)

Facilities. There are 12 ramadas (some with electricity) serving up to 350 people, and many uncovered picnic tables. Some areas are reserved, others first-come. Washrooms and drinking water are located at the large parking area at the park office near the Pima Ramada (Area 4). There are also

washrooms at the Yavapai Ramada (Area 10). There are 4 orienteering courses, with a master map available at the park office. As is true of other Phoenix Mountain Parks, hours are limited to 5:30 a.m. through 12:30 a.m.
  The Shaw Butte area has facilities at Mountain View Park only.

Recommended Hikes and Trail Rides. The entire North Mountain area is honeycombed with trails, but many of them have no legal access points. We have described those which are recreationally significant and are legally accessible. (The Shaw Butte area has fewer trails.) Numbers used are either official City of Phoenix numbers or our own letters. Officially numbered trails are listed first, and the North Mountain Area is covered before Shaw Butte. The easiest approach to North Mountain is the National Trail [44]; to Shaw Butte, the route from Central Avenue [306]. The Christiansen Trail [100] is easy, but all in the valley. Peak 1700 (trail [G]) offers good views for little effort, as does the knob reached by a branch of [B] near the North Mountain Road. Trail [60] also has some good views. There are many other view-points.

Cautions. Many of the trails are steep and rocky.

North Mountain Area

Lower North Mountain Road

General Description. The entire paved road is 0.87 mile long, with a short trail to the actual summit bringing the total ascent (650') to 0.89 mile. The upper section is part of the National Trail [44] (see that description for the ascent of North Mountain). The approach described here is not highly recommended because of very limited parking at the access point. There are several junctions with trails. The ascent to the National Trail is 210' and the distance is 0.32 mile.

Access. *From the north:* the road leaves 7th Street about 1.1 miles south of Thunderbird Road, just before the two sets of lanes rejoin. When approaching *from the south,* you will have to pass the area, then double back because of the dual roadway. There is very limited parking at the base of the road before the gate. *(Park authorities are not encouraging use of this parking area.)*

Read Down	Detailed Road Description	Read Up
0.00	Leave 7th Street (elevation 1450').	0.32
0.02	Gate (pass on R).	0.30
0.04	**Junction:** gravel road on L.	0.28
0.07	Road bends to L; narrow trail ascends draw on R.	0.25
0.10	Road bends to R (poor track ascends on L).	0.22
0.19	Switchback to L (faint trail on R leads to knob; deteriorates).	0.13
0.21	Gate.	0.11

| 0.25 | **Junction:** trail ascending steeply to R [B] leads to knob and to CMC. Continue ascending to S. .... | 0.07 |
| 0.32 | **Junction:** trail dropping L down steps is National Trail [44] to Maricopa Ramada in 0.17 mi. (Road continues ahead as National Trail [44], see below.) (Elevation 1,660' here.) .... | 0.00 |

[44] National Trail NORTH MOUNTAIN FROM THE NORTH

General Description. From the Maricopa Ramada Area, this trail ascends the side of a dry wash to a prominent trail junction and view at 0.15 mile, then up a short pitch to the North Mountain Road at 0.17 mile. It then follows the road and a short trail for 0.57 mile to the summit for a total distance of 0.74 mile. (This is the easiest approach to North Mountain.) Total ascent is 170' to the road, 615' to North Mountain summit. The Trail then continues south to the Quechan Ramada (see reverse of next description).

Access. From Maricopa Ramada near the Recreation Area entrance.

Read Down	Detailed Trail Description	Read Up
0.00	Leave R side of Maricopa Ramada, elevation 1,490'. From signpost, ascend along side of wash.	0.74
0.14	**Junction (4-way):** trail L is alternate [A] back to start (narrower). Trail R leads onto knob with view in 170'. Go straight.	0.60
0.15	Pass (VP to N). Switchback to L and up steps.	0.59
0.17	**Junction:** North Mountain Road (1,660'; sign. (To R, paved road descends 0.32 mile to 7th St.) From here, trail follows road up North Mountain.	0.57
0.25	Road turns sharp L; overlook.	0.49
0.44	**Junction:** wide trail to L quickly deteriorates. A branch ascends knob on L; another bad track drops steeply down to Tewa Ramada (not recommended).	0.30
0.47	Road bends to L, then to R.	0.27
0.56	**Junction:** where road turns L, a trail [C] drops down to the R (descends to valley and CMC).	0.18
0.67	Hairpin turn to L; good view of Shaw Butte.	0.07
0.71	**Junction:** where road turns sharp R and passes through fence ahead, ascend L (SW) on trail.	0.03
0.74	*Summit*, North Mountain, 2,104'. **Junction:** trail along crest to L is continuation of National Trail [44] from the south (see below). Straight ahead parallel to fence is steep trail down ridge to **junction** where two trails lead W to CMC [not recommended for descent].	0.00

[44] National Trail NORTH MOUNTAIN FROM THE SOUTH

General Description. This major trail ascends from the Quechan Ramada onto the ridge crest where there are several side-trails. It then takes a circuitous route along the east flank of North Mountain, finally ascending the crest to the summit at 0.57 mile where there are fine views in all directions. (It continues north to the Maricopa Ramada; see previous section.) Total ascent is 715'.

Access. Take the trail from the right side of the ramada which immediately crosses a wash.

Read Down	Detailed Trail Description	Read Up
0.00	From Quechan Ramada at 1,400', bear R and cross wash, ascending.	0.57
0.10	On R is orienteering post.	0.47
0.10	**Junction (5-way):** (Only 20' beyond last point.) Pass in ridge crest (1,523'). To L, trail [G] leads onto summit of Peak 1700 or down to Ak-Chin Ramada. Even sharper L, poor trail leads up crest toward Peak 1700. Ahead, a short trail drops to a cul-de-sac in new housing development (no public access). To continue, go N along sharp rocks, then bear L, to W of crest, up a draw.	0.47
0.18	Bear R.	0.39
0.19	Reach minor crest with trails of use. From here, ascend to E of crest, with ramadas and parking area in view below.	0.38
0.23	**Junction:** poor trail on R descends 0.14 mi to park drive between Tewa and Quechan Ramadas (not recommended).	0.34
0.26	Ascend more steeply; here there are 2 trails that rejoin ahead, beyond a tree.	0.32
0.28	**Junction:** just off main trail to R is knob with good view. Turn L here, ascend.	0.29
0.30	Views S to center of city. Turn R here.	0.26
0.34	With rocks ahead, switchback to R.	0.23
0.36	Trail of use joins from R (on descent, keep R here).	0.21
0.37	Reach main crest (1,910') and head N, climbing steep, braided trail.	0.20
0.41	Switchback to R.	0.16
0.46	**Junction:** trail L (obscure here) descends to [60] in 0.33 mi. Almost level trailway ahead, marked with rocks on L. Towers in view ahead.	0.11
0.57	*Summit of North Mountain* (elevation 2,104'). Fence surrounds towers. **Junction:** to L 110' is start of [E] & [F]. National Trail [44] passes to E of tower fence, drops to road bend, continuing to Maricopa Ramada. (See previous description.)	0.00

[60] Shaw Butte Nature Trail FROM MOUNTAIN VIEW PARK

General Description. This trail's name is possibly confusing: it looks out on Shaw Butte, but nestles along the side of North Mountain. It incorporates a new and some old segments. It leads from Mountain View Park to 0.51 mile, where it turns east to cross a wash and then meet a track heading south. At 0.85 mile it descends steadily to pass the north side of a retention dam and meets the previous trail at 1.10 miles. (The circuit back to Mountain View Park is 1.37 miles.) There are views across the valley toward Shaw Butte. (An interpretive brochure is planned.)

Access. From Mountain View Park at the Christiansen Monument, or walk east on the paved path for 125', turning left for 35' to post #1. In 145' more you will join the trail from the Christiansen Monument.

Read Down	Detailed Trail Description	Read Up
0.00	Leave Mountain View Park from sidewalk just E of CMC Monument.	1.10
0.22	**Junction (4-way):** R is track 0.29 mi back to Mountain View Park; L goes up-hill.	0.88
0.23	**Junction:** track L up hillside.	0.87
0.27	**Important junction:** on R is [60] returning; continue straight.	0.83
0.51	**Important junction:** where trail [E] continues up steepening track, turn R on new trail.	0.59
0.54	Cross small, rocky wash and another wash in 250'.	0.56
0.62	**Junction:** on L is narrow trail 0.33 mi up ridge to [44] on North Mountain and 0.11 mi further to summit *[steep in spots]*.	0.48
0.69	Trail becomes road.	0.41
0.85	**Junction:** on crest, narrow trail ahead leads 195' up hump with VP. Turn R and descend steadily on rocky track.	0.25
0.97	Pass fence on L, level out, passing north of dam.	0.13
1.06	**Junction:** sharp L is trail along top of dam. Bear R.	0.04
1.10	**Junction:** you are now back at [60]. Mountain View Park is 0.27 mi to L.	0.00

[100] Charles M. Christiansen Trail EASTBOUND

MOUNTAIN VIEW PARK TO 7th STREET

General Description. The Christiansen Trail starts at Mountain View Park and leads through a flood works area, following an old road with an ascent of 160' through the wide valley separating North Mountain from Shaw Butte. It intersects many trails along the way, joins the Shaw Butte Trail [306], reaching a major junction with an old road east toward 7th Street at 1.36 miles. Here it leaves the Shaw Butte Trail and circumnavigates a minor summit and heads east to 7th Street at 1.67 miles, where it enters a tunnel and ends at 2.15 miles, just beyond its eastern opening, adjacent to the parking lot of the Pointe at Tapatio Cliffs. Total ascent is 160'.

Access. *Western end:* from the park at 6th Drive and Cheryl Drive, just east of 7th Avenue. *Eastern end:* from the Pointe's public parking area east of 7th Street, just east of their tennis courts.

Read Down	Detailed Trail Description	Read Up
0.00	Leave Mountain View Park at road bend where Cheryl Drive turns south to become 6th Drive (1,290'). Head north.	2.15
0.02	Monument to Charles M. Christiansen. **Junction:** trail heading NE is [60] to North Mountain (and access to [E]). Continue straight ahead.	2.13
0.15	**Junction:** minor trail to R.	2.00

0.17	**Junction:** wide track enters on L, from 7th Avenue. Bear R here.	1.98
0.30	Enter flood works, with fences on both sides. Old road crosses	1.85
0.63	**Junction:** trail sharp L leads back to Desert Cove Ave. and 7th Avenue in 0.17 mi. Ascend gradually.	1.52
0.70	**Junction:** in open area, sharp L is the Shaw Butte Trail [306], which joins here (leads 0.51 mi onto road on Shaw Butte).	1.45
0.76	Old gate posts on either side. Ascend.	1.39
0.88	**Junction:** old road joins on L.	1.27
1.00	**Junction:** narrow trail R leads around knob to meet [F].	1.15
1.08	**Junction:** track to R (old road) is [F] ascending North Mountain.	1.07
1.26	**Junction:** trail on L ends on slopes of Shaw Butte.	0.90
1.36	**Junction:** wide trail [B] leads R to North Mountain area and to 7th Street.	0.79
1.43	**Junction:** trail on R parallels previous trail. Cross wash.	0.72
1.46	**Junction:** road angles off to L.	0.70
1.49	**Junction:** poor trail angles off to L.	0.66
1.59	**Junction:** sharp R is a short-cut trail.	0.56
1.61	**Junction:** poor trail on L.	0.54
1.65	**Junction:** trail R parallels CMC and joins it in 0.17 mi.	0.50
1.67	**Major junction:** *CMC turns R here.* Trail ahead ([306]) leads to flood works and Central Avenue trail-head in 0.50 mi.	0.48
1.77	**Junction:** road turns sharp L (orienteering post on L).	0.39
1.85	**Junction:** trail enters from R at acute angle.	0.30
1.89	**Junction:** wide track leads R and ascends. Descend here.	0.26
1.92	**Junction:** ignore road bearing L.	0.23
1.99	**Junction:** track goes R here. Pass signpost in 90'.	0.16
2.02	**Junction:** trail joins at acute angle on L. Pass trail map in 50'.	0.13
2.04	Gate. 30' beyond, turn L, descending into small wash where road continues ahead.	0.11
2.06	**Junction:** bear R; trail ahead leads to W side of 7th St. [location of future parking lot and access point].	0.09
2.09	Enter tunnel under 7th Street.	0.06
2.15	**Junction:** trail R leads a few feet to Pointe's public parking area (1,440').	0.00

[A]

This is a short trail parallelling [44], less well worn, slightly longer and rougher. Ascent is 110' to the pass and junction. From Maricopa Ramada, ascend on the left (west) side of the wash. (The more distinct National Trail [44] is visible on the other side.) At around 0.11 mile there are several alternate trails leading to the same point. The trail junction is reached at 0.16 mile. (North Mountain Road is 0.03 mile to the left; a knob and view are only 170' ahead; to the right trail [44] descends back to Maricopa Ramada in 0.14 mile.)

[B]

General Description. This is a wide trail; the main trail ascends easily for 0.40 mile from the Christiansen Trail to a junction with [C], then ascends more steadily to 0.51 mile where there is a spur trail to a knob with a good view of

North Mountain towering above the valley. It reaches the North Mountain Road at 0.54 mile. Ascent is 210'.

Access. *Lower end:* junction with the Christiansen Trail at 0.79 mile from 7th Street or 1.36 miles from Mountain View Park. *Upper end:* from 0.25 mile on the North Mountain Road, a deeply worn trail climbs onto the crest.

Read Down	Detailed Trail Description	Read Up
0.00	Leave CMC at 0.77 mi from 7th St. (1,430'), heading E.	0.54
0.11	**Junction:** trail L 195' to alternate track parallelling this one. Ascend gradually along wash on L.	0.43
0.18	**Junction:** alternate track is 80' to L.	0.36
0.38	**Junction:** track enters sharp L (0.17 mi to alternate track, then 0.19 mi E to 7th Street, but no parking there).	0.16
0.40	**Junction:** trail [C] to R (1,520') to North Mountain Road. Bear L, cross wash.	0.14
0.41	**Junction:** track L is poor, wide track steeply ascending knob.	0.13
0.51	**Junction:** branch trail L to knob (1,710', good view of North Mountain) in 600' (100' ascent). Turn R here, then drop down deeply worn trail.	0.03
0.54	**Junction:** North Mountain Road (1,610') at 0.25 mi from bottom.	0.00

[C]

General Description. This short, steep trail ascends from the valley to join the North Mountain Road [44] 0.18 mile below the summit. Ascent is 400'.

Access. *From the north:* take the Christiansen Trail and then [B]. *From the south:* the junction is at 0.56 mile on the North Mountain Road 0.18 mile below the summit.

Read Down	Detailed Trail Description	Read Up
0.00	From 0.40 mi on trail [B] at junction (1,520'), ascend.	0.31
0.04	Bear R and ascend more steadily.	0.27
0.15	Reach crest of ridge (1,700'). Bear L (S).	0.16
0.22	Reach main crest (1,800'); continue ascending.	0.09
0.31	**Junction:** this trail ends at the National Trail [44] (North Mountain Road) at elevation 1,920'. It is 0.18 mi to top of North Mountain.	0.00

[D] (incorporated into [306])

[E] North Mountain from the Southwest

General Description. This trail is not recommended for descent because of its steepness and loose rock. It ascends steadily and then steeply to 0.12 mile where there is a choice of two routes, reaches the ridge at 0.19 mile and then a scramble leads to the top and the National Trail at 0.33 mile. Ascent is 615'.

Access. From the Shaw Butte Nature Trail [60] at 0.49 mile.

Read Down	Detailed Trail Description	Read Up
0.00	From **junction** at 0.27 mi on [60], continue straight,ascending away from wash. ...	0.33
0.02	Cross minor wash, parallel it on L. Bear R away from it in 65', then ascend over loose rock; trail braids.	0.31
0.12	**Junction:** choice of trails -- straight ahead leads to ridge in 465', then turns R over hump to meet main trail at 665' (0.13 mi). Better way is to R *(use care with route-finding).*	0.21
0.19	**Junction:** trail joins from L (alternate route). Go R, up ridge.	0.14
0.27	**Junction:** trail joins from CMC (northwest approach, [F]).	0.06
0.31	Corner of enclosure around towers on North Mountain. Road can be reached by going L around fence (caution) to gate. For National Trail [44], continue up (past actual summit, 2,104'), parallelling fence on L.	0.02
0.33	**Junction:** National Trail [44] to R to Quechan Ramada (0.57 mi). Trail L leads down to North Mountain Road (trail [44] to Maricopa Ramada in 0.74 mi or bottom of road in 0.89 mi).	0.00

Charles M. Christiansen memorial plaque near Mountain View Park

[F] North Mountain from the Northwest

General Description. North Mountain may also be approached from the Christiansen Trail on the northwest side. This approach is not recommended for the descent because of its steepness and loose rock near the very top. The lower section is in good shape and offers excellent views along the ridge. The first portion is a wide mining track leading 0.32 mile to the ridge. It then narrows to a trail that ascends the ridge to a junction with the trail from the southwest [E] at 0.55 mile. The summit and National Trail [44] are reached at 0.61 mile. Ascent is 655'.

Access. From the Christiansen Trail at 1.08 mile north of its start at Mountain View Park. From the north, at 1.07 miles west and south of 7th Street.

Read Down	Detailed Trail Description	Read Up
0.00	Leave CMC at 1.08 mi, heading E on wide track (elevation 1,440').	0.61
0.11	**Junction:** alternate trail joins from R (1.00 mi on CMC). Small knob on R can be ascended in 180'. Ascend steadily along wash on L, then ascend steeply to R, away from it.	0.50
0.32	**Junction:** crest of ridge, poor trail on R. Go L here on narrow trail.	0.29
0.47	Final ascent starts, with zigzags but no switchbacks.	0.14
0.55	**Junction:** trail from Mountain View Park and CMC [E] enters on R. Turn L here, *use care* on loose rock.	0.06
0.57	Scramble over rocks, then just to R of crest line.	0.04
0.59	Fence corner near towers. Follow fence line straight ahead.	0.02
0.61	**Junction:** National Trail [44] to R to Quechan Ramada (0.57 mi). Trail L leads down to North Mountain Road (trail [44] to Maricopa Ramada in 0.57 mi or to bottom of road in 0.89 mi).	0.00

[G] Peak 1700

General Description. This is the southernmost hump on North Mountain's ridge. There are two approaches via this loop: (1) From the Ak-Chin Ramada, the trail ascends to the ridge at 0.21 mile, joins the ridge route, and reaches the summit at 0.28 mile. (2) It is an easy ascent from the Quechan Ramada via the National Trail [44]: from the pass at 0.10 mile on that trail, this wide trail starts at an almost level grade, then switchbacks up at 0.10 mile. From there a steady ascent leads to the ridge crest at 0.14 mile, where the summit of Peak 1700 is just 0.12 mile ahead (0.36 mile total). Ascent is 230'. (It is planned to include this trail in the park system as a maintained trail, at which time it will have an official name and number.)

Access. Start just west of the Ak-Chin Ramada, southernmost of the park's ramadas. Or take the National Trail [44] from the Quechan Ramada up to the pass in the ridge at 0.10 mile, then turn left, contouring along the western slope of the ridge.

Read Down	Detailed Trail Description	Read Up
0.00	From Ak-Chin Ramada, ascend W, passing trails of use (elevation 1,370').	0.40
0.18	Switchback to L; ascend steadily up side of ridge..	0.22
0.21	**Junction:** on crest, narrow rough trail L leads to summit [pass first hump in 110', reach Peak 1700 with fine views at 0.28 mi]. To continue, turn R, along ridge	0.19
0.25	Top of hump is just to R.	0.15
0.26	**Junction:** straight ahead is poor trail generally following crest to pass in 420'. Turn L here for main trail, switchbacking down.	0.14
0.31	Level off, turn R (N).	0.09
0.40	**Junction (5-way), in pass** (1,523'): sharp R is poor trail up crest of ridge to Peak 1700. Ahead is [44] up North Mountain. To L is trail descending to private land. Go R to reach Quechan Ramada in 0.10 mi, and another 440' to R along park drive to Ak-Chin Ramada at start of this loop.	0.00

Shaw Butte Area

[306] Shaw Butte from Central Avenue

General Description. This circuit trip is the main approach, popular for joggers and local residents walking their dogs as well as for hikers. It is used frequently by service vehicles (move well off the road when they pass, to avoid being hit by flying rocks.) The views from the summit are excellent. First it ascends Shaw Butte to reach a spur road to the summit at 1.23 miles (total to summit, 1.36 miles). At 1.40 miles the road reaches the sag between the two summits and turns south, zigzagging down a ridge past the old Cloud 9 site to 1.93 miles, where trail drops into the valley to reach the Christiansen Trail at 2.37 miles. It turns north on that trail to 3.29 miles, where it leaves it to return to this trail (first around a retention dam) at 3.79 miles. Total ascent is about 800'.

Access. From Thunderbird Road drive 0.2 mile south on Central Avenue to its end, where there is an obvious parking area on the right (capacity limited).

Read Down	Detailed Road Description	Read Up
0.00	Leave gate near end of Central Avenue (elevation 1,390').	3.79
0.03	**Junction (4-way):** on L is this trail returning (0.50 mi to CMC).	3.76
0.11	Road steepens.	3.68
0.25	**Junction:** trail R descends to private land.	3.54
0.27	Hairpin turn to L.	3.52
0.33	Bend to R; grade steepens, paving starts & ends again.	3.46
0.63	Paving ends.	3.16
0.65	**Junction:** track L 575' (100' ascent) to top of hump on ridge (1,890').	3.14
0.69	**Junction:** track L onto crest.	3.10

0.72	**Junction:** track L along crest to hump.	3.07
0.84	**Junction:** ignore old track ascending on L (peters out).	2.95
1.03	**Junction:** at crest (1,980), with views, is trail sharp L onto ridge in 175' and ending in 500'.	2.76
1.23	**Junction** (elev. 2,060'): to L is road spur to summit of highest peak *[details: in 160' rough track diverges to L; in 430' is a junction -- a loop road returns on L, go straight 0.13 mi to top and relay towers. On R is black-top area for hang gliders on weekends and VP. Continuing, loop road rejoins at 0.20 mi.]* Continue on main road (paved here), descending.	2.56
1.40	**Junction:** in sag, [J] goes straight, to western summit and Sweetwater.	2.39
1.43	Metal barriers on road.	2.36
1.61	**Junction of roads:** straight ahead, branch road descends to 15th Ave. Keep L.	2.18
1.64	**Junction:** on L is road up to old Cloud 9 site; sharp L is steep track toward tower.	2.15
1.87	**Junction:** straight ahead road descends mountain; go sharp L, almost level, on branch of road.	1.92
1.93	**Junction:** where road [H] turns R to descend mountain (0.41 mi to 15th Avenue), go sharp L (E), descending on trail.	1.86
2.09	**Junction:** old road ascends valley to L; sharp R is road descending toward housing development; go half-R, descending.	1.71
2.18	Pass track on R, bear L to **junction:** track R descends to valley. Ascend.	1.62
2.20	**Junction:** track L ascends ridge, then heads E to intersect old road to CMC in 0.34 mi.	1.59
2.24	**Junction:** at top of rise, trail R leads 175' to VP. Descend steeply.	1.55
2.37	**Junction (4-way):** track R to 7th Ave.; track L to CMC in 0.22 mi. Continue straight, cross major wash.	1.42
2.44	**Junction:** CMC [100]. To R, Mountain View Park is 0.50 mi; turn L, joining CMC here.	1.35
2.50	Old gate posts on both sides. Ascend.	1.29
2.62	**Junction:** old road joins on L.	1.17
2.74	**Junction:** narrow trail R leads around knob to meet [F].	1.05
2.82	**Junction:** track to R (old road) is [F] ascending North Mountain.	0.97
3.00	**Junction:** track on L ends on slopes of Shaw Butte.	0.79
3.10	**Junction:** wide trail [B] leads R to North Mountain area and to 7th St.	0.69
3.17	**Junction:** trail on R parallels previous trail. Cross wash.	0.62
3.20	**Junction:** road angles off to L.	0.59
3.23	**Junction:** poor trail angles off to L.	0.56
3.27	**Junction:** trail R parallels CMC, joins it in 0.17 mi.	0.52
3.29	**Major junction:** *CMC turns R here* (0.48 mi to 7th St.). Go straight (1,390').	0.50
3.33	**Junction:** trail R leads back to Central Avenue.	0.46
3.38	**Junction:** trail R is short-cut over dam (not much shorter). Keep L around flood works, then head E.	0.41
3.59	**Junction:** track R to top of retention dam (short-cut). Turn L.	0.20
3.63	**Junction:** obscure track bears R in open area.	0.16
3.66	Fence line and Preserve signs.	0.13
3.71	Cross wide wash.	0.08
3.77	**Junction:** trail R leads toward Central Avenue.	0.02
3.79	**Junction:** back at start of [306]; trail-head 170' to R.	0.00

[H] Shaw Butte from 15th Avenue

General Description. Road access from the south consists of an old way to the defunct Cloud 9 restaurant site (now on [306]). There are some good views, though not so fine as from trail [306]. The rocky road, with several alternates, ascends steeply for 0.18 mile to a junction. Here an alternate diverges west. Going right, there is another alternate at 0.22 mile. Taking the longer route, the road reaches a junction with [306], where this segment ends. One can continue on [306] past the Cloud 9 site in another 0.29 mile (total of 0.60 mile), and reach the service road at the sag between the summits in a further 0.24 mile, for a total of 0.84 mile. From that junction, either branch road can be taken to Shaw Butte's summits (0.30 mile to right to the highest summit, a total of 1.14 miles; or 0.21 mile to the left to the western summit on [J], a total of 1.05 miles).

Access. Drive east on Desert Cove Avenue from 19th Avenue for 0.4 mile to 15th Avenue, then left (north) on it, to its end at a barrier at 0.7 mile. Take the obvious road heading up the mountain.

Read Down	Detailed Road Description	Read Up
0.00	Leave 15th Avenue at barrier, ascending steeply (1,390').	0.41
0.18	**Junction of roads:** alternate (western) road ascends sharp L, 0.43 mi to [306] ahead. Go straight.	0.23
0.22	**Junction:** where short-cut goes sharp L (steeper, 0.13 mi shorter), bear slightly L for main route, ascending steadily.	0.19
0.41	**Junction:** at switchback, on R, trail [306] descends to CMC in 0.51 mi.	0.00

[J] Shaw Butte from Sweetwater

General Description. This narrow, unmaintained trail is hard to see at either end. It can be used as part of a circuit trip by taking [306] up the Butte and walking the roads (Sweetwater to Thunderbird, then Central back to the start, about 1.7 miles). There are good views and the way is easy. Ascent is 660'.

Access. *From the bottom:* head south from Sweetwater, just east of the Fraternal Order of Police building, picking up the trail ahead. (Access at the south end of the FOP parking lot may be negotiated in the future.) *From the top:* at the sag on the ridge, at 1.40 miles on [306]. Once reaching the western summit, be sure to head for the power poles descending the broad ridge to pick up the trail heading west.

Read Down	Detailed Trail Description	Read Up
0.00	From Sweetwater Rd. just E of Fraternal Order of Police building and its parking area (1,300') head S without defined trail, crossing track that parallels Sweetwater toward first power pole.	0.98
0.01	**Junction (4-way):** cross track parallelling Sweetwater (parking area to E).	0.97
0.17	**Junction:** trail on R leads to FOP building (private land). Ascend.	0.81
0.20	**Junction:** at crest, switchback to L. End of ridge is 250' to R.	0.78
0.23	Jog R & L, off of crest, descending gradually. Use care. Another trail is below.	0.75
0.26	**Junction:** to L is pass and 150' further N is top of bump on ridge. Turn R here. ...	0.72
0.31	**Junction:** trail of use enters on R (leads down draw, to private land). Ascend.	0.67
0.37	**Junction:** spur trail R 45' to hump on ridge. Turn L here, up crest, then keep L of crest in 65'.	0.63
0.43	Sag in ridge. Keep to R of rocks ahead.	0.55
0.44	Ascend twisting route up ridge, which broadens. *Use care finding trail.*	0.54
0.46	Steadier ascent begins.	0.52
0.72	Cross under power line; follow it generally SE to a track.	0.26
0.77	**Junction:** end of road loop on western summit of Shaw Butte (1,960'). From here it is 1.40 mi to Central Avenue, 0.78 mi to 15th Ave. via [306] & [H]. Keep L, pass windsocks, then pass tower on L.	0.21
0.80	**Junction:** on R is crossover to other side of road loop.	0.18
0.86	Tower on L.	0.12
0.89	**Junction:** on R is end of road loop. Descend.	0.09
0.98	**Junction:** in sag on ridge, [306] goes R to CMC in 1.04 mi; straight ahead to Central Ave. trail-head in 1.40 mi. (Elevation 1,900').	0.00

City of Phoenix

Shadow Mountain Area

Shadow Mountain from Peak 1845

Introduction. Shadow Mountain is an unofficial name applied to an isolated group of summits east of Lookout Mountain. The mountain has three parts. On the north is a rounded low summit 1,779' high, here designated "Peak 1779." The central peak is the highest and steepest, Peak 1928. It has a steep-sided ridge trending south, leading to a 1,670' pass. Furthest to the south is the second-highest summit, Peak 1845. All offer good views of the valley and other nearby mountains. Ascents are 280' to 450', but some are quite steep for short distances. (Peak 1928 on the topo map has been re-measured at 1926.5'.)

Maps. *Our map 4.* The USGS Sunnyslope 1:24,000 topo (1965, photorevised in 1982) shows the topography, but none of the trails.

Access. There are several access points: (1) from the reservoir access road east of Cave Creek Road; (2) three trails off Avenue Joan d'Arc (north of 24th Street and Sweetwater) on the southeast; (3) a trail off 26th Place and Rue de l'Amour; and (4) at the northwest corner of the area at Peter Bob's Bar on Cave Creek Road.

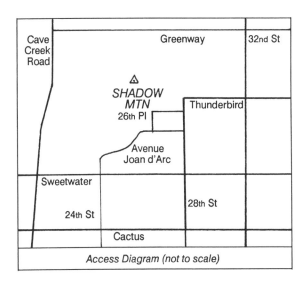

Access Diagram (not to scale)

Facilities. This is a completely undeveloped area of the Phoenix Mountains Preserve: there are no ramadas, toilets, water fountains, or trail signs.

Recommended Hikes and Trail Rides. Indicator letters and names used are our own. No trail is presently designated or maintained. The area is so criss-crossed with trails and 4-wheel drive tracks that full description of all of them would only be confusing. We have therefore chosen a few logical sequences and destinations and indicated the short links from each of these to other trails. Most trails on the east slope of Peak 1928 are in poor condition. Several trails receive frequent horse usage, especially parts of the Perimeter North [G] and Perimeter South [H] Trails.

Cautions. Preserve land often does not extend to the adjacent roads. This has resulted in trails that lead almost all the way around the recreation area, partly on private but still undeveloped land; access may be denied at any time by sign-posting or actual development. (Some of this land may be acquired subsequently for the Preserve.) Although our general policy is not to describe trails that cross private land, in this instance we have included some such trails where there is no current substitute. This has been indicated both on the map and in the text. *Be prepared to alter your plans if access is denied.*

In several locations trails have deteriorated and a double trail has resulted, with the lower of the two usually having less loose rock. The mountains in this area have steep slopes with tilted rock strata (shale) resulting in sharp-pointed rocks that can make a fall hazardous. The ridge of Peak 1928 is especially steep, as is Peak 1845 on the east side. Old four wheel drive tracks on the east-facing slopes are often steep and slippery on the descent.

[A] Peak 1928 via Reservoir

General Description. A paved road ascends 0.36 mile to a covered reservoir and trail junction. From there a wide trail leads up to the ridge at 0.57 mile and a narrower trail then leads onto the summit at 0.65 mile. Ascent is 440'.

Access. On Cave Creek Road 0.25 mile north of Shadow Drive, this gated, narrow paved road heads east. There is no parking along the shoulder of Cave Creek Road.

Read Down	Detailed Road and Trail Description	Read Up
0.00	Leave Cave Creek Road at gate (elevation 1,490').	0.65
0.03	**Junction:** in open area on L, trail [G] leads N.	0.62
0.07	**Junction:** trail [G] on R; departure point is unclear in open area.	0.58
0.22	**Junction:** Shed on L. Poor old roads ascend slope on R.	0.43
0.30	Huge reservoir tank on L. Fence starts -- keep to R (outside it).	0.35
0.36	**Junction:** trail ascends steeply on R (elev. 1,620'). (Fence ends on L in 310'; no trail beyond at that point.)	0.29
0.42	**Junction:** trail [B] on R (leads 0.10 mi to ridge, 0.24 mi to summit). Bear L, ascend.	0.23
0.45	**Junction:** narrow trail L [E] along ridge to Peak 1779 in 0.10 mi. Continue on old road on a level grade.	0.20
0.53	Turn R, ascend.	0.12
0.57	**Junction (4-way):** at crest of ridge (1,620'), trail L and straight is Perimeter Trail North [G]. Go R, along crest.	0.08
0.63	**Junction:** [C] enters on L. Final ascent begins along crest to summit.	0.03
0.65	*Summit* (USGS bench mark here indicates 1926.5'). Trail ahead along ridge is [B]. Good views.	0.00

[B] Peak 1928 via Reservoir (Alternate)

Follow [A] to 0.42 mile. At the junction (0.00 mile), ascend to the right on a good trail. Reach a junction at the crest at 0.10 mile (ahead 110' is another junction - a good horse trail descends to the south to join the Ridge Trail [F], and straight ahead a trail leads 480' along the crest, then descends 0.13 mile further to join the Perimeter North Trail [G]). From the junction, head east to 0.13 mile where [F] enters on the right, then to the summit at 0.24 mile, where it meets [A] again. Ascent is the same as [A], or 440' from Cave Creek Road. Total distance from Cave Creek Road is 0.66 mile.

[C] Peak 1928 from the East

General Description. Another (shorter) way to reach the summit ascends to a low pass, then attacks the summit ridge by way of a steep trail to 0.29 mile. Total ascent is 390'.

Access. From 26th Place where it bends east to become Rue de l'Amour. There is very limited parking along the road.

Read Down	Detailed Trail Description	Read Up
0.00	Leave bend where 26th Place becomes Rue de l'Amour, ascending between private homes.	0.29
0.05	**Junction:** trail R leads up, past a home, reaching another trail in 415'.	0.24
0.12	**Junction (4-way):** narrow trail to R [G] descends for 460' to a junction. On L, horse trail [G] ascends 550' to Ridge Trail [F]. Continue ascent.	0.17
0.21	**Junction:** in pass, a small hump is a 40' steep scramble to R, where a poor trail descends to E. Turn L here and ascend steadily.	0.08
0.25	Come out onto rocks, continuing steep ascent.	0.04
0.27	Ridge crest. In 30', reach **junction** with [A]. Go L on it to reach summit.	0.02
0.29	*Summit.* Ahead is [B] along crest (0.24 mi to [A], 0.66 mi to Cave Creek Road).	0.00

[D] Peak 1845 from the Southeast

General Description. Peak 1845 can be reached by the Ridge Trail [F] from the north; this is an alternate. A climb of only 0.31 mile leads to fine views, but note that sections are quite steep. Total ascent is 350'.

Access. From Avenue Joan d'Arc 350' (0.07 mile) east of its start at 24th Street, take the trail north, uphill.

Read Down	Detailed Trail Description	Read Up
0.00	Leave Avenue Joan d'Arc (limited road-side parking); take trail N (1,500').	0.31
0.04	**Junction:** Perimeter Trail South [H]; go L on it. (To R, roundabout route to summit of Peak 1845 takes 0.41 mi.)	0.27
0.09	**Junction (4-way):** go R (trail L to private land; trail straight ahead is Perimeter Trail South [H]). Ascend steeply with some loose rock.	0.22
0.17	**Junction:** trail on L descends to [H]; continue ascent.	0.14
0.25	**Junction:** ignore poor trail on R.	0.06
0.26	**Junction:** trail bearing L bypasses summit, leads to [F].	0.05
0.29	**Junction:** trail joins on L; go R, switchbacking up ridge. (L descends 50' to junction, then goes R 435' to connect with Ridge Trail [F].)	0.02
0.31	**Junction on crest at Peak 1845:** R leads along bumps on ridge for 385', then ends. L (N) is Ridge Trail [F] to Peak 1928 (0.57 mi away).	0.00

[E] Peak 1779

Follow [A] to 0.45 mile from Cave Creek Road, where this trail (much narrower) diverges to the left (northwest) on an easy grade. Ignore a poor trail to the right at 250'. Reach the crest of the connecting ridge at 410' (0.08 mile) and the summit at 0.10 mile. Ascent is 80'.

[F] Ridge Trail NORTH to SOUTH

General Description. Peak 1928 is connected to Peak 1845 to its south by a steep-sided ridge with several passes or sags. Use care -- some sections are quite steep. Ascent is 200'.

Access. From the crest of Peak 1928, 0.11 mile west of the summit.

Read Down	Detailed Trail Description	Read Up
0.00	Leave [B] on crest of Peak 1928, 0.11 mi to W of summit. Descend to S. Short-cut trail from [B] soon enters on L.	0.43
0.05	**Junction:** poor trail on L ascends back up ridge crest.	0.38
0.08	**Junction:** horse trail enters R from ridge.	0.35
0.09	**Junction (4-way):** Perimeter North Trail [G] L & R in pass (1,730'). Ascend to S.	0.34
0.13	**Junction:** trail splits; go either way.	0.30
0.16	**Junction:** branches rejoin.	0.27
0.18	**Junction:** in sag, wide, steep track descends L & R (both very poor). Ascend over hump.	0.25
0.23	**Junction:** poor track descends on L. Descend.	0.20
0.26	**Junction (4-way):** rocky track crosses (Perimeter South Trail [H] descends R for 0.17 mi to church; on L, Perimeter South Trail leads to Avenue Joan d'Arc in 0.15 mi).	0.17
0.29	**Junction:** trail S joins Perimeter South [H] in 385'.	0.13

0.34	**Junction:** poor track descends to R, then another within 40'.	0.09
0.36	**Junction:** trail ahead to [D] in 435' (0.08 mi).	0.07
0.38	Reach crest; continue SW on it.	0.04
0.43	**Junction at Peak 1845:** straight ahead 385' leads over bumps on crest and ends; to R is [D], 0.31 mi to Avenue Joan'd'Arc.	0.00

[G] Perimeter North Trail COUNTERCLOCKWISE

General Description. Around the northern section of the recreation area is a network of trails. This one encounters the least private land and connects with many others leading to ridges and makes possible several circuit trips around Peak 1928 for a total of 1.86 miles. There are two ascents of about 200' each.

Access. On the east side of Cave Creek Road at Peter Bob's Bar; park off the road shoulder, taking a spur trail heading southeast for 200' to the main trail.

Read Down	Detailed Trail Description	Read Up
0.00	Leave spur trail junction 200' from Cave Creek Road, heading counter-clockwise (elev. 1,480'). Parallel Cave Creek Road (private land here).	1.86
0.34	**Junction:** turn L (E) on paved reservoir access road [A] just E of gate.	1.57
0.41	**Junction:** leave paved road to SW over E end of large cleared area with trail route not distinct at first (if you go too far, the cleared area ends -- go back).	1.45
0.43	**Junction:** before open area ends, bear slightly L on narrower trail, crossing slopes to S.	1.43
0.67	**Junction:** join track that runs E-W. Parallel church parking area to S.	1.19
0.73	**Junction:** wide, steep & rocky track to L ascends past barrier to ridge in 0.13 mi and joins [B] there at 0.22 mi (0.38 mi total to Peak 1928). Turn R (S) here.	1.13
0.78	**Junction:** trail ahead is Perimeter South Trail [H]. Turn L, ascending (also Perimeter South Trail here).	1.08
0.84	**Junction:** turn L, ascend (Perimeter Trail South turns R). Parallel wash; take lower of two trails where it splits.	1.02
0.96	**Junction (4-way):** cross Ridge Trail [F]; descend with lower of two alternate routes the better one.	0.90
1.06	**Junction (4-way):** [C] crosses; R 0.12 mi to Avenue Joan d'Arc. Continue on narrower trail.	0.80
1.15	**Junction (4-way):** poor track ascends on L and descends on R (in 40' keep straight where steep track descends R to private land).	0.71
1.20	**Junction:** wide track on R descends 350' to valley and junction where trails lead E to private land.	0.67
1.22	**Junction:** narrow trail ascends L to ridge crest and [A].	0.65
1.26	**Junction:** trail R leads to private land. Continue straight.	0.60
1.29	**Junction:** trail R descends 435' to junction (where trail R leads to private land, trail L leads back up ridge).	0.57
1.31	**Junction:** trail R toward private land; bear L.	0.55
1.34	**Junction (4-way):** [A] ahead to Cave Creek Road in 0.57 mi; sharp L to Peak 1928 in 0.52 mi. Turn sharp R here onto wide track on ridge.	0.52

1.38	**Junction:** trail sharp R to bump on ridge (1,693') in 460' and several trails to private land. Turn L here, descending.	0.48
1.62	**Junction:** main trail in open area; go L here (R to private land).	0.24
1.86	**Junction:** spur trail R leads 200' to Cave Creek Road (back at start).	0.00

[H] Perimeter Trail South COUNTERCLOCKWISE

General Description. This description starts arbitrarily at the northernmost spur to Avenue Joan d'Arc, counterclockwise to lead near Peak 1845. Ascent is about 250' around the flanks of Peak 1845 for a total of 0.90 mile.

Access. Start from Avenue Joan d'Arc near where it bends to the east, ascending a steep, rocky trail. In 75' a short-cut leads southwest 315' to the Perimeter South Trail [H] southbound. Continue to 265' to intersect [H].

Read Down	*Detailed Trail Description*	*Read Up*
0.00	Leave 4-way **junction** heading N on narrower trail. Wider track (slightly L) leads 385' to Ridge Trail [F]. (This section is frequently used by horses.)	0.90
0.09	**Junction (4-way):** in sag, Ridge Trail [F] to R heads N, and to L to Peak 1845 in 0.17 mi. Continue straight ahead, descending wide, rocky track.	0.81
0.14	**Junction:** poor track ascends R to ridge. Continue rocky descent.	0.76
0.20	**Junction:** sharp R is Perimeter North Trail [G]. Join it, bearing L.	0.70
0.26	**Junction:** at church parking area, Perimeter North Trail heads N. Turn sharp L here, parallelling parking area.	0.64
0.30	**Junction:** where poor track bears L, bear R across open area, then toward church itself on narrower trail, parallelling parking area.	0.60
0.42	**Junction:** where wide track continues ahead, turn L (S) onto narrower trail.	0.48
0.51	**Junction:** where trail continues R, toward area being developed, bear L on narrower trail, ascending.	0.39
0.55	**Junction:** trail joins from R.	0.35
0.56	**Junction (4-way):** trail to R goes up, then down to area being developed in 200'; to L, trail ascends 530' to [D] on ridge.	0.34
0.65	**Junction:** trail L is [D] up Peak 1845 in 0.27 mi. Descend.	0.25
0.70	**Junction:** on R is [D] leading 195' down to Avenue Joan d'Arc.	0.20
0.79	**Junction:** spur trail R 220' to Avenue Joan d'Arc.	0.12
0.86	**Junction:** short-cut R 315' to 75' spur trail to Avenue Joan d'Arc. Ascend.	0.04
0.90	**Junction:** back at starting point: R leads down 340' to Avenue Joan d'Arc.	0.00

City of Phoenix

Squaw Peak Area

Introduction.   Squaw Peak (2,608') is the highest point in the Phoenix Mountains Preserve.[1] Its views are superb. The Summit Trail is one of the nation's most popular hikes, but there are many other attractive options. Many subsidiary peaks, humps and valleys have good trails, so that much variety is available for the hiker and trail rider. The Charles M. Christiansen Trail passes through the northern section.

History.   Squaw Peak's name was conferred by Dr. O. A. Turney in 1910. Originally the area was used for grazing and mining. The City of Phoenix obtained a long-term lease on it from the State in 1959.

Geology.   Much of this area's rock is a metamorphic type of granite known as *schist*. The mountain tops are relatively young, poking up above the valley floors, covered with varying layers of material eroded from the summits. There is no gold in the area, but many old prospect holes and pits give evidence of past mining activity. Mercury (cinnabar) mines worked in the early 1900s are alleged to have resulted in the name "Dreamy" Draw from its mental effects. Kyenite (a combination of schist and quartz) was mined during World War II. You will find many examples of *desert varnish* on rocks (see Geology chapter).

Maps.   *Our maps 7-8.* The USGS Sunnyslope topo (1965, photorevised 1982) shows a few of the trails and old roads.

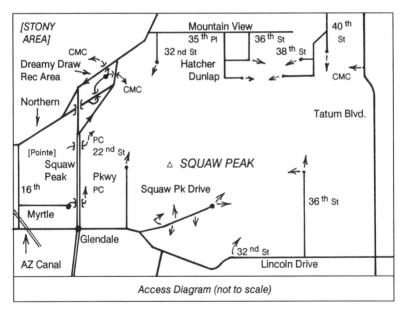

Access Diagram (not to scale)

[Previous page: Squaw Peak from Stony Mountain]

---

[1]Camelback is the highest peak in the Phoenix Mountains, but is not in the Preserve.

Access. There are 15 access points, arranged clockwise from (1) Squaw Peak Drive; (2) the Arizona Canal at 16th St., and Myrtle Trail-head [Perl Charles Trail]; (3) 22nd St.; (4) from E. Pleasant Drive through the tunnel under Squaw Peak Parkway; (5) Dreamy Draw; (6) 32nd St.; (7) 36th St. and Hatcher; (8) Dunlap east of 34th Way; (9) Hatcher west of 38th St.; (10) Dunlap west of 38th St.; (11) 38th St.; (12) 40th St.; (13) Tatum Boulevard; (14) 36th St. and Lincoln Drive; and (15) 32nd St. and Lincoln Drive. *Each of these access points is a separate section in this chapter [except (7) - (10), which have been combined].* See the **index** below to find trails.

Index. The trail descriptions are organized around "access points," clockwise from Squaw Peak Drive. (Some trails deep in the area are included under the section on the Perl Charles [1A] *"PC,"* or Charles M. Christiansen Trails [100] *"CMC."*) *All trails are indexed below:*

Designated Trails:			Trails:		
Trail	Access Point	Page	Trail	Access Point	Page
[1A]	AZ Canal/16th St./Myrtle	77	[304]	Squaw Peak Drive	71
[1A]	E. Pleasant Drive	78	[A]-[G]	Squaw Peak Drive	72
[8]	Squaw Peak Drive	66	[H]-[O]	E. Pleasant Drive	80
[100]	Dreamy Draw, 40th St.,		[P]	Dreamy Draw	87
	Tatum Blvd	84	[Q]-[R]	32nd St.	88
[200]	Squaw Peak Drive	68	[S]-[T]	Hatcher	89
[200A]	Squaw Peak Drive	68	[U]-[Z]	Dunlap	90
[220]	Dreamy Draw	86	[AA]	38th St	92
[220A]	Dreamy Draw	87	[BB]-[DD]	40th St	93
[300]	Squaw Peak Drive	68	[EE]-[GG]	36th St/Lincoln	96
[302]	Squaw Peak Drive	70	[HH]	32nd St/Lincoln	97

Facilities. Squaw Peak Drive is reached from Lincoln Drive between 16th and 24th Streets. It gives access to 17 ramadas, a ranger station, restrooms, and trails. Picnic ramadas serve up to 600, with electricity, drinking water, and firepits (8 ramadas first-come, 9 reserved).

Recommended Hikes. Trail indicators used here are either official City of Phoenix numbers, or our own arbitrary letters for non-designated trails.

> *The overwhelming number of trails in this area has required simplification or the length of the chapter would be prohibitive. Where there is a maze of trails with many alternates, we have chosen those that are most important or best-used and have indicated the others on the maps IN BLACK.*

The immensely popular Squaw Peak Summit Trail [300] is 1.20 miles long (ascent of 1,190'). Good views are obtained at points along the ridge without having to proceed all the way to the summit. The less crowded Circumference Trail [302] starts from the Summit Trail and leads all the way around the mountain over four passes (a long, strenuous trip). There is a Nature Trail [304] from the end of Squaw Peak Drive and one [220] from Dreamy Draw, with an associated shorter Children's Nature Loop [220A]. The Quartz Ridge Trail [8] leads from the Squaw Peak Nature Trail to the Charles M. Christiansen Trail through an attractive area. From the south side of the drive, short trails such as the Mohave [200] ascend the lower peaks which offer close-up views of Squaw Peak. These are linked up with various other segments. New trails are planned there.

The easiest access to good views is from the end of 22nd Street north of Glendale. This is also a short-cut onto the Circumference Trail without climbing over the Squaw Peak ridge. From the north, access is good from several points.

Important Note. The Squaw Peak Parkway (State Route 51) is being constructed through Dreamy Draw, with completion to Shea Boulevard scheduled for 1993. Parking will not be allowed on the road shoulder; only official access points can be used. The approach to Dreamy Draw from Northern will undergo change as the Parkway is completed. The new Myrtle Trail-head adjacent to the Perl Charles Trail [1A] will provide another main access point, especially for equestrians. The three new trail tunnels under the Parkway are wider and have much better lighting.

Squaw Peak Drive Access Points

[8] Quartz Ridge Trail SOUTH to NORTH

General Description. From the pass north of the end of Squaw Peak Drive on the Nature Trail [304] the Quartz Ridge Trail descends a valley, then crosses the divide between two major washes and heads east to a junction with [EE] at 1.01 miles. Here it turns north, ascending to a pass at 1.09 miles. It then makes a long descent past a quartz outcrop to reach the Christiansen Trail at 2.01 miles, 0.44 mile south of 40th Street. Total ascent is 220'.

Access. Take the Nature Trail [304] from the end of Squaw Peak Drive for 0.36 mile to the pass. This trail starts just 30' beyond, angling off to the right.

Read Down	*Detailed Trail Description*	*Read Up*
0.00	Leave Nature Trail [304] just 30' N of pass.	2.01
0.43	**Junction:** half-L is spur 100' to old road, then 290' L to [N].	1.58
0.53	**Junction:** join old road on L, head E.	1.48
0.62	**Junction:** short-cut trail L to [N].	1.39
0.65	**Junction:** old road sharp L 0.20 mi to [N]. Follow road to R.	1.36
0.74	**Junction:** sharp L is crossover across wash 250' to [DD].	1.27
0.75	Turn R in wash, following it.	1.26

0.77	**Junction:** trail R is [GG] heading S to [FF]. Continue in wash, then ascend R, out of it.	1.25
0.95	**Junction:** old track sharp L [DD].	1.07
1.01	**Junction:** road [EE] on R (leads S to 36th St in 0.62 mi). Turn sharp L.	1.00
1.06	Road ends; descend on trail briefly.	0.95
1.08	Ascend, level off briefly in 100'.	0.94
1.19	Pass (1,860'). Good views, especially off trail to E.	0.83
1.24	**Junction:** trail splits, alternate on R.	0.77
1.29	Cross wash.	0.73
1.30	**Junction:** alternate rejoins on R. Pass field of cactus.	0.71
1.48	**Junction:** at cairn, obscure trail ascends to join [BB].	0.53
1.50	Cross small wash.	0.51
1.54	Approach wash; reach level area along it on L in 150'.	0.48
1.65	**Junction:** trail of use half-L.	0.36
1.68	Flat area.	0.34
1.69	**Junction:** cat road leads steadily up to R, 0.12 mi to [BB].	0.32
1.75	**Junction:** obscure trail L.	0.26
2.01	**Junction:** CMC L & R. To R it is only 0.07 mi to the junction of entrance spurs to 40th St. and Tatum Blvd.	0.00

On the Circumference Trail

[200] Mohave Trail

General Description. Access to several scenic areas is possible from this short trail leading up the ridge south of Squaw Peak, including [E] or [F] up Peak 1920. The views of Squaw Peak are very fine. Ascent is 270'.

Access. Leave Mohave Ramada (off Squaw Peak Drive at 0.8 mile) near its eastern end. Use care because of several alternate routes and steep slopes.

Read Down	Detailed Trail Description	Read Up
0.00	Leave Mohave Ramada (paved loop off Squaw Peak Drive, elevation 1,500'), ascending S from upper ramada.	0.38
0.08	**Junction:** on R is alternate trail back to Mohave Ramada in 0.08 mi. From this point ascent eases as trail contours around minor 1,700' summit.	0.30
0.09	**Junction:** trail on L ascends steeply 165' to crest, then 250' further to minor peak (1,700'). Above are very sharp rock formations. Head into valley with very good views of Squaw Peak.	0.29
0.21	**Junction:** in pass (1,610'), to R, poor trail descends toward Navajo Ramada. To L, wide old trail descends 460' to join [D]. To continue up Peak 1788, cross pass, bear slightly L (W) and up, keeping to L of crest.	0.17
0.24	**Junction:** alternate trail rejoins.	0.14
0.29	Switchback to R (*use care*, trail appears to continue ahead, but ends).	0.09
0.32	Switchback to L at crest. (Poor trail to R descends.)	0.06
0.37	**Junction:** this trail turns R. (Wide trail ahead here leads onto flat area, then trail [B] descends ridge to Squaw Peak Drive in 0.56 mi.) Go R.	0.01
0.38	**Junction:** narrow trail ahead leads toward actual summit (can be scrambled up); trail to L on flat leads 40' to hitching post.	0.00

[200A]

From the Mohave Ramada (1,500'), this short trail ascends southeast for 0.09 mile (130'). Ignore a trail of use in 260', and other alternate, rutted routes. At the top is a pass (1,630') and 4-way junction. Narrow trail [F] to the left leads up Peak 1920 in 0.30 mile. Ahead, there is a narrow, deeply rutted trail [D] descending to the valley. To continue, turn right (west), contouring along the side of the ridge. In 150' more (at 0.13 mile), this trail ends at [200], which leads sharp right, back to the ramada in 0.08 mile, or ahead toward Peak 1788.

[300] Squaw Peak Summit Trail

General Description. The popularity of this trail is legendary. Hundreds of hikers and runners use it every day, thousands on weekends. (Trail rehabilitation was under way in 1991.) The trail starts from either end of the parking area; a sign indicates the park rules. Switchbacks are numerous. At 0.23 mile the crest of the first ridge is reached and a junction with side-trails (one to a hump on the ridge, the other [G] returns to Squaw Peak Drive). From here the trail swings from one to the other side of the ridge, reaching a major junction at 0.57 mile where the Circumference Trail [302] descends north. The crest becomes rougher, with frequent steep rock bluffs so that the trail only occasionally crosses it. Steepness increases after 0.90 mile, with occasional handrails. At 1.14 miles the grade steepens to some scrambling over open rocks and finally a notch is reached. To the left is the peak usually climbed; to the right, a scramble leads to the true summit, both at 1.20 miles from the start. Views are fantastic! Ascent is 1,190'.

Access. After entering the Recreation Area on Squaw Peak Drive, take the first left turn (spur road) to the parking area. The prominent trail leaves either end, with a green and yellow sign near their junction. (Maintenance is by the Squaw Peak Hiking Club.)

Read Down	*Detailed Trail Description*	*Read Up*
0.00	Leave parking area at sign (1,420').	1.20
0.04	**Junction:** trail from E end of parking area joins from R.	1.16
0.13	Switchback to R, then to L.	1.07
0.18	VP (1,500'). Turn R (N).	1.02
0.23	**Junction:** trail L leads onto hump on ridge in 600' with good views (1,540').	0.97
0.24	**Junction:** trail L [G] descends side-valley to return to Squaw Peak Drive in 0.33 mi (it also intersects previous trail to hump on ridge).	0.96
0.27	Switchback to L.	0.94
0.29	Turn R, onto ridge, then R again.	0.92
0.32	First of 4 switchbacks in next 250'.	0.89
0.41	Switchback to L (SW). Elevation 1,700'.	0.80
0.43	**Junction:** reach subsidiary ridge crest; short trail to L leads to rocky outcrop. Turn R here, then bear L.	0.77
0.48	Level area on crest; in 150' switchback to R (N).	0.73
0.57	**Junction (4-way):** Circumference Trail [302] drops to L. Sharp L is old trail 0.32 mi down to Circumference Trail (avoid it). Elevation 1,890'.	0.63
0.60	First of 6 switchbacks in next 0.11 mi.	0.60
0.72	Reach crest just N of outcrop, then drop over side, following ridge to W of it.	0.49
0.86	Switchback to R over to crest, then zigzag up.	0.34
0.90	Brief level area on crest (2,190'), with tree providing some shade.	0.30
0.92	Switchback to R (SE), then L, then R. Continuous steep switchbacks beyond.	0.28
0.98	Reach crest (2,270').	0.22
1.02	Switchback to L, between rocks.	0.18
1.04	Railing on R. Good views.	0.17
1.07	Switchback to R (E), then to L, with railing.	0.13
1.09	On crest, switchback to R. Grade eases.	0.11
1.10	Switchback to L.	0.11
1.11	Reach crest again, head N. Grade eases.	0.09
1.14	Final ascent begins over very steep rocks, some of which are loose. *Use care*.	0.06
1.19	Notch between two summits. Turn L for one usually ascended.	0.01
1.20	*North Summit, Squaw Peak* (elev. 2,580'). For highest (S) summit (2,608'), head SE from notch, descending on E side of crest, then cautiously work your way up to the peak over sharp rocks.	0.00

[302] Circumference Trail CLOCKWISE

General Description. This is one of the finest trails in this guidebook. It starts on Squaw Peak's ridge and makes a long (0.39 mile) switchbacking descent to the valley from Squaw Peak's ridge. You then head north, crossing several washes, to a minor ridge crest and then a pass where the Perl Charles Trail joins at 0.91 mile. From there it starts a long 500' ascent to the highest pass at 1.68 miles. The Perl Charles Trail and Nature Trail [304] then diverge at 2.07 miles. The route winds southward through the valley to the end of Squaw Peak Drive (which is reached via the Nature Trail at 2.64 miles from the start) and continues along the west side of the parkway to return to the Summit Trail parking area at 3.17 miles (3.74 miles total if the first part of the Summit Trail is included).

Access. From 0.57 mile on the Squaw Peak Summit Trail, or from junctions on the Perl Charles Trail [1A] at 2.78 miles and 3.97 miles and on the Nature Trail [304] at 0.06 mile and 0.62 mile. It can also be reached from the Hopi and Navajo ramadas on the north side of Squaw Peak Drive.

Read Down	*Detailed Trail Description*	*Read Up*
0.00	From 0.57 mile on Squaw Peak Summit Trail [300] (1,890'), descend to N. Switchbacks start in 80'.	3.17
0.12	Switchback #7, to L. Makes a long traverse, followed by 10 switchbacks.	3.05
0.36	Bear R (W).	2.81
0.37	**Junction:** near here is obscure junction to old trail leading back onto Squaw's ridge -- avoid it.	2.80
0.39	**Junction:** trail L leads to private land (no sign here). Turn R, ascending gradually to N.	2.78
0.44	Cross a wash.	2.73
0.53	Shade tree on R. Ascend steadily.	2.64
0.56	Cross a wash, then another in 0.04 mi.	2.61
0.65	Turn R, into a wash, then L out of it.	2.52
0.66	Switchback R, ascend steadily, then L.	2.51
0.71	Reach ridge crest (1,660') with good views. Grade levels.	2.46
0.75	Trail zigzags L and R, descending, then levels out.	2.42
0.83	Cross a wash, bear L, then descend gradually.	2.34
0.91	**Junction in pass** (1,610'): trail descending ahead is Perl Charles Memorial Trail (junction in valley is 0.23 mi away; leads W to 22nd St. access point). Bear R here (with Perl Charles coinciding), ascending away from pass.	2.26
0.98	Top of rise (1,630') in level, pleasant area.	2.29
1.06	Cross wide wash, then climb N out of it.	2.21
1.17	Switchback to R, ascending steadily.	2.10
1.19	Level area, cairn. Head into valley (not the one trail finally climbs).	2.18
1.22	Turn L, ascending steadily to N, then turn R.	2.15
1.29	Top of rise (1,840'); descend.	2.08
1.30	Cross a wash and ascend, then another wash in 0.16 mi.	2.07
1.49	**Junction:** trail to L [M] ascends to pass, drops to meet CMC & PC trails. Final pass now in view ahead. Elevation here 1,920'.	1.68
1.54	Switchback to L, then to R in 150',then ignore trail of use crossing.	1.63

1.59	Switchback to L (VP just off trail to R). Start final ascent over loose rock; use care.	1.58
1.68	**Junction in pass:** here, at elevation 2,120', a wide un-numbered trail to W ascends to a crest at 300', then tops a rise at 500' with good views (deteriorates beyond and is not recommended). To continue, descend 200' in elevation from pass on loose, rocky trail with 9 switchbacks.	1.49
1.89	Turn L (N), then bear R.	1.28
1.90	**Junction:** [O] diverges L. Elevation 1,900'.	1.27
1.97	Cross wash.	1.20
2.07	**Junction:** PC/Nature Trail [304] go R; Nature Trail coincides from here.	1.10
2.14	Post #6 on Nature Trail.	1.03
2.15	**Junction:** sharp L is crossover to Nature Trail in 480'. Ascend gradually to S.	1.02
2.20	Post #5 on Nature Trail; then reach **junction** on L with crossover trail 0.23 mi to Nature Trail.	0.97
2.26	Trail diverges, then rejoins in 125'; take either branch.	0.91
2.30	Post #3 on Nature Trail.	0.87
2.32	Cross wash.	0.85
2.40	Descend S-curve. Trail of use and steep-walled canyon on L.	0.77
2.58	**Junction:** trail post for [302]. [Straight ahead, Nature Trail descends into wash at 200', bears L and ascends up a concrete, walled path, reaching signboard at NW corner of parking area at end of Squaw Peak Drive in 350', for total of 2.64 mi (3.21 mi from start of Squaw Peak Summit Trail).]	0.59
2.64	Cross wash, bear L and level out.	0.53
2.75	**Junction:** trail straight ahead leads to Hopi Ramada in 110'. Bear R here, ascend gradually.	0.42
2.77	Pass large rock on R.	0.40
2.78	**Junction:** trail on L descends to parking area. Bear R, ascend more steadily.	0.39
2.79	Sign-post (trail of use descends here).	0.38
2.80	**Junction (4-way):** cross a wide track, then level out.	0.37
2.92	Bear R, ascend; then cross a wash, descend again, crossing 2 small washes.	0.25
3.07	**Junction:** cross track ascending sharp R, and narrow trail of use half-R.	0.10
3.12	**Junction:** at E end of parking lot, a trail ascends to join Summit Trail.	0.05
3.17	W end of parking lot, Summit Trail start (1,440').	0.00

[304] Squaw Peak Nature Trail CLOCKWISE

General Description. This is a 1.52 mile long loop trail with several short-cuts. There are 21 numbered posts keyed to a nature brochure. It provides access to the Perl Charles Trail [1A] from Squaw Peak Drive. (In 1988 it was adopted by the Mountaineers for maintenance.)

Access. Head north from the end of Squaw Peak Drive down a paved path (or from the Apache Ramada, descend 100' to wash, joining trail in 100').

Read Down	Detailed Trail Description	Read Up
0.00	Leave end of Squaw Peak Drive at signboard where steps lead down into wash. ...	1.43
0.06	**Junction:** Circumference Trail [302] L to base of Squaw Peak and other ramadas. Go straight.	1.37

0.32	Cross wash.	1.11
0.34	Post #3 on Nature Trail.	1.09
0.38	**Junction:** trail splits, rejoins.	1.05
0.44	**Junction:** trail of use on R, then Post #5.	0.99
0.49	**Junction:** crossover on R to Nature Trail in 0.23 mi. Keep L, with Circumference Trail.	0.94
0.54	**Junction:** short-cut bears R; turn L here, with Circumference Trail.	0.89
0.62	**Junction:** go sharp R on PC [1A] where Circumference Trail goes L.	0.81
0.71	**Junction:** where short-cut goes sharp R, bear L, crossing wash.	0.72
0.73	**Junction:** old mine road on L [N]; go R on it, with PC.	0.70
0.77	**Junction:** PC leaves this trail, ascending L. Continue on road.	0.66
0.82	**Junction:** poor trail of use R, crossing wash.	0.61
0.85	**Junction (4-way):** trail of use L joins PC in 0.10 mi; ahead is [N] to CMC. Turn R, cross wash in 200'.	0.58
0.98	**Junction:** crossover trail enters, sharp R.	0.45
1.07	**Junction:** Quartz Ridge Trail [8] sharp L; pass (1,790') 30' beyond.	0.36
1.21	**Junction:** trail splits briefly, rejoins.	0.22
1.24	Descend to cross wash, then ascend out of it.	0.19
1.30	**Junction:** on L, trail leads up to pass and [FF] in about 0.36 mi (360' ascent, good views), and other trails of use.	0.13
1.34	**Junction (4-way):** on R, trail of use leads to edge of wash; on L trail (not well-defined) joins maze of trails leading E, up toward pass.	0.09
1.38	**Junction:** trail of use straight ahead; bear L, cross wash in 100'.	0.05
1.43	Squaw Peak Drive (1,610'). Original start is just to L.	0.00

[A]

This formerly undesignated trail has now been absorbed into the extension of [200] from the Mohave Ramada (see that description).

[B] Peak 1788 from the West

General Description. This is an old trail, now eroded and brushy in spots, that was originally constructed for equestrian use. It offers very good views. For 0.27 mile it heads south on an easy grade, then turns up the ridge by means of 7 switchbacks to reach the junction near the summit of Peak 1788 at 0.56 mile. Ascent is 360'. From here, descent can be made via [200] back to Squaw Preak drive.

Access. From Squaw Peak Drive, at the first paved parking area on the south side (0.2 mile from the start of the desert area), 0.5 mile from its start.

Read Down	Detailed Trail Description	Read Up
0.00	Leave Squaw Peak Drive at parking area (1,400').	0.56
0.01	**Junction:** trail [C] on R; keep L.	0.55
0.05	**Junction:** poor track sharp R. Ascend gradually.	0.51
0.10	**Junction:** near top of rise, leave track by ascending L (SE) at small cairn. *[use care here -- junction is not obvious in open area.]* (Ahead is [C].)	0.46
0.26	Hitching post on L.	0.30
0.27	**Junction (4-way):** in open area, trail ahead is to private land. Turn sharp L on eroded trail. (Ahead is [D] back to either end of [200].)	0.29
0.31	Switchbacks (7 of them) start.	0.25
0.37	**Junction:** trail splits: go straight (rejoins in 60').	0.19
0.53	Level out (note striations on rocks to L).	0.03
0.56	**Junction:** at top of rise (1,760'), trail [200] leads NE down to Squaw Peak Drive (0.38 mi). (On L is short, unclear route to top of Peak 1788.)	0.00

[C] COUNTERCLOCKWISE LOOP

From a parking area 0.2 mile from the edge of the Preserve on Squaw Peak Drive, take a trail east from the far end of the lot for 150', dropping into a wash and joining a track 195' from Squaw Peak Drive. (At 60' from the Drive, tracks diverge.) Keep right, along a wash at an easy grade, gradually bearing left around a ridge. At 0.28 mile from the road there is a junction: sharp right leads to the wash and private land (keep left). Reach the top of a rise at 0.40 mile. Descend for only 135' and turn left off the track onto a faint trail for 135', then go left again, away from the fence ahead. Join another old track at 0.50 mile, heading northeast around the other side of the ridge. At 0.66 mile, just past a low pass, trail [B] diverges sharp right and leads straight ahead 0.10 mile back to the Drive for a total of 0.76 mile. Ascent is 50'.

[D] SOUTHWEST to NORTHEAST

General Description. From trail [B] this old horse trail connects with the pass above the Mohave Ramada on [200] and makes several circuit trips possible.

Access. *At the southwestern end:* from trail [B] at 0.27 mile; *at the northeastern end:* from [200], 0.06 mile above Mohave Ramada.

On the Christiansen Trail near Dreamy Draw

On the Quartz Ridge Trail

Read Down	Detailed Trail Description	Read Up
0.00	Leave junction with [B], heading NE (elev. 1,500').	0.50
0.08	**Junction:** go L, then in 30' switchback to L, then R.	0.42
0.11	**Junction:** trail splits briefly, rejoins in 80', then switchback to L.	0.39
0.13	Switchback to R; reach top of rise in 0.08 mi.	0.37
0.23	**Junction:** trail continuing on leads 460' to a junction (trail [200] on L, and 50' further to pass on [200].) Go R here, then switchback to R and L.	0.27
0.27	**Junction:** ignore trail sharp R descending to private land. Keep straight on, ascending.	0.23
0.44	**Junction:** trail [E] leads sharp R to Peak 1920. Continue up to L, switchbacking to R in 30'.	0.06
0.50	**Junction:** this trail ends in pass at [200A] (1,630'). Descent may be made from here to Mohave Ramada in 0.09 mi.. On the R, Trail [F] ascends to Peak 1920.	0.00

[E] Peak 1920 From SOUTHWEST via LOOP

General Description. An excellent circuit trip leads over a scenic ridge to Peak 1920, then loops back with fine views of the Squaw Peak range. Total distance is 1.76 miles. Ascent is 420'.

Access. From pass on ridge on [200A] (0.09 mile from the Mohave Ramada), take [D] south for 330' to junction, then turn sharp left. This is 0.15 mile from Mohave Ramada.

Read Down	Detailed Trail Description	Read Up
0.00	Leave junction with [D] (1,540'), turning R in 30'.	1.54
0.14	Top of rise.	1.40
0.22	**Junction:** trail straight ahead is this trail returning. Ascend by bearing L. *Note: corner here is overgrown.* Start series of 6 switchbacks in 80'.	1.32
0.36	Top of rise, descend briefly.	1.18
0.37	Pass (1,620'). Ascend brushy trail. In 135' 7 switchbacks start.	1.17
0.45	VP; switchback to L, then turn R on crest.	1.10
0.48	Pass (1,710'). In 60' switchbacks (7 in all) start.	1.07
0.58	Top of rise; cross to R of crest on rocks.	0.96
0.60	Switchback to L, then 2 more.	0.94
0.63	**Junction:** trail descending on L is [F]. Turn sharp R and up (2 switchbacks).	0.91
0.69	Summit, Peak 1920. (55' further is hitching rail.) Turn R, descend switchbacks.	0.85
0.75	Pass (1,870'), **junction:** trail of use to N. Descend to S.	0.79
0.85	Switchback to R (trail of use on L).	0.69
0.87	**Junction:** obscure trail on L; keep R.	0.67
0.90	Cross small wash with eroding sides. Descend switchbacks on very attractive trail	0.64
1.06	**Junction:** descend sharp R where there is an alternate.	0.48
1.08	**Junction:** short-cut enters on R.	0.46

1.09	**Junction:** go sharp R, switchbacking down. (Straight ahead up ridge leads to private land.)	0.45
1.19	**Junction:** trail to private land on L. Go R, ascending.	0.36
1.26	Cross wash. Trail is very pleasant.	0.28
1.37	Switchback to L, descending, then to R.	0.17
1.42	**Junction:** keep straight (avoid old road on L).	0.12
1.49	**Junction:** go slightly R.	0.05
1.54	**Junction:** you are back at 0.22 mi junction (1,500'). Total to start of trail is 1.76 mi.	0.00

[F] Peak 1920 from Northwest

From pass on ridge on trail [200A] at 0.09 mile from Mohave Ramada, head southeast up the ridge. The way consists of 17 switchbacks. The ridge is reached at 0.24 mile. Here is trail [E]. Turn left up it for only 0.06 mile to the summit. Ascent is 240' to junction with [E], 290' to summit.

[G]

If you want some variety and solitude for the lower part of the Squaw Peak Summit Trail [300], or just a quick circuit trip with views, try this trail. From the entrance of Squaw Peak Drive into the Preserve, the base of this trail is 600' (0.11 mile) to where there is an unpaved parking area on the right (south). [If you go too far, there will be a paved parking area (for [C]) in 400'.] The trail starts as a rather indistinct track on the north side of the Drive, heading northwest for 260', where it bears right (north) toward a valley. It narrows and starts to parallel the wash and ascend at 0.12 mile, then more steadily at 0.25 mile. It is then steady all the way to a junction at 0.32 mile where a spur trail leads right to a hump on the ridge in 200'. Continue on for another 40' to the Squaw Peak Summit Trail [300] at 0.33 mile. Ascent is 230'.

22nd Street Access Point

This is an excellent access point for the Perl Charles Trail [1A] and to get views from passes in the ridge or from the tops of minor peaks. Drive north from Glendale Avenue on 22nd Street to its end (there is limited on-street parking). The trail leads 270' to the Perl Charles junction, where it is 0.28 mile left, over a ridge, to Monument Junction, and only 0.16 mile right to the pass (views). The Circumference Trail is 0.63 mile to the right.

Arizona Canal/16th St./Myrtle Access Points

The Sun Circle Trail will eventually loop around the entire Phoenix area, connecting with numerous minor and major parks. Its development is being overseen by the Maricopa County Parks and Recreation Department. A section follows the northeast bank of the Arizona Canal, connecting with the Phoenix Mountains Preserve via the Perl Charles Trail [1A] from 16th Street *[see description below]*. (For more information about the Perl Charles Trail, and its main loop, see the E. Pleasant Drive Access Point.)

[1A] Perl Charles Trail

FROM ARIZONA CANAL to "MONUMENT JUNCTION"

General Description. This section leads north along a right-of-way constructed next to the sidewalk on the east side of 16th Street to Myrtle, then east along the north side of Myrtle until it enters Myrtle Wash. It passes the end of Myrtle Road where there is a trail-head parking area on the south side, and enters a long tunnel under the Squaw Peak Parkway. It then heads north, between the Parkway and 20th Street. The houses are rounded at 1.06 miles and the monument is reached at 1.25 miles, 300' south of the access point. *For the continuation of this trail, see the E. Pleasant Drive Access Point.*

Access. *From the south:* from the point where 16th Street crosses the Arizona Canal. *From the north:* just east of the tunnel under the Squaw Peak Parkway from E. Pleasant Drive, a total of 0.19 mile, then south 300' to junction.

Read Down	Detailed Trail Description	Read Up
0.00	Leave Arizona Canal at 16th St. (N-side paved bike route), paralleling 16th St, heading N on its E side - Perl Charles Monument here.	1.25
0.13	Cross Myrtle to N side, turn R along it.	1.12
0.25	Cross N. Dreamy Draw Drive, then enter Myrtle Wash.	1.00
0.50	Parking area above (to S) at end of Myrtle. Go thru long tunnel.	0.75
0.55	Turn L (N) on E side of tunnel, paralleling Parkway & 20th St.	0.70
1.06	Round corner of housing development on R.	0.19
1.09	**Junction:** in open area where track heads N, ascend half-R (NE).	0.16
1.12	**Junction:** track R over pass leads to Peak 1570 and to 22nd St; head N.	0.13
1.14	**Junction:** track on R joins previous track.	0.11
1.22	**Junction:** go half-L to join parallel road. Sharp R is PC loop returning.	0.02
1.25	**Monument Junction:** trail sharp R leads to higher-level track in 100'. Straight ahead 300' on service road (PC) is trail & road L, 0.19 mi to E. Pleasant Drive & Pointe at Squaw Peak via tunnel.	0.00

E. Pleasant Drive Access Point

There is a tunnel under the Squaw Peak Parkway just east of the end of E. Pleasant Drive (there is very limited on-street parking). Here horses from local stables and horses and hikers from The Pointe at Squaw Peak enter the Preserve. This approach follows the service road south from the east end of the tunnel to the Perl Charles Trail (here the service road) for a total of 0.19 mile. "Monument Junction" is 300' south on the trail. The Perl Charles Trail northbound first heads briefly northeast, then east and north to the "cookout area" above a major wash. This is used periodically by The Pointe (by permit), and Pointe vehicles service the area.

The plaque on the Perl Charles Trail monument near E. Pleasant Drive has this inscription: "Dedicated to one who worked endlessly for the preservation of the mountains he loved." It was erected on April 10, 1982, by the Phoenix Mountains Preservation Council, Park Foundation of Phoenix, and the City of Phoenix Parks, Recreation and Library Department. *The photo on the right is of Perl Charles and his horse River Mac marking the "Squaw Peak Corner" of the original Squaw Peak Park.*

[1A] Perl Charles Trail CLOCKWISE

General Description. From Monument Junction the trail follows horse paths north past the "cookout area" at 0.40 mile, then ascends east up a valley past two mine shafts, turns north over a pass, and descends to reach the Charles M. Christiansen Trail at 1.15 miles. It coincides briefly with that trail, then heads southeast for higher country, rising along the flank of Squaw Peak and several passes to reach the Nature Trail [304] at 2.63 miles which it briefly joins, then joins the Circumference Trail at 2.78 miles and coincides with it over a high pass (at 3.17 miles), descends "Hidden Valley" and leaves the Circumference Trail at 3.97 miles to cross the valley. It then ascends over another pass to reach the 22nd Street Access at 4.55 miles and makes a final rise over a ridge to rejoin itself at Monument Junction at 4.83 miles. *[Add 1.25 miles to distances below for travel to or from the Arizona Canal at 16th St.]*

Access. From "Monument Junction," 0.19 mile east of the end of E. Pleasant Drive, via the tunnel under the Squaw Peak Parkway, then 300' south.

Read Down	Detailed Trail Description	Read Up
0.00	Leave Monument Junction, head N.	4.83
0.02	**Junction:** trail L rejoins spur to Monument.	4.81
0.09	**Junction (4-way):** on R trail connector ascends to join PC (counterclockwise) in 415'. Trail L descends to cross road, reaches junction at E end of tunnel at 530' (0.10 mi). Continue straight.	4.74
0.11	**Junction (4-way):** on R is [H] to ridge in 795'; on L, trail leads to horse tunnel in 0.12 mi. Head N, *keeping L where trail doubles (later it triples).*	4.72
0.19	**Junction (on parallel trail):** trail sharp R back to connector to ridge in 315'.	4.64
0.40	**Junction:** ahead 180' on trail [J] is cookout area (and toilets in wash, beyond).	4.43
0.44	**Junction (5-way, complex):** L leads back to cookout area, sharp R is parallel trail to S, half-L is track into valley (385'; poorer route leads up it, parallelling PC). PC bears R, with steady ascent.	4.39
0.62	**Junction (4-way):** at mine shaft, sharp L is poor trail descending to valley; half-L is trail 60' down to valley. Continue straight along hillside.	4.21
0.68	**Junction:** poor steep, rocky track descends mine tailings to L.	4.15
0.69	**Junction:** at second mine shaft, on R steep trail ascends 0.12 mi to crest and junction with [K] (descends to [L] in 0.16 mi).	4.14
0.71	**Junction:** eroded trail of use descends to valley trail in 120'. Start rocky ascent, switchbacking.	4.12
0.80	Pass (1,699'), **junction:** trail R is [K] to [L] in 0.32 mi. Descend.	4.03
0.88	**Junction:** at sharp bend in mine road, L leads down to [J] in 0.16 mi. Continue along easy old road, ascending gradually past trail of use on L.	3.95
1.21	**Important junction:** CMC L & R. Go R on it.	3.62
1.24	**Junction:** L to Dreamy Draw Nature Trail [220] in 0.10 mi.	3.59
1.34	**Junction:** R is trail [L] over pass to PC in 0.73 mi.	3.49
1.37	**Important junction:** PC leaves CMC by ascending to R.	3.46
1.46	**Junction:** trail R (spur to [M]) in 100'.	3.37
1.51	**Junction (4-way):** old mine road, L, & R [M] to PC/Circumference Trails in 0.40 mi. Continue straight. Pass cut-off L (N) to road in 40'.	3.32
1.55	**Junction:** mine road on R. Bear L.	3.28
1.60	**Junction:** mine road on R; join it, heading L. In 250' road ends, trail starts. Cross several washes.	3.23
1.72	**Junction (4-way):** poor track descends on L; on R, [O] leads up to junction in 0.20 mi, then over pass to PC/Circumference/Nature Trails.	3.11
1.88	**Junction:** where poorer trail ascends R, keep L; cross trail of use in 120'.	2.95
1.92	**Junction:** trail on L descends to CMC in 0.17 mi. Turn R here, descend.	2.91
1.99	**Junction (5-way):** track descends on L, ascends on R (joins [O] in 0.20 mi.; trail comes in just ahead, sharp R. Continue straight, passing poor trail of use on R.	2.84
2.15	**Junction (4-way):** track L & R. From here, PC ascends along hillside.	2.68
2.40	Pass (1,727') with knob to E. Descend S.	2.43
2.49	**Junction:** ahead, trail descends to old mine road [N] in 0.10 mi. Turn sharp R, uphill, then descend to valley.	2.34
2.63	**Junction:** Nature Trail [304] on L. Join it and go R.	2.20
2.67	**Junction:** where old road [N] ascends on R, leave it on L, descending to cross major wash.	2.16
2.69	**Junction:** short-cut trail L to Nature Trail and end of Squaw Peak Drive; go R.	2.14
2.78	**Junction:** Nature Trail [304] leaves, sharp L. Turn R here, uphill, joining Circumference Trail [302], ascending switchbacks and rocky trail.	2.05
2.95	**Junction:** trail [O] on R over pass joins PC in 0.49 mi.	1.88
3.17	Pass. Trail L to VP in 500'. Descend.	1.66

3.36	**Junction:** trail [M] on R, descends to cross wash, then ascends over pass to PC in 0.40 mi.	1.47
3.97	**Important junction:** Circumference Trail [302] bears L in pass; go sharp R, descending toward valley (1,645').	0.88
4.16	Leave poor track ahead, switchback R and down to cross major wash.	0.67
4.18	**Junction:** trail of use on R splits and leads around minor hump ahead to connect with [L] in 0.16 mi. Go sharp L here along wash.	0.65
4.25	**Junctions:** 2 trail junctions are 45' apart. At upper one, trail straight ahead [H] leads over pass to reach ridge above PC trail in 0.30 mi.; trail R is [L], up valley and over pass to PC. Turn sharp L, ascend hillside.	0.58
4.39	Pass (1,593'). Switchback down, avoiding eroded track directly ahead.	0.44
4.55	**Junction:** on L is 22nd St Access in 270'. Turn R, uphill.	0.28
4.64	**Junction:** track R leads up ridge. Ascend steadily.	0.19
4.67	Pass (1,483'), **junction:** trail R is connector 175' to [H]; to L, two trails rejoin and ascend Peak 1570 in 350', or side-hill S to reach pass in 400' and descend to PC in 0.28 mi. Descend.	0.16
4.73	**Junction:** track R descends to PC in 415'. Go L.	0.10
4.83	**Monument Junction 20' to R.**	0.00

[H]

From Perl Charles Trail at 0.11 mile (1,368'), ascend east up the ridge. A trail joins on the left in 290' (315' north to the Perl Charles Trail). Swing around to the south. At 0.10 mile there is a junction where a poor, rocky track ascends sharp left to the crest. Keep right here, ascending to the crest (1,492') and a 4-way junction at 0.15 mile. (Ahead, a track descends 120' to the Perl Charles Trail. On the right, a trail leads 175' past a knob to a 5-way junction on the ridge and the Perl Charles trail at 4.50 miles.) Turn left, ascending along the side of the ridge. At 0.23 mile there is a junction with the track that diverged at 0.10 mile. Continue rising until the pass is reached at 0.36 mile. Here there are trails of use up both sides, with fine views if one scrambles up to the north. A short descent leads to the end of this trail at 0.53 mile, at 1,510' at the Perl Charles Trail (at 4.08 miles). Ascent is 290', descent is 160'.

[J]

General Description. From the Perl Charles Trail just south of the cookout area, head north, crossing a deep wash and around the flank of the mountain to an old mine road at 0.23 mile. There are many junctions before it reaches the Christiansen Trail at 0.76 mile. Ascent is 160'.

Access. From the Perl Charles Trail at 0.40 mile or the Christiansen Trail at 0.74 miles.

Read Down	Detailed Trail Description	Read Up
0.00	Leave PC at 0.40 mi from Monument Junction, head N.	0.76
0.01	**Junction (4-way):** road crosses. Bear L toward cookout area.	0.75
0.03	Cookout area (1,412'). At far side, descend past toilets to cross wash.	0.73
0.07	**Junction:** track R leads up valley for 0.12 mi to join track ascending valley bottom. Ascend N.	0.69
0.20	**Junction (4-way):** in pass (1,446'), spur L leads to hump in 250'; on R is old mine road. Continue straight, on narrower trail parallelling track on L.	0.56
0.23	**Junction:** join mine road from R; other trails of use join. Bear E.	0.53
0.33	**Junction:** straight ahead, trail leads E, then N into confusing maze. Keep R, around mountain side, then keep to L where alternate tracks ascend.	0.43
0.46	**Junction:** tracks sharp R toward mine workings. Turn L across wash on road.	0.30
0.63	**Junction:** road bears L, around loop in 345'. Take short cut straight.	0.13
0.65	**Junction:** road rejoins on L; sharp R is road ascending to PC in 0.16 mi. Continue E along road.	0.11
0.70	**Junction (4-way):** trail sharp L to road loop; half-R to junction above CMC. Stay on road.	0.06
0.75	**Junction:** short-cut L in 90' to CMC (N to Dreamy Draw). Keep R.	0.01
0.76	**Junction:** CMC (PC is 450' to R here).	0.00

[K]

From the Perl Charles Trail at 0.80 mile in the pass (1,699'), this narrow trail side-hills to the south, with good views, to the next crest (1,810') at 0.16 mile. Here there is a junction (to the southwest, a sketchy trail switchbacks steeply down the ridge to the Perl Charles Trail at the second mine site in 0.12 mile). Turn southeast and descend a good trail for 0.31 mile (total of 0.32 mile) to reach [L] in the valley. (The Perl Charles Trail is to the R here.) Ascent is 110', descent is 210'.

[L] WEST to EAST

General Description. From the Perl Charles Trail, this good trail makes a long ascent of "Hidden Valley", topping a pass at 0.57 mile and descending to the Christiansen Trail (at 0.79 mile from Dreamy Draw), which is also at 3.49 miles on the Perl Charles Trail. Ascent is 350', descent is 270'.

Access. *From the west:* at the Perl Charles Trail at 1.34 miles. *From the east:* at 3.49 miles on the Perl Charles Trail or the Christiansen Trail 0.96 mile from Dreamy Draw.

Read Down	Detailed Trail Description	Read Up
0.00	Leave PC Trail (1,516'). Ascend up valley.	0.79
0.01	**Junction:** short-cut L from [H].	0.78
0.14	**Junction:** trail sharp R narrows, descends to PC in 600' near wash.	0.64

0.15	**Junction:** on L is [K]. On R is spur up minor hump in 140'.	0.77
0.17	**Junction:** in pass (1,591'), trail R leads down to PC in 0.16 mi near wash.	0.62
0.38	**Junction:** trail of use on R. Ahead, ascend side-valley.	0.41
0.57	Pass (1,817'). Descend.	0.22
0.61	Turn L.	0.16
0.70	**Junction:** connector R leads 210' to [M]. Descend.	0.09
0.79	**Junction:** CMC/PC Trails (1,590') by either branch of trail.	0.00

[M] SOUTH to NORTH

General Description. A circuit trip can be made with this trail from Squaw Peak Drive by taking the Circumference Trail [302] over the highest pass, then this trail north to the Perl Charles Trail [1A] which is taken east to either [O], [N], or the Perl Charles itself, back to either branch of the Nature Trail [304]. Ascent is 65'; descent is 200'.

Access. *From the south,* at 1.49 miles on the Circumference Trail. *From the north,* from the Christiansen Trail at 1.21 miles, or the Perl Charles Trail at 1.51 miles.

Read Down	Detailed Trail Description	Read Up
0.00	Leave Circumference [302]/PC Trails. Descend, cross wash in 95', ascend.	0.50
0.08	Pass (1,959'). Descend.	0.42
0.17	**Junction:** poorer trail on R descends to mine road in 0.11 mi, to PC in 0.18 mi. Go sharp L here.	0.33
0.27	**Junction:** on L is crossover trail to [L] in 210'. Go R.	0.23
0.35	**Junction:** poor trail descends on L to PC in 100'. Keep R.	0.15
0.39	**Junction:** trail on R ascends back to this trail. Go straight.	0.11
0.41	**Junction:** PC Trail (1.51 mi L, 3.15 mi R to Monument Jct.	0.09
0.43	**Junction:** sharp R is mine road back to PC in 115'.	0.07
0.45	**Junction:** trail of use L over hill to CMC in 175'. Turn R here.	0.05
0.49	**Junction (4-way):** on L, trail of use leads over hill to CMC in 215'; half-L poor track leads to CMC in 90'. Continue straight.	0.01
0.50	**Junction:** CMC sharp L and straight. This trail ends.	0.00

[N] EAST to WEST

General Description. This loop leads from the Charles M. Christiansen Trail up a valley to 0.92 mile, where the Perl Charles [1A] and Nature Trail [304] diverge, then steepens and climbs a pass to join trail [O] at the ridge at 1.23 miles. Ascent is 350'; descent is 180'.

Access. *At the eastern end,* from 2.23 miles on the Charles M. Christiansen Trail. *At the western end,* from trail [O] just north of the pass.

Read Down	Detailed Trail Description	Read Up
0.00	Leave CMC at 2.23 mi (1,570').	1.23
0.05	**Junction:** trail L 0.14 mi to CMC. Go R.	1.19
0.10	**Junction:** trail sharp L back to CMC in 0.15 mi.	1.13
0.14	**Junction:** trail R parallels CMC to the west for 0.44 mi.	1.10
0.40	**Junction:** trail L leads to Quartz Ridge Trail [8] in 0.20 mi. Ascend gradually with wash on L.	0.83
0.65	**Junction:** sharp L is crossover 290' to trail parallelling Quartz Ridge Trail [8], and 100' further to latter S-bound or 390' N-bound.	0.58
0.78	**Junction (4-way):** on R trail ascends to PC in 0.10 mi; on L is Nature Trail [304], 0.15 mi to crossover on R or 0.24 mi to Quartz Ridge Trail [8].	0.45
0.86	**Junction:** PC on R.	0.37
0.92	**Junction:** PC/Nature Trail [304] on L. Continue on rough track.	0.31
1.05	**Junction:** poor track ascends steeply on R. Ascend on trail with loose rock.	0.19
1.20	**Junction:** in pass (1,920'), faint trail L goes around S side of hump 180' to [O]. Take trail on N side of hump.	0.04
1.23	**Junction:** this trail ends at [O] just N of pass. L to Circumference Trail [302] in 0.20 mi; R to PC in 0.33 mi.	0.00

[O] NORTH to SOUTH

General Description. From the Perl Charles Trail an ascent up open slopes and ridges leads to a pass with views at 0.35 mile. The Circumference Trail/PC Trail is reached at 0.49 mile. Ascent is 200'; descent is 60'.

Access. *From the north,* at 1.72 miles on the Perl Charles Trail. *From the south,* from 2.95 miles on the Perl Charles Trail (1.90 miles on the Circumference Trail [302]).

Read Down	Detailed Trail Description	Read Up
0.00	Leave PC at 1.72 mi from Dreamy Draw. Ascend.	0.49
0.13	**Junction:** trail of use on L.	0.36
0.17	**Junction:** trail of use on R.	0.32
0.20	**Junction:** trail sharp L to PC in 0.20 mi. Ascend.	0.29
0.35	**Junction:** just before pass, [N] enters on L. Descend.	0.14
0.40	**Junction:** on L is side-trail to VP (another trail joins it 35' ahead.	0.09
0.49	**Junction:** PC/Circumference Trails.	0.00

Dreamy Draw Access Point

[100] Charles M. Christiansen Trail WEST to EAST

DREAMY DRAW to ENTRANCE SPUR JUNCTION

General Description. This is a long and varied section of the Trail. It leaves the junction 100' north of the Dreamy Draw parking area, runs in a tunnel under the Squaw Peak Parkway, and then heads south past a mine site. Crossing a major wash, it then heads generally east to its junction with the Perl Charles Trail at 0.82 mile. (This is a complex route, with dozens of junctions). It then follows the valley north and east to a junction with the Quartz Ridge Trail [8] at 2.85 miles and reaches the junction of entrance spurs at 2.92 miles. Here there is a choice of routes: 40th Street is reached at 3.29 miles, or Tatum Boulevard at 4.00 miles. Ascent is 340', descent is 220'.

Access. *At the western end:* from the junction 100' north of the Dreamy Draw parking area (reached off Northern Avenue). *At the eastern end:* 0.37 mile south of 40th Street, or 1.08 miles west of Tatum Boulevard.

Read Down	Detailed Trail Description	Read Up
0.00	**Junction** 100' N of parking area (1,380'). Head R here, following wash, entering tunnel at 0.10 mi.	2.92
0.15	**Junction:** Nature Trail [220] on R, across wash. Ascend to L.	2.77
0.16	**Junction:** sharp L is track to highway.	2.76
0.20	**Junction (4-way):** on L is new trail (0.21 mi to old road); on R is short connector to Nature Trail [220] in 80'. Go straight, uphill.	2.72
0.22	**Junction (4-way):** [220] goes straight; sharp R to [220]; go half-R.	2.70
0.29	Top of rise (1,497').	2.63
0.42	**Junction:** on L is [220A]. Descend.	2.50
0.44	**Junction:** trail to peak on L (170' to junction where trail ascends to top).	2.48
0.46	Mine tailings in flat area on R. Ascend.	2.46
0.54	Cross wash, then pass trail of use on R in 45' and switchback to L through pass.	2.38
0.57	**Junction:** trail on L leads to [220] in 190'. Bear R.	2.35
0.61	**Important junction:** Nature Trail [220] straight ahead (back to Dreamy Draw in 0.52 mi). Turn L here; in 35' cross wash.	2.31
0.62	**Junction:** trail of use on R.	2.30
0.66	**Important junction:** sharp L is [220], just 30' before top of rise.	2.26
0.68	Cross deep wash.	2.24
0.69	**Junction:** on R is trail of use leading 0.27 mi through maze to [J] Switchback to L here, ascend rocky trail.	2.23
0.72	**Junction:** on R is short-cut to [J] in 90'. Keep L.	2.20
0.74	**Junction:** sharp R (track) is [J]. Keep L.	2.18
0.75	**Junction:** on L is poor alternate. Bear R.	2.17
0.76	**Junction:** sharp R is trail W to [J] in 385'. Continue straight.	2.16
0.82	**Junction:** sharp L is old road (poor) (0.11 mi back to CMC).	2.10
0.82	**Important junction:** 35' past previous junction PC leaves this trail sharp R.	2.10

0.86	**Junction:** trail on L passes white rocks, ascends to junction with trail of use in pass at 460', reaches [220] at 0.10 mi. Trail improves past 0.91 mi.	2.06
0.96	**Junction:** on R is [L], ascending steeply.	1.96
0.97	**Junction:** on R is alternate for [L].	1.95
0.99	**Important junction:** PC on R, uphill. Continue on easy track.	1.93
1.09	**Junction:** on R, poor trail of use ascends over hill 175' to [M].	1.83
1.12	**Junction:** track [P] diverges L; 30' further there is a 4-way junction on R: trail of use leads over hill to [M] in 215'; on L is start of [P].	1.80
1.13	**Junction (4-way):** trail L to [P] in 80'; on R, track over hill to [M].	1.79
1.17	**Junction:** on L is track switchbacking up to join [P] in 0.11 mi. Pass cut-off trail on L.	1.75
1.18	**Junction:** on L is trail to [P] in 0.22 mi. Bear R.	1.74
1.19	**Junction:** poor track goes R; bear L here.	1.73
1.21	**Junction:** track [M] sharp R uphill.	1.71
1.31	**Junction:** on L is old CMC; go R here (8 MI marker in 15').	1.61
1.32	**Junction:** on R is alternate for CMC, 0.26 mi. Bear L, cross wash.	1.60
1.35	**Junction:** old CMC on L. Turn R.	1.57
1.38	**Junction:** trail on L, 0.17 mi to [P].	1.54
1.41	**Junction:** poor trail on R (150' to CMC alternate).	1.51
1.49	**Junction:** on L, uphill, is trail to [P] in 0.21 mi. Descend into wash.	1.43
1.52	**Junction:** on L is poor trail; leave wash, go R up bank, pass poor trail on L, turn sharp R.	1.40
1.57	**Junction:** trail sharp L is [Q].	1.35
1.67	**Junction:** alternate trail uphill on R (0.26 mi back to CMC).	1.25
1.73	**Junction:** on R is wide track up hill popular with horse parties in 300' and beyond to PC in 0.13 mi. At top of hill, trail leads E 0.38 mi to [N].	1.19
1.76	**Junction:** on L is short-cut to [Q].	1.16
1.78	**Junction (4-way):** on L is [R]; on R, top of hill is 315'.	1.14
1.88	**Junction:** on R is trail of use.	1.04
1.93	**Junction:** on the L, trail crosses wash, ascends to [AA] in 0.14 mi.	0.99
1.98	**Junction:** on R is alternate 250' to CMC ahead; bear L.	0.94
2.02	**Junction:** trail sharp L crosses wash in 160', ascends to mine site on [AA] in 0.12 mi.	0.90
2.03	**Junction:** trail on R leads back to CMC in 260'. Cross wash.	0.89
2.07	**Junction:** R is [N] to Quartz Ridge Trail [8] in 0.55 mi.	0.85
2.23	**Junction:** track sharp R to [N] in 0.17 mi. Cross wash.	0.69
2.26	**Junction:** [DD] sharp R to Quartz Ridge Trail [8] in 0.68 mi.	0.66
2.40	**Junction:** L is crossover to [AA] in 320'.	0.52
2.41	**Junction:** L is crossover to [AA] in 490'.	0.51
2.57	**Junction:** L is crossover to spur trail in 80', then L to [AA] in 330'.	0.35
2.61	**Junction:** sharp L is spur to [AA] in 0.10 mi.	0.31
2.85	**Junction (4-way):** on R is Quartz Ridge Trail [8]; on L is poor track. Continue straight, passing poor track on R in 65'.	0.07
2.92	**Important Junction (4-way):** *here there is a choice.* Spur to 40th St. goes N 0.37 mi *[see 40th St. Access]* for a total of 3.29 mi from Dreamy Draw. Tatum Boulevard spur *[see that access for details]* goes straight ahead, 1.08 mi, for a total of 4.00 mi. To the R, [BB] heads S to Peak 2429 (Elevation 1,543').	0.00

[220] Dreamy Draw Nature Trail

General Description. From the Dreamy Draw access point, go through the tunnel and then head south, ascending a ridge. At 0.52 mile there is a junction with the Charles M. Christiansen Trail, from which it diverges shortly to climb a pass and a crest with fine views at 0.92 mile. It then descends north and west back to its beginning. Ascent is 380'; descent is the same. There are signs for points of interest, and a brochure has been published.

Access. One hundred feet north of the Dreamy Draw parking area this trail starts at the signboard and coincides with the Charles M. Christiansen Trail heading east through the horse tunnel. It then immediately diverges to the right.

Read Down	Detailed Trail Description	Read Up
0.00	Leave signboard (1,380'), heading E through tunnel.	1.64
0.15	**Junction:** where CMC ascends L, this trail crosses minor wash.	1.49
0.17	**Junction:** track sharp R to highway.	1.47
0.20	**Junction:** track on L crosses wash, ascends to [220]/CMC in 200'. Turn R, ascend.	1.44
0.24	**Junction:** track on R. [7 more junctions on R, ahead, along ridge.]	1.40
0.50	**Junction:** last track on R.	1.14
0.52	**Important junction:** CMC and Children's Loop [220A] go straight. Turn sharp R, cross wash.	1.12
0.55	**Important junction:** turn sharp L (narrow trail); CMC goes straight.	1.09
0.61	**Junction:** trail on L crosses wash to CMC in 120'. Turn R, ascend.	1.03
0.70	**Junction:** trail on R leads over low pass 0.10 mi to CMC. Turn L, ascend eroded trail.	0.94
0.72	**Junction:** keep R where abandoned route diverges L.	0.92
0.77	**Junction:** on L is eroded abandoned route.	0.87
0.85	**Junction:** at pass, 40' to R is [P], descending. Turn L up crest.	0.79
0.92	Top of rise on crest with fine views. Descend.	0.72
1.02	**Junction:** trail of use on R.	0.62
1.05	**Junction:** on L trail descends 0.16 mi to junction where CMC/Nature Trail [220A] are 170' to L or 190' straight ahead. Turn R here.	0.59
1.18	**Junction (4-way):** straight ahead leads around to loop; on R, trail leads back to [P]. Go L.	0.46
1.43	**Junction:** on L is [220A], Children's Nature Loop. Go straight.	0.21
1.45	**Junction:** track ascends on R, rejoins ahead.	0.19
1.52	**Junction:** track ascends on R.	0.12
1.57	**Junction (4-way):** sharp L is CMC; half-L is short-cut. Join CMC, straight ahead.	0.07
1.59	**Junction:** new trail on R, 0.11 mi up to loop [see map].	0.05
1.64	**Junction:** on L is start of [220] -- end of this Nature loop.	0.00

[220A] Children's Nature Loop

General Description. A short series of trail segments reduces the length and ascent of the main Dreamy Draw Nature Trail [220]. Total distance is 1.25 miles from Dreamy Draw and back to it. Ascent is 200'; descent is 140'.

Access. Description starts from 0.52 mile on [220], but access can be considered to also be at Dreamy Draw.

Read Down	Detailed Trail Description	Read Up
0.00	Leave Nature Trail [220] at 0.52 mi from Dreamy Draw. Head E, following CMC.	0.58
0.03	**Junction:** on R is trail to [220] in 190'. Ascend over low pass.	0.55
0.06	**Junction:** poor trail of use straight ahead. Turn sharp R, cross wash, ascend to L.	0.52
0.14	Mine tailings on L.	0.44
0.19	**Junction:** on R is trail of use.	0.39
0.21	**Important junction:** CMC is straight ahead. Go R.	0.37
0.22	**Junction:** trail on R ascends summit to join [220] in 0.20 mi. Turn L.	0.36
0.36	**Junction:** [220] L & R. Go L.	0.22
0.39	**Junction:** track on R (rejoins ahead).	0.19
0.46	**Junction:** track on R (rejoining).	0.12
0.51	**Junction:** CMC sharp L. Continue straight.	0.07
0.53	**Junction (4-way):** new trail on R, 0.11 mi to top of track loop; short-cut on L.	0.05
0.58	**Junction:** [220] on L. Dreamy Draw is 0.15 mi ahead.	0.00

[P] SOUTH to NORTH

General Description. An ascent up an old mine road to good views is the chief feature of this trail that makes connections between the Charles M. Christiansen Trail and 32nd Street. Ascent is 80'; descent is 220'.

Access. *From the south:* at 1.12 miles on the Charles M. Christiansen Trail. *From the north:* at 0.21 mile on [R].

Read Down	Detailed Trail Description	Read Up
0.00	Leave CMC, ascend on wide track (1,640').	0.99
0.02	**Junction:** on R trail leads to CMC in 80'.	0.97
0.04	**Junction:** on R is track descending. Ascend.	0.95
0.10	**Junction:** on R trail descends to old mine road.	0.89
0.17	**Junction:** on R is trail of use descending past mine pits and tailings to junction in 200', where trail of use descends R to trail in 300'. Trail continues up to hump at 430', then descends 290' to valley (360' back to CMC).	0.82
0.18	**Junction:** on L, 40' up to pass and [220]. Descend narrow trail.	0.81
0.35	**Junction:** trail sharp R back to CMC in 0.16 mi.	0.64
0.41	**Junction:** trail R to CMC in 0.17 mi.	0.58

0.45	**Junction (4-way):** on L is trail of use to [220] in 0.36 mi. On R is trail to CMC in 0.21 mi.	0.54
0.52	**Junction:** on L is trail of use to private land.	0.47
0.59	**Junction:** on R is trail of use to [Q] in 350'.	0.40
0.66	**Junction (4-way):** [Q] L & R. On L it is 0.28 mi to 32nd St.	0.33
0.82	**Junction (4-way):** [R] on L, short-cut to [Q]. On R, it is 0.13 mi on [R] to ridge. Bear L, then R.	0.17
0.99	**Junction:** sharp R is [R] (elev. 1,490'). Dunlap is 0.21 mi ahead.	0.00

32nd Street Access Point

[Q] NORTH to SOUTH

General Description. A short, easy (0.56 mile) access to the Christiansen Trail. Ascent is only 60'.

Access. *From the north:* from the south end of 32nd Street. *From the south:* from the Charles M. Christiansen Trail at 1.57 miles from Dreamy Draw.

Read Down	Detailed Trail Description	Read Up
0.00	Leave 32nd St. (1,500').	0.56
0.08	**Junction (4-way):** sharp L to Dunlap in 0.48 mi; straight ahead connects with [P] in 350'. Turn R here.	0.48
0.11	**Junction:** cross track.	0.45
0.17	**Junction:** sharp L leads 475' to [P].	0.39
0.23	**Junction:** trail R to private land.	0.33
0.28	**Junction (4-way):** [P] crosses.	0.28
0.41	**Junction:** on L, trail leads to [R] N-bound & [AA] in 0.17 mi; or R S-bound in 0.18 mi.	0.15
0.50	**Junction:** 150' ahead is CMC. Turn L here.	0.06
0.52	**Junction:** poor trail of use on R.	0.02
0.56	**Junction:** CMC, 1.57 mi from Dreamy Draw.	0.00

[R] NORTH to SOUTH

General Description. Ascends end of ridge to good views, then drops to the Christiansen Trail at 0.71 mile. Ascent is 280'; descent is 180'.

Access. *At the northern end,* leave the south end of 32nd Street. *At the southern end,* from the Christiansen Trail at 1.78 miles.

Read Down	*Detailed Trail Description*	Read Up
0.00	Leave 32nd Street (1,500).	0.56
0.08	**Junction (4-way):** on R is [Q]; on L trail of use leads to Dunlap E of 34th Way in 0.48 mi.	0.48
0.13	**Junction (4-way):** cross track - R to [Q] in 475'. On L is [P] to Dunlap in 0.47 mi. In 40' there is another junction: On L is [P], a steep, rocky trail.	0.45
0.19	**Junction:** trail on L leads 295' to junction where trail descends N 0.16 mi to [P].	0.39
0.28	**Junction:** sharp L trail descends to valley. Turn R, ascend ridge on better trail. ...	0.33
0.45	**Junction:** trail on R leads 260' to Peak 1781. Turn L, descend.	0.28
0.52	**Junction:** trail splits; go L (R descends to pass below).	0.21
0.54	**Junction (4-way):** on L is [AA]. On R it is 0.17 mi to [Q].	0.15
0.60	**Junction:** alternate on R.	0.06
0.71	**Junction:** CMC L & R. Dreamy Draw is 1.78 mi to R.	0.00

Hatcher Access Points

This pair of access points is less likely to be used than the Dunlap pair to the south. A complicated trail system is spread over low Peak 1601.

[S] WEST to EAST

From Hatcher at 36th Street, head east, taking a wide track uphill. In 100' trail [T] angles off to the right. Just after that another trail goes sharp right, crossing the previous trail and leading back to [T] in 460'. Ascend to a low pass (1,507') at 0.07 mi, where there is a 4-way junction: on the right is [W] to Peak 1601 and Dunlap. Half-right is narrower [U], leading around the flank of the peak to Dunlap west of 38th Street in 0.22 mile. Descend to Hatcher cul-de-sac at 0.15 mile, where there is good parking. Ascent is 40'.

[T] NORTH to SOUTH

From the bend in the road, head southwest. In 220' there is a junction sharp left (back to [S] in 460'). Head around the flank of Peak 1601 to a 4-way junction at 0.22 mile. Here trail [W] ascends sharp left up the peak and back to Hatcher. On the right, the cul-de-sac is 230'. Continue descending. In another 115' there is a trail of use on the left to [T]. Another 110' leads to trail's end at [V].

Dunlap Access Points

Dunlap can be reached from 34th Way on the west, or from 38th Street on the east. This access is convenient for Peak 1601 and points south.

[U] SOUTH to NORTH

From the bend in the road on Dunlap west of 38th Street, 195' east of the cul-de-sac, head northeast, in 170' passing a trail of use on the left that parallels [V] at a higher elevation. Continuing north, pass a junction with a trail half-left at 505' (leads up to intersect [W]). Continue northwest, ending at [S] at 0.22 miles. Hatcher is 420' right or 385' left. Sharp left is [W] up Peak 1601.

[V] EAST to WEST

Head straight west from Dunlap, passing a stile and fence at 70'. A narrow trail of use branches left at 130', and 30' further there is a rock barrier. The wide track reaches a 4-way junction at 420' (to the right is [T] to [S] in 0.27 mile; to L is [Y] and [Z]) and the cul-de-sac at 0.14 mile. Just before the fence at the end [W] leads sharp right up Peak 1601. There is no elevation change.

[W] Peak 1601

From Dunlap east of 34th Way head east, uphill. In 230' there is a 4-way junction with [T] left and right. Go half-left, uphill, reaching junction with [X] at 0.14 mile. (To right, trail descends to [V] in 445'.) Turn right here to another junction in 55' at 0.15 mile ([X] continues straight ahead to [S] in 0.15 mile). Turn right, uphill here. At 0.17 mile a spur trail leads right 100' to the summit with good views. Begin the descent at 0.22 mile and reach a junction in a sag on the ridge crest at 0.24 mile. ([U] goes right.) At 0.31 mile is trail's end on the ridge at [S].

[X]

From the cul-de-sac at Dunlap west of 38th Street, head north, uphill, crossing a trail of use in 100'. At 445' there is a junction with [W] left, down to the road end. Continue 55' more to a junction with [W] on the right (to the summit). Continue north on a level trail, then descend starting at 0.12 mile (ignore a trail of use straight ahead). With rocks ahead, bear R and descend at 0.14 mile. At 0.24 mile cross trail [T] and at 0.25 mile reach [S] just 150' east of Hatcher and 36th Street.

[Y] Peak 1928

General Description. Peak 1928 has good views and this is a fairly easy 0.53-mile ascent for hikers. Ascent is 440'.

Access. From [V] between Dunlap access points (295' east; 420' west).

Read Down	Detailed Trail Description	Read Up
0.00	Leave road [V] (1,490'), heading S, pass cross trail in 25'.	0.53
0.04	**Junction:** where [Z] continues straight ahead, turn R.	0.49
0.06	**Junction:** trail ahead to [P] in 0.16 mi. Turn L here, ascend.	0.47
0.30	**Junction:** in pass, L descends 380' to [Z]. Turn uphill here on narrow trail.	0.23
0.42	Trail turns sharp R.	0.11
0.45	Grade steepens; no horses beyond this point.	0.08
0.53	*Summit, Peak 1928*, VP. On L, poor trail descends 260' to pass and [Z].	0.00

[Z] Peak 1951

General Description. The summit itself is a rough scramble, not suitable for horses. A minor peak can be reached from a side-trail at 0.19 mile. A pass is reached at 0.49 mile before the final ascent to 0.53 mile. Ascent is 460'.

Access. From the Dunlap access points.

Read Down	Detailed Trail Description	Read Up
0.00	Leave [V], pass cross-trail in 25'; continue straight up.	0.53
0.04	**Junction:** [Y] diverges R. Continue straight S.	0.49
0.19	**Junction (4-way):** in pass, trail sharp L leads 115' to top of rise and junction -- 300' scramble L (CAUTION!!) up gully to Peak 1690, and 0.41 mi back E and N to Dunlap. Half-L leads 0.27 mi to [AA]. Continue straight.	0.34
0.29	**Junction (4-way):** on R is trail 380' to [Y]; L leads up onto Peak 1705 in 165'.	0.24
0.33	**Junction:** on L, trail ascends, then descends for 0.22 mi to [AA] in valley.	0.20
0.49	**Junction:** in pass (1,863'), poor trail leads R to Peak 1928 and [Y]. Turn L and make steep ascent here.	0.04
0.53	Peak 1951.	0.00

38th Street Access Point

[AA]

General Description. From the gate at 38th Street a wide track (used at times by service vehicles) leads south along a major wash to a flat, open area at 0.48 mile. There are several short crossovers to the Charles M. Christiansen Trail. A trail then leads past a rocky area below cliffs and ascends to an old mine pit at 0.90 mile, then along the hillside to intersect trail [R] at 1.12 miles, close to the Christiansen Trail (0.11 mile) and to Peak 1781 (0.12 mile).

Access. From the south end of 38th Street, off 39th Street at Shea Blvd.

Read Down	Detailed Trail Description	Read Up
0.00	Leave 38th Street (1,500'). Cross over stile next to gate. Just beyond is trail of use to L & R (L leads to 40th St in 0.28 mi).	1.12
0.05	**Junction:** track enters on R (to private land).	1.07
0.31	**Junction:** track sharp L.	0.81
0.32	**Junction:** trail L leads 330' to spur on R 80' to CMC W-bound, or total of 0.10 mi to CMC E-bound.	0.80
0.34	**Junction:** trail of use sharp R.	0.78
0.42	**Junction:** track half-L descends to cross wash, joins CMC in 490'.	0.70
0.47	**Junction:** track half-L parallels this track, then crosses wash to CMC in 320'.	0.65
0.48	**Junction:** poorly-defined track to R leads to trail [Z] in 0.23 or 0.27 mi *[see map]*. Beyond, track narrows to trail, goes up and down over rocks above major wash, then leads above wash until it climbs hillside.	0.63
0.90	**Junction:** at mine site, trail L descends to CMC in 0.12 mi.	0.22
0.96	**Junction:** trail sharp L descends, crosses wash to CMC in 0.14 mi.	0.16
1.12	**Junction:** this trail ends at trail [R], leading L 0.11 mi to CMC in valley, R to Peak 1781 in 0.12 mi, or 32nd St in 0.49 mi.	0.00

40th Street Access Point

[100] Charles M. Christiansen Trail

40th STREET ENTRANCE SPUR

General Description. The Trail enters a broad valley on an old mining road, then joins the spur from the east (Tatum Boulevard) at 0.37 mile. *Note that this is the shorter of the two entrances to the Christiansen Trail heading west.* Ascent is 90'. There are many trails of use.

Access. From 40th Street and Shea Boulevard head south on 40th Street. The paving ends at 1.0 mile. Continue on a gravel road for 0.1 mile where a parking area is obvious on the left before a gate. Continuation of the road is the Christiansen Trail.

Read Down	Detailed Trail Description	Read Up
0.00	Head S on road at gate (1,450'). (To W is trail along fence line that leads to parallel trail S.) Ascend gradually.	0.37
0.07	Preserve sign.	0.30
0.15	Top of rise. Descend very gradually with open valley on R.	0.22
0.17	Cross small wash.	0.20
0.24	**Junction:** trail angles to L (crossover to CMC spur to Tatum Blvd. in 0.19 mi).	0.13
0.26	Cross moderate wash.	0.11
0.37	**Junction:** alternate spur to Tatum Blvd. on L (1.08 mi). Trail turns R (W) here. Ahead, road & trail continue to Peak 2429 [BB] in 1.08 mi. (Elev. here 1,543').	0.00

For continuation of this trail to the west, see the Dreamy Draw Access Point.

[BB] Peak 2429

General Description. The road that starts as the Charles M. Christiansen Trail spur south of 40th Street continues south of where the main trail turns west (and the other spur enters from Tatum Boulevard to the east). Gradually, then steadily, the old mining road ascends the slope west of Peak 2429, making a switchback to the north at 0.50 mile where the way diverges and becomes a foot and horse trail, ascending a draw. This is well constructed with many switchbacks. At 0.57 mile there is a junction with a minor trail joining the Quartz Ridge Trail [8] below. Switchbacks continue all the way to 0.88 mile just below the ridge crest. The main trail heads north around the peak on an easy grade to 0.99 mile, where the trail turns south again and ascends to the summit at 1.08 miles. Views are excellent. The ascent is 890'.

Access. The trail leaves the Charles M. Christiansen Trail 0.37 mile south of the 40th Street access point, or 1.08 miles west of Tatum Boulevard access point. Head south on the old mining road.

Read Down	Detailed Trail Description	Read Up
0.00	Leave CMC Trail junction heading S (1,543').	1.08
0.05	**Junction:** faint trail on L is alternate to CMC Trail and Tatum Blvd.	1.05
0.07	**Junction:** poor trail on L leads onto side of mountain (N end of this trail is at 0.23 mi, ahead). Road soon steepens.	1.01
0.23	**Junction:** track ascends steeply on L (leads onto ridge top at 490'; poor horse trail descends N side, returning to main trail at 0.07 mi, a total of 0.30 mi.)	0.85
0.33	**Junction:** broad trail descends on R to valley (leads to Quartz Ridge Trail [8] in 0.12 mi).	0.74

0.35	On L is cairn with old cross in it.	....	0.73
0.50	**Important junction:** where road steepens and makes hairpin bend to L (N), take trail R; there is another faint trail on R from road ahead (road ends at boulder field in 380'). Elevation 1,840'. Trail starts out level, crosses a minor wash, then ascends parallelling wash.	....	0.57
0.56	Use care to avoid side route on R that ends; keep on top of rocks, then bear R.	....	0.52
0.57	**Junction:** at level area, trail ahead descends 0.26 mi to Quartz Ridge Trail [8], deteriorating as it drops (not recommended). Elevation here is 1,880'.	....	0.51
0.59	Switchbacks (21 of them) begin.	....	0.49
0.88	**Junction:** main trail heads N, contouring along side of Peak 2429. Ahead 35' is crest (2,320') with views of Camelback, South Mountain, Squaw Peak. (There is no trail along rough ridge to S.)	....	0.20
0.99	**Junction:** at crest N of Peak 2429, poor trail leads 350' toward next summit; from there a 250' scramble leads to its top. Turn sharp R here, ascending on good trail.	....	0.09
1.01	Switchback to L, then to R.	....	0.06
1.03	**Junction:** at white cairn, continue straight ahead; trail sharp L crosses over ridge and in 410' descends side ridge to private land.	....	0.05
1.08	*Summit, Peak 2429.* Fine views.	....	0.00

[CC] Peak 1987

Good views may be had from this outlying summit, the high point of a ridge trending southwest-northeast, at the northeastern edge of the Squaw Peak area. (Part of it has been used by horses, but the last section is much too steep.)

From the end of 40th Street, walk back to the north end of the parking area; here a trail angles northeast through the fence. At 365', with private property ahead, take a right turn in an open area, heading toward a broad track, slightly uphill. The track starts at 565' (0.11 mile) and soon ascends steadily up a valley, then narrows, reaching the crest at 0.37 mile, where there are views and a fire ring (1,880'). To the right, a bump on the ridge is only 65' away without trail. For best views, turn left and take a narrow, steep trail with loose rock, zigzagging up to the summit at 0.46 mile (use care, there are some steep drop-offs).

[DD] NORTH to SOUTH

General Description. From the Christiansen Trail this old track ascends along a major wash to the Quartz Ridge Trail [8] at 0.82 mile. Ascent is 140'.

Access. *From the north,* at 2.26 miles from Dreamy Draw on the Charles M. Christiansen Trail, or 0.66 mile from the junction of entrance spurs. *From the south,* at the Quartz Ridge Trail [8] at 0.95 mile.

Read Down	Detailed Trail Description	Read Up
0.00	Leave CMC (1,550').	0.82
0.43	**Junction:** sharp R is trail of use.	0.39
0.50	Cross wash.	0.32
0.62	**Junction:** poor trail of use on L. Turn R, descend to cross wash.	0.20
0.64	**Junction:** trail on R crosses wash to [8] in 250'. .	0.18
0.68	**Junction:** trail on R across wash to [8] in 215'. Ascend steadily.	0.14
0.72	**Junction:** on L is poor trail of use. Ascend.	0.10
0.82	**Junction:** ends at [8], sharp R (1,690').	0.00

Tatum Boulevard Access Point

[100] Charles M. Christiansen Trail

TATUM BOULEVARD ENTRANCE SPUR

General Description. This link follows a strip of land in a wash between developed areas for a little over half a mile, then gradually ascends 130' on the north side of the wash to a low pass at 0.86 mile. Finally a gradual descent leads to the spur from 40th Street at 1.08 miles. (There are also two narrower alternate trails on the south side of the wash.)

Access. On Tatum Boulevard there is a small parking area opposite Tomahawk Trail on the east; this is 1.3 miles south of Shea Boulevard and 2.25 miles north of Lincoln Drive.

Read Down	Detailed Trail Description	Read Up
0.00	Limited parking at Tatum Blvd.; Preserve sign. Elevation 1,380'.	1.08
0.02	Charles M. Christiansen Trail sign.	1.06
0.08	Flood control channel on R.	1.00
0.18	Flood control channel on R.	0.90
0.25	Bear R where private trail continues ahead.	0.83
0.29	**Junction:** trail crosses (L leads to private road). Go straight.	0.79
0.36	Cross wash and ascend.	0.72
0.37	Bear L on bank of wash, parallelling wash.	0.71
0.52	Wall on R ends.	0.56
0.61	**Junction:** alternate trail descends on L to cross wash [see 0.93 mi]. Bear R, ascend.	0.47
0.64	Cross small wash.	0.44
0.80	"10 MI" sign.	0.36
0.86	Two large saguaros on R. Continue ascent.	0.28
0.89	Cross wash.	0.19

0.93   Pass (1,550') and **junction:** trail angling R is short-cut to 40th Street spur
        in 0.19 mi. On L, in open area, alternate trail from 0.61 mi enters but is
        not very obvious. Continue on CMC at arrow, descending gradually. 0.15
1.08   **Junction:** 40th St. Spur of CMC on R (to 40th St. in 0.37 mi). Road on L [BB]
        to Peak 2429 (1.08 mi). *CMC westbound continues straight ahead* (1,543'). 0.00

36th Street/Lincoln Drive Access Point

Drive north on 36th Street (mostly gravel) to a locked gate (1,740'). *There is
no legal parking here.* 375' north of the gate is a junction: the old road to the
right leads to private property. There is a choice of two routes:

[EE]

Straight ahead is a paved section past the white house (an inholding in the
Preserve), then a gravel road (partly deteriorated and by-passed by trail at 200'
for 195') to the junction with the Quartz Ridge Trail [8] at 0.55 mile. There is a
120' ascent.

[FF]

To the west (left), a rough road ascends to a junction on the left at 450' where
a side-trail leads up the ridge for 345' and turns left another 40' to a hump with
a fine cliff view-point. (This ridge can be descended without trail to join [HH] in
about 0.32 mile, above 32nd Street). In another 570' at top of rise there is
another junction on the right (short-cut to [GG] in 410'). In another 540' there
is a junction on the right where trail [GG] leads north 0.60 mile to the Quartz
Ridge Trail [8]. On the left is a short spur loop trail up to another hump
(1,970') in 100'. The road becomes steep and rougher as it ascends 540' to
the top of the high pass (1,950') at a total of 0.40 mile and a 5-way junction. (A
trail to the southwest ascends a ridge for 290' to a better view-point.) At this
point a trail starts down the valley to the west and then diverges into a complex
and confusing set of trails of use, all of which eventually end at the Nature Trail
[304] above Squaw Peak Drive in about 0.36 mile. (To the north the trail
shortly ends.) Total ascent is 200'.

[GG] From [FF] to Quartz Ridge Trail SOUTH to NORTH

General Description. From the road [FF], descend a valley, generally along
the course of a wash, with some pleasant walking for 0.60 mile to the Quartz
Ridge Trail [8] in a deep wash. Descent is 200'.

Access. *At the southern end:* from [FF] 0.30 mile west of the gravel road [EE], and 0.37 mile above gate on 36th Street; *at the northern end:* from [8] at 0.77 mile.

Read Down	Detailed Trail Description	Read Up
0.00	Leave [FF], descending.	0.60
0.13	**Junction:** trail sharp R crosses wash, returns to [FF] in 410'.	0.47
0.29	**Junction:** alternate trails: go L for shortest way (R is 105' longer).	0.31
0.34	**Junction:** alternate rejoins on R. Easy trail from here.	0.26
0.60	**Junction:** Quartz Ridge Trail [8] in wash.	0.00

32nd Street/Lincoln Drive Access Point

[HH]

A dead-end trail starts from the north side of Lincoln at 32nd Street. Head northeast, pass a trail of use on the right, turn left at 440', and head up the valley with the main wash on your right. Cross this wash at 0.37 mile and turn left up the valley where a rough road joins on the right at 0.41 mile. Pass a large boulder on the left at 0.53 mile; the trail splits at 0.56 mile (on the right is the lower route). Keep left to go over the top of a hill and rejoin the alternate at 0.61 mile, then turn east, uphill, to a pass at 0.75 mile, where the trail ends at a white boulder (1,590') near the Preserve boundary. Ascent is 250'. Ahead are private homes. The ridge above can be ascended without trail for about 0.32 mile to join [FF].

City of Phoenix

Stony/Echo Mountain Area

Introduction. Stony Mountain is an unofficial name for a long, steep-sided ridge west of Squaw Peak. For the purposes of this guidebook we have defined the "Stony Area" as bounded by 7th Street on the west, 24th St. and Dreamy Draw on the east, Thunderbird and Cactus on the north, and Northern Avenue on the south. (There is no significant named feature in the pie-shaped area between Cave Creek and 7th Street.) The highest peak is 2,020' high. Peaks rise 400-500' above the surrounding valley. On the south there is a section locally known as Echo Mountain (highest summit 1,845').

The section west of Cave Creek Road has one north-south trending steep-sided summit at 1,833'. On its north, parallelling Thunderbird, are a series of ridges and bumps from 1,500' to almost 1,700' in elevation. Most summits in the northern area have trails. In the Cave Creek-Dreamy Draw area there are a few *very* steep trails to or along the ridge crest where great care must be exercised.

Maps. *Our Map 6.* The USGS Sunnyslope 1:24,000 topo (1965, photorevised 1982) shows a few old roads but almost none of the trails.

Access. There are many access points; these can be confusing. Only the most important are shown on the access diagram below.

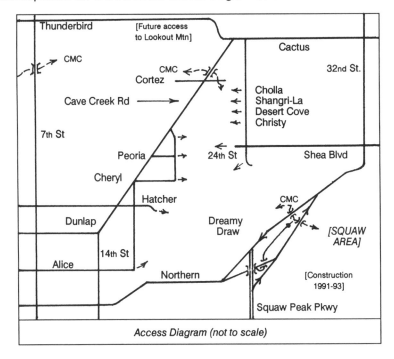

Access Diagram (not to scale)

[Opposite page: Looking east from Peak 1871]

Recommended Hikes and Trail Rides. Letters used for designation are our own, so as not to confuse designated (numbered) trails with these. The Charles M. Christiansen Trail is abbreviated "CMC" in tabular detailed text. This is the best trail for both hikers and trail riders *and is described in two sections.* (Because there are many confusing junctions, considerable detail is provided.) [Q], [R], and [T] are easy trails.

Cautions. The tilted rock strata have resulted in a very steep spine to this range. Trails ascending the ridge or its subsidiary ridges tend to be excessively steep, definitely unsuitable for horses. Where this is the case, we have described the trail as "very steep."

[100] Charles M. Christiansen Trail EASTBOUND

7th STREET to CAVE CREEK ROAD

General Description. From 7th Street a public corridor is followed around the north side of The Pointe at Tapatio Cliffs, then a low hill ascended. A wide track is then followed up a valley before climbing over a pass at 0.71 mile and following a complex route over the hills and down to, and under, Cave Creek Road at 1.92 miles. Ascent is 200', descent 240'.

Access. *From the east:* leave Cortez Road just east of Cave Creek Road, heading north. There is limited parking. *From the west:* at present, this section ends just east of 7th Street at the public parking area of the Pointe at Tapatio Cliffs, just east of their tennis courts. A new public parking area on the west side of 7th Street, with a connecting trail down to the Christiansen Trail, is planned.

Read Down	Detailed Trail Description	Read Up
0.00	Leave side-trail to Pointe parking area, near map & sign (elevation 1,440').	1.92
0.06	**Junction:** private road on L; Pointe parking on R. Head uphill on narrow trail.	1.86
0.13	**Junction (4-way):** cross trails of use L & R on top of hill (VP).	1.79
0.17	**Junction:** cross private road.	1.75
0.36	**Junction (4-way):** join 2 tracks from L; keep R on wide track.	1.56
0.44	**Junction:** on L is [R] to picnic area and beyond.	1.48
0.50	**Junction:** bear R from track [T] on ascending trail.	1.42
0.53	**Junction:** sharp L is spur trail to [T] in 170'. Ascend, avoiding trail on L.	1.38
0.64	Turn sharp L here.	1.27
0.69	Pass (1,550'). Descend.	1.23
0.71	**Junction:** trail L descends 0.14 mi to [T] in valley. Bear slightly R, descending past short-cut R to [U] in wash, then ascend.	1.21
0.73	**Junction:** [U] on R; trail L descends 0.11 mi to [T] in valley. Bear L, ascend.	1.19
0.79	**Junction:** poor tracks join from L. Keep R, uphill.	1.13
0.82	**Junction (5-way):** on R is [S] to Sunnyside Access, returning to this trail at 1.14 mi; sharp R is [U]; on L is poor track. Continue ahead on easy track, narrowing to trail.	1.09

0.88	**Junction (4-way):** track crosses diagonally.	1.04
0.92	**Junction (4-way):** on L, to [T] in 380'; on R is rough pipeline road descending to [S] in 0.10 mi. Continue on trail.	1.00
0.98	**Junction:** sharp R is poor track that ends. Turn L here onto track.	0.93
1.00	**Junction:** track sharp L descends 300' to [T]. Turn R here.	0.92
1.06	**Junction:** bear L where poor track enters on R.	0.86
1.11	**Junction:** short-cut trail L, 75' to [T]. Bear R.	0.81
1.12	**Junction (4-way):** sharp R is [S] to Sunnyside Access, then back to this trail at 0.82 mi; sharp L is [T]. Continue straight ahead on wide, level track.	0.80
1.21	**Junction:** where [R] continues to ridge, turn R, descending parallel to wash on L, passing several trails of use.	0.71
1.63	**Junction:** trail on L joins Loop Trail [Q] in 80'.	0.29
1.72	**Junction:** road on R.	0.20
1.73	**Junction:** trail on R; descend.	0.19
1.77	Turn R, parallelling Cave Creek Road, above.	0.15
1.82	W end of tunnel.	0.10
1.84	Turn R on E side of tunnel.	0.08
1.92	**Junction:** Cortez Road (1,400'). Cave Creek Road is just to R here. Go across road, diagonally L, to continue.	0.00

[100] Charles M. Christiansen Trail EASTBOUND

CAVE CREEK ROAD to DREAMY DRAW

General Description. An old road is followed along the west side of some hills to 0.39 mile, where the trail ascends over a shoulder and reaches Shea Access. A circuitous route around the developed land to the east leads to a side trail to 24th Street. The next section again leads past private homes before climbing over a pass at 2.00 miles and rounding the flank of a minor summit to reach Dreamy Draw at 2.97 miles. *[NOTE: the last section descending into Dreamy Draw was being re-routed at the time of publication, making the distance slightly longer - see map.]* Ascent is 450', descent is also 450'.

Access. *From the west:* leave Cortez Road just east of Cave Creek, heading southeast at the junction. *From the east:* leave the Dreamy Draw parking area heading north 100' to a junction, then left (west) through the tunnel under the Squaw Peak Parkway.

Read Down	*Detailed Trail Description*	*Read Up*
0.00	Leave Cortez Road E of Cave Creek Road (1,400'). Climb bank onto trail heading SE.	2.97
0.04	**Junction (4-way):** trail L back to Cortez. Go half-L along old road [J] parallelling Cortez.	2.93
0.07	**Junction:** turn R off [J], past barrier, on wide, easy trail (ahead leads 0.63 mi to Cholla Access and points E).	2.90
0.39	**Important Junction:** track ahead is [H] to Sahuaro Access in 0.48 mi. Turn L here, onto ascending trail.	2.57

0.41	**Junction:** in open area, keep L where track continues, ascending trail.	2.56
0.55	**Junction:** trail L is [G]. Bear R and descend.	2.42
0.58	**Junction (4-way):** track crosses diagonally.	2.39
0.66	**Junction (5-way):** sharp R is old CMC ascending; on R is [F] to [H] and Sahuaro Access; track continues on L to Christy Drive Access in 0.19 mi. Bear half-L on level track.	2.31
0.69	**Junction:** sharp L is [E] over minor summit (1,750') and Desert Cove Access. Pass fence line and other tracks.	2.28
0.77	**Junction:** track on L.	2.20
0.84	**Junction (4-way):** track crosses diagonally.	2.13
0.93	**Junction (4-way):** Shea Access is 335' to L; on R is very steep trail [D] up ridge of Stony Mountain in 0.27 mi. Continue level, above homes.	2.04
1.33	**Junction:** poor track descends on L. Ascend over low pass.	1.64
1.36	**Junction:** on L is [C] to 24th St. in 0.18 mi (elev. 1,580').	1.61
1.45	**Junction:** trail ahead to private land; go uphill to R on trail, circling around private homes.	1.52
1.61	Descend.	1.36
1.78	**Junction (4-way):** L leads to private land; R is very steep, narrow trail [B] (upper portion a scramble) up Stony Mountain in 0.18 mi.	1.19
1.82	**Junction:** bear R where trail enters on L.	1.15
1.90	**Junction:** bear R, joining ascending track.	1.07
1.96	**Junction:** alternate trail on R rejoins here.	1.01
2.00	Pass (1,600). Descend steeply, passing loop track on L.	0.97
2.23	**Junction:** poor, rocky track ascends on L.	0.74
2.26	**Junction:** on R is [A]. Bear L on trail.	0.71
2.29	**Junction:** on R 135' is junction in open area with Hatcher Access [A]. Pass mine shaft on R.	0.68
2.41	**Junction:** turn L from track onto trail.	0.56
2.53	**Junction:** spur trail descends on R. Ascend, then descend.	0.44
2.67	**Junction:** at top of rise, track descends on R. Turn L here and descend.	0.30
2.72	**Junction:** turn L from track onto trail.	0.25
2.74	**Junction:** join track at barrier; bear R, down-hill.	0.23
2.76	**Junction:** wide track joins on L. Bear R onto track.	0.21
2.82	**Junction:** trail of use on L to 19th St. in 325'. Descend steadily.	0.15
2.85	W end of tunnel.	0.12
2.87	Emerge from E end of tunnel.	0.10
2.90	**Junction:** cross track, keep R.	0.07
2.97	**Junction:** spur trail R to Dreamy Draw parking area in 100' (1,400'). CMC continues E by turning L here.	0.00

[A] Hatcher Access NORTH to SOUTH

HATCHER DRIVE to 17th PLACE and ORCHID LANE

General Description. The first part of this trip is an old road into the center of the Preserve area near the Christiansen Trail, where it turns south and descends into a rather confusing complex of washes. From there it ascends past an enclosed private area to a pass (1,505') and viewpoint junction at 0.66

mile, then descends to end at the road at 0.84 mile. Ascent is 90' over the pass.

Access. *From the north:* at Hatcher Road at 16th Street, Hatcher Drive bears south. Take it to its end, an unpaved parking area. *From the south:* at 17th Place just north of Orchid Lane.

Read Down	Detailed Trail Description	Read Up
0.00	Leave Hatcher Drive (1,495'), descending.	0.84
0.03	**Junction:** steep track uphill to L leads to pass in ridge (1,523'). From there, a trail descends 450' to the water tower at end of Hatcher Road. Another steep trail heads R, up the ridge, to Peak 2016 (550' ascent).	0.81
0.05	**Junction:** poor track descends on R.	0.80
0.07	**Junction:** in wide open area, poor track descends R.	0.77
0.13	**Junction:** in messy area, poor track descends R.	0.72
0.16	Bear R.	0.69
0.21	**Important 4-way junction:** straight ahead is track crossing over to CMC in 325'; to R is poorer approach to S; for Orchid and 17th Place, continue sharp R.	0.63
0.37	**Junction:** in open area where there are wide tracks ahead, descend into wash, then turn R on track, ascending gradually away from wash.	0.48
0.38	Cross wash.	0.47
0.44	**Junction:** where track continues ahead through fence, turn L on narrow trail along fence line for 80', then follow fence to R.	0.40
0.50	**Junction:** where trail rejoins track from fenced-in area, turn L (S) onto trail. Cross wash in 185' on mostly level trail.	0.35
0.58	**Junction (4-way):** track on L descends into valley, on R ascends but does not lead anywhere of significance. Go slightly R, ascending on track.	0.26
0.61	**Junction:** track to L descends to cross wash; joins parallel track on far side of wash.	0.23
0.63	**Junction:** bear L, cross wash and ascend.	0.21
0.66	Pass (1,505') and **junction (4-way):** sharp L is track descending along wash; to L is 290' trail to top of bump on ridge (1,576') with views. Descend, passing washes and several poor trails. This track widens, passes messy area on L (E).	0.18
0.84	This trail ends at 17th Place (1,375'). Orchid Lane is 100' ahead.	0.00

[B] Stony Mountain Ridge from the Southeast

1.19 miles west of Dreamy Draw on the Christiansen Trail this *very steep*, hiker-only trail leads up the side of Stony Mountain. (It is not advised for children or those fearing steep slopes.) In 360' the old mining road ends and trail continues easily to 455', then it steepens. At 445' take the left fork, reaching a sag at the top of a small subsidiary ridge at 0.14 mile. Here there are some good views except to the west. To the right 250' (at 0.18 mile) is a fine view. To the left, a narrow and progressively steepening trail traverses loose rock, levels off briefly at 0.23 mile, then reaches the very fine view-point on the crest at 0.27 mile (1,920'). *Use great care.* Ascent is 350'.

[C] 24th St. to Charles M. Christiansen Trail

General Description. A short side-trail provides an excellent access to the Christiansen Trail and views on the way. Total ascent is 120'.

Access. From the bend in 24th Street south of Shea Boulevard, ascend trail southwest up the slope.

Read Down	Detailed Trail Description	Read Up
0.00	At 24th St. head S and SW, steadily uphill (elevation 1,480').	0.18
0.09	Ease ascent.	0.09
0.12	Top of rise on top of gently-curving ridge crest. Descend gradually.	0.06
0.18	**Junction:** CMC is to L and R (elevation 1,580').	0.00

[D] Stony Mountain Ridge from Shea Blvd

General Description. From Shea Access at the Christiansen Trail, ascend west up a steep track to a side-ridge at 0.21 mile. A poor, very steep trail then leads to the crest of Stony Mountain at 0.27 mile, a total ascent of 320'.

Access. From the Christiansen Trail at 2.04 miles west of Dreamy Draw, or 335' west of the end of Shea Boulevard, at the Trail junction.

Read Down	Detailed Trail Description	Read Up
0.00	Leave CMC (1,590'), ascend track to W.	0.27
0.05	**Junction:** poor track enters on R (avoid it).	0.22
0.13	Grade steepens; use care.	0.14
0.21	Top of side-ridge. Take poor trail steeply L (W).	0.06
0.27	Crest of Stony Mountain (1,910') with excellent views. Ridge can be followed S (rough) to [D].	0.00

[E] SOUTHWEST to NORTHEAST

General Description. From the Christiansen Trail, this trail ascends 200' to a minor summit (views), then descends to a valley and heads east to Desert Cove Access at 0.51 mile. Ascent is 200', descent is 230'.

Access. *From the southwest:* at the Christiansen Trail 2.28 miles west of Dreamy Draw, 0.69 mile east of Cave Creek Road. *From the northeast:* at Desert Cove Access.

Read Down	Detailed Trail Description	Read Up
0.00	Leave CMC (1,550').	0.51
0.02	**Junction (4-way):** track crosses. Ascend.	0.49
0.09	**Junction:** trail L 80' to CMC W-bound. Ascend.	0.41
0.13	Use care with steep section: head E, then N.	0.38
0.16	Crest (1,750'), VP. Jog L on it, then descend steadily to N.	0.35
0.24	**Junction (4-way):** on L & straight is [G]. Turn R, descend along wash.	0.27
0.37	**Junction:** poor trail L crosses wash. Bear slightly L.	0.14
0.41	**Junction:** poor track crosses.	0.10
0.42	**Junction:** track on R. Continue, then bear L from track, crossing wash.	0.09
0.46	**Junction (4-way):** cross track.	0.05
0.49	**Junction (4-way):** in open area, L [G] leads back to CMC on other side of wash. Ahead, [M] leads N along edge of private homes. Turn sharp R here.	0.02
0.51	Desert Cove cul-de-sac, limited parking (1,520').	0.00

[F] WEST to EAST

General Description. This is an 0.29-mile connector between the trail from Sahuaro and the Christiansen Trail east-bound.

Access. *At its western end,* it leaves [H] 0.38 mile from Sahuaro Access. *At its eastern end,* it leaves the Christiansen Trail 0.66 mile from Cave Creek Road and 2.31 miles from Dreamy Draw.

Read Down	Detailed Trail Description	Read Up
0.00	Leave [H], ascend (1,510'). In 90', track from L is part of previous triangular junction.	0.29
0.09	**Junction:** narrow trail R to [H] in 530'. Ascend steadily for 315' on rocky, wide track, then ascent eases.	0.20
0.19	**Junction:** at top of rise, trail L leads 75' to VP on hump. Descend.	0.10
0.21	**Junction:** narrow level trail R. Descend.	0.08
0.25	With open area ahead, keep to R.	0.03
0.29	**Junction (5-way):** CMC E-bound to R, half-L is W-bound; straight ahead leads to NE access points; L is old CMC ascending.	0.00

[G] WEST to EAST

General Description. From the Christiansen Trail, this trail ascends a low ridge, then parallels [E] on the north side of a wash, descending to Desert Cove Access at 0.37 mile. Along the way it gives access to several other trails. Ascent is 60', descent is 100'.

Access. *At the western end:* at the Christiansen Trail 2.42 miles west of Dreamy Draw (0.55 mile east of Cave Creek Road). *At the eastern end:* at the western end of Desert Cove.

Read Down	Detailed Trail Description	Read Up
0.00	CMC heads W. Ascend (1,550').	0.37
0.05	**Junction:** At top of rise, [K] bears slightly L over bare rock.	0.32
0.10	**Junction (4-way):** sharp R is [E] over ridge and back to CMC in 0.16 mi. Slightly R is [E] into valley, to Desert Cove Access in 0.27 mi. Keep L, parallelling wash on R.	0.27
0.18	**Junction:** track (and then trail) on L [L] ascend to summit in 0.16 mi.	0.19
0.20	**Junction:** poor trail L up ridge.	0.17
0.24	**Junction:** diverge L from wider track that descends roward wash.	0.13
0.31	**Junction:** trail slightly L; keep straight on.	0.06
0.33	**Junction (4-way):** trail L joins previous trail, leads to [M] in 475'; sharp R is poor track.	0.04
0.35	**Junction:** in open area, [M] heads NE; [E] is on R. Continue straight.	0.02
0.37	**Junction:** Desert Cove cul-de-sac, limited parking (1,520').	0.00

On Stony Mountain's ridge

[H] Sahuaro Access to Charles M. Christiansen Trail

WEST to EAST

General Description. Access via Sahuaro is an old road ascending to cross many other trails and tracks. There is one high point, otherwise it is an ascent all the way (260' total).

Access. *From the west:* take Sahuaro off of Cave Creek Road just north of Peoria, and drive to the very end of the road where Preserve signs will be seen. *From the east:* on the Christiansen Trail 0.39 mile from Cortez near Cave Creek Road, 2.57 miles from Dreamy Draw.

Read Down	Detailed Road Description	Read Up
0.00	Leave E end of Sahuaro, near maintenance office of NE District Parks (1,360').	0.48
0.02	**Junction:** trail on R is being revegetated -- ignore. Go straight.	0.46
0.08	**Junction (4-way):** sharp R is trail to Peoria access in 945', S to Cheryl Access; half-L is track in open area. Go straight.	0.40
0.11	**Junction:** track joins on L. This trail narrows, descends gradually.	0.37
0.13	**Junction (4-way):** trail R leads S to Peoria/Cheryl Accesses, track half-R is poor. Bear L here, ascending gradually.	0.35
0.31	**Junction:** at top of rise, narrow trail R connects to [F], heading S & E (short-cut to CMC W-bound). Descend, then level out on wide trail.	0.18
0.38	**Junction:** R is [F] (old road) to CMC in 0.29 mi.	0.10
0.40	**Junction:** in open area, track to R joins previous trail; L is poor track to flood control area. Go straight, descending. Pass trail on L in 130' descending to W.	0.09
0.44	**Junction (4-way):** in open area, track to R peters out, on L poor track descends toward flood works.	0.04
0.48	**Junction:** CMC W-bound to Cave Creek Rd ahead, E-bound sharp R (1,560').	0.00

[J] WEST to EAST

General Description. An old road and sections of trail lead from the Christiansen Trail just south of Cortez Road on the west, over a rise and past mine pits at 0.38 mile to near the Preserve boundary at 0.49 mile. Here there is a junction with the main trail [M] along the boundary to various access points. Ascent is 120'.

Access. *From the east:* at various northeast access points (Cholla, Shangri-La, Desert Cove, Paradise Drive) on [M]. *From the west:* at 0.04 mile east of Cave Creek on the Christiansen Trail.

Read Down	Detailed Trail Description	Read Up
0.00	Leave CMC trail, heading E, ascending easily past open area (1,410').	0.49
0.21	Bear slightly L (NE) through open area to find trail .	0.28

0.25	**Junction:** cross paved water tank road [K] (L leads back along Cortez to CMC in 0.27 mi; R 0.10 mi to [G]. This trail continues on a good grade.	0.24
0.33	Top of rise; follow wider, level track ahead.	0.16
0.36	**Junction:** straight ahead is rockier track leading in 35' to another junction where track to R leads 0.21 mi to junction with [M] and a further 270' to Cholla Access (total = 0.27 mi). Go L here; in 25' pass top of previous track descending to Cholla. Continue, descending gradually past mine pits on R (1,520').	0.13
0.41	**Junction:** poorer track joins on R.	0.09
0.47	**Junction:** in open area, sharp L is old road back to water tower road in 0.21 mi. Continue in same direction.	0.02
0.49	**Junction:** join [M] near Preserve boundary with private homes ahead. L leads to Desert Vista and Paradise Drive Accesses. R leads in 0.26 mi to Cholla, further S to Shangri-La and Desert Cove Accesses (1,470').	0.00

[K] NORTH to SOUTH

General Description. From the water tank road (extension of Cortez) this narrow trail ascends over a low pass to join [G] in 0.24 mile. Ascent is 90', descent 100'.

Access. *From the north:* on [J] at 0.25 mile (water tank road). *From the south:* at 240' north of the Christiansen Trail at the junction with [G] (2.42 miles west of Dreamy Draw, or 0.55 mile east of Cave Creek Road).

Read Down	*Detailed Trail Description*	*Read Up*
0.00	Leave [J], follow water tank road 0.10 mi to S, ascending.	0.34
0.10	Leave water tank road, ascending S on rocky trail.	0.24
0.19	Pass (1,710'). Descend.	0.15
0.34	**Junction:** [G] in pass. *In reverse direction: trail start is obscure because it is over bare rock.* (CMC is 240' ahead.)	0.00

[L] Peak 1871 WEST to EAST

General Description. From [G] leads over steep Peak 1871 at 0.21 mile, connecting with several other trails, descending to eastern access points via [M] at 0.41 mile. Ascent is 310', descent 350'.

Access. *Western end:* at 0.18 mile on [G]. *Eastern end:* at [M] at 0.20 mile.

Read Down	*Detailed Trail Description*	*Read Up*
0.00	Leave [G] at 0.18 mi, ascending NE.	0.41
0.06	Track ends, trail starts.	0.35
0.07	Go R, cross very small wash, ascend steeply in brushy area.	0.34

0.11	Join very steep wash.	0.30
0.16	**Junction at crest:** to L, minor summit VP is 160' on sketchy trail; Turn R (E) along rocky ridge (1,760').	0.25
0.18	Bump on ridge.	0.23
0.21	Summit (1,871'). Head SE, descending.	0.20
0.25	**Junction:** trail ahead 100' onto minor summit, and poor trail in 35' descends R to join [G]. Go L (NE) here.	0.16
0.35	**Junction (4-way):** on L & R trail connects with other trails, parallels [M]. Continue descent.	0.06
0.41	**Junction (4-way):** [M] L & R at 0.20 mi N of Desert Cove. Ahead 325' is Cholla Access.	0.00

[M] SOUTH to NORTH

General Description. This is a connector trail leading around the developed areas and connecting a number of access points. From Desert Cove Access to Paradise Drive Access is 0.66 mile. Ascent is 20', descent is 60'.

Access. *From the south:* at west end of Desert Cove. *From the north:* at Paradise Drive off Poinsettia, or at other intermediate points.

Read Down	*Detailed Trail Description*	*Read Up*
0.00	Leave Desert Cove Access, limited parking (1,520').	0.66
0.02	**Junction:** L is [E]; straight is [G]. Go sharp R (NE) here.	0.64
0.06	Go L, uphill.	0.60
0.09	**Junction:** sharp L leads back to trails W of Desert Cove.	0.57
0.16	**Junction:** faint trail R to Shangri-La Access in 245'.	0.50
0.17	**Junction (4-way):** R to 23rd St. in 245'; L to [L] in 530' by turning R in 315'. Go straight.	0.49
0.20	**Junction (4-way):** half-R, trail leads 325' to Cholla Access; L is [L] over hump and back to valley and CMC.	0.46
0.24	**Junction:** half-L to [J] in 0.20 mi.	0.42
0.25	**Junction:** R to Cholla Access in 270'; L to trail from previous junction. Pass NW toward corner of developed housing.	0.41
0.40	**Junction:** sharp L is track S, joining parallel trail in 285'. Continue N along developed area.	0.26
0.46	**Junction:** [J] on L.	0.20
0.52	**Junction:** lane on R.	0.14
0.58	**Junction:** access on R to Poinsettia Drive in 200'.	0.08
0.66	**Junction:** Paradise Drive Access on R, to Poinsettia, 23rd St., and out to Cactus Road.	0.00

[N] Stony from the West

General Description. A rough trail leads up Stony's ridge from the west. The first part is fairly good, but soon it steepens, reaching the crest at 0.38 mile with fine views. (The ridge can be followed north to [D] by some scrambling.)

Access. From 17th Street and Cinnabar turn north, following Cinnabar, then east, then north where it becomes Gold Dust Avenue. The access point is on the right at the end of paving. The trail starts northeast, crossing a track.

Read Down	Detailed Trail Description	Read Up
0.00	Leave Gold Dust Ave. (1,460'), cross track, then 2 small washes.	0.38
0.09	**Junction (4-way):** L leads back to Cheryl Access in 0.19 mi. Straight ahead to Peoria Access in 0.29 mi. Turn sharp R (E) here, onto an indistinct track. Ascend steadily, then steeply.	0.29
0.19	**Junction:** track ahead ends in 60' at rocks in wash. Turn R here, on narrow trail, up rocks. Switchback to L in 60', ascending with care.	0.20
0.26	Ease grade at top of rise, then turn R and ascend. In 40', go up subsidiary crest, then in 40' more, bear R, steeply up rocks.	0.13
0.32	Ease grade.	0.06
0.34	Go around head of ravine, head N.	0.04
0.38	Top of ridge (1,910'), excellent VP. Poor trail on R descends toward Shea Access. Ridge can be followed N to [D].	0.00

[O] Peak 1721

General Description. From [P], this trail ascends the end of a ridge, then heads east to old mine workings at 0.13 mile. Here trails diverge with one heading up a pass and the ridge trail to the peak, the other switchbacking directly up to the peak. The total ascent is 0.19 mile, and the elevation change is 225'.

Access. From [P] at 0.11 mile.

Read Down	Detailed Trail Description	Read Up
0.00	From junction on [P] at 580' (0.11 mi), head N.	0.13
0.02	**Junction:** short-cut trail from [P] enters on L.	0.11
0.06	**Junction:** near top of rise, poor trail tops small pass and descends ahead to N. Bear R here, along mountain-side, ascending.	0.07
0.13	**Junction (4-way):** steep track descends L to valley in 350' and in 655' more reaches Dunlap via obscure route heading straight N. To R, up steep track, is old mine shaft in 50' and pit in another 30'. There are two choices of route here: *see below.*	0.00

Here there are two choices: (1) Go straight for 75', then sharp R and up to the mine shaft in 65'. From there it is 470' steeply onto the ridge, and another 400' to Peak 1721, for a total of 0.19 mile. (2) Go straight for 75', then continue along the side of the valley, reaching a junction with a trail on the left (back to the valley) and continue up to reach the pass (1,603') at 0.15 mile, then turn right for 675' up a steep, rough ridge to Peak 1721 (total of 0.27 mile). From the pass, a very rough, poor and sketchy trail heads 0.18 mile northeast along the ridge to Peak 1845.

[P] Peak 1677

General Description. This is a low peak in the Echo Mountain area, reached by a steep trail to 0.31 mile, where one can scramble up to the actual summit.

Access. From 14th Street just 100' north of Alice (between it and Lawrence Lane).

Read Down	Detailed Trail Description	Read Up
0.00	Leave 14th St. on old track heading E, ascending.	0.31
0.10	**Junction:** trail angling L joins trail [O] in 180'.	0.21
0.11	**Junction:** trail L [O] to Echo Mountain (1,721'). Continue straight ahead.	0.20
0.15	Trail braids. Enter small ravine valley in 110'.	0.16
0.17	Cross ravine to R (S), then ascend steadily.	0.14
0.18	Level out and head S.	0.13
0.19	Ascend toward pass in ridge ahead.	0.12
0.21	**Junction:** trail of use on R (alternate route).	0.10
0.22	Switchback to L, then R.	0.09
0.23	Ease grade of ascent.	0.08
0.24	**Junction:** trail of use ascends L to poor ridge trail.	0.07
0.25	Pass (1,605'). Poor trail to W is alternate. Head S on E side of crest.	0.06
0.29	**Junction:** trail of use descends on L. Switchback up to R.	0.02
0.31	**Junction:** below summit knob on L (E), rough trails on L lead 140' to peak, with excellent views (1,677').	0.00

[Q] Loop Trail CLOCKWISE

General Description. From near the Christiansen Trail, this trail runs north, then east above Thunderbird Road, south along Cave Creek Road to a viewpoint at 0.62 mile, then back west again to its start at 0.83 mile. Ascent is 160'.

Access. From the Christiansen Trail 0.29 mile west of Cave Creek Road, take spur trail across wash for 80' to junction.

Read Down	Detailed Trail Description	Read Up
0.00	Leave junction, head N, ascending gradually (1,420').	0.83
0.06	**Junction:** alternate narrow trail on L, 15' shorter. Keep R.	0.77

0.12	**Junction:** join alternate from L.	0.71
0.15	**Junction:** on L is trail to hills to NW. Go R on good trail.	0.68
0.22	**Junction:** with ruined building ahead, turn R, cross wash, descend.	0.61
0.31	**Junction:** poor track to L to ruin. Keep straight on.	0.52
0.36	**Junction:** bear R where obscure trail descends on L. Reach top of rise and descend.	0.47
0.41	**Junction:** track descends L to Thunderbird.	0.42
0.43	**Junction:** track slightly L ahead to private property. Turn R on wide old road, almost level, with views over Cave Creek Road.	0.40
0.58	**Junction:** track descends to private property on L. Swing around to L.	0.25
0.62	**Junction:** in pass (1,510'), track ends, side trail L leads to VP on bump in 155'. Descend steep, rocky trail.	0.21
0.73	Turn R, parallel wash on L, on easy trail.	0.10
0.83	**Junction:** this trail ends at its start; CMC is 80' to L.	0.00

[R] Ridge Trail EAST to WEST

General Description.   From the Christiansen Trail and back to it, this hiker/horse trail gives good views from the northern ridge. Ascent is 200', descent same.

Access. *From the east:* at the Christiansen Trail 0.71 mile west of Cave Creek Road. *From the west:* at the Christiansen Trail 0.44 mile from 7th Street.

Read Down	*Detailed Trail Description*	*Read Up*
0.00	Leave CMC and turn sharp R, ascending gradually.	0.93
0.16	**Junction:** trail R connects to Loop Trail ([Q] (in 0.16 mi there is a junction: keep R. In another 0.21 mi there is another, turn R (S). In 0.43 mi reach [Q].) Turn L, continue rocky ascent.	0.78
0.22	Summit (1,690'). Descend W with good footway.	0.71
0.29	Second summit (1,680'). Descend good trail along crest.	0.64
0.40	Trail loops, rejoins in 55'.	0.53
0.60	Open area. Descend rocky trail.	0.33
0.70	**Junction:** on R trail heads N to valley.	0.24
0.71	**Junction (4-way):** R leads to valley and future crossing under Thunderbird to Lookout Mountain. Straight ascends to pass in 235', then R 140' to VP on bump (1,550'), and beyond to private land. Go L here, descending.	0.22
0.75	**Junction:** R is crossover 130' to parallel trail on other side of wash. Descend, parallelling wash on R.	0.19
0.88	**Junction (4-way):** sharp R 120' to parallel trail; half-L 70' to junction (crosses wash, in another 180' crosses open area where picnic areas are to L, then in another 315' joins [T] for total of 0.11 mi). Continue straight ahead.	0.05
0.89	**Junction (4-way):** L to picnic area and [T]; R to parallel trail in 90' and top of knob in 0.13 mi.	0.04
0.93	**Junction:** cross wide track L to picnic area (joins trail from previous junction); continue 40' more to end at CMC.	0.00

[S]
Sunnyside Access to and from Charles M. Christiansen Trail
EAST to WEST

General Description. A looping route can be taken from the Christiansen Trail, past the Sunnyside access and close to the Sierra Access. Leaving the Christiansen Trail it heads south to pass the road access points, then leads west across the valley and back up to the Christiansen Trail at 0.62 mile. It is not very scenic and much of the footway is rough and rocky. Ascent is 200'.

Access. *From the east:* at 0.80 mile from Cave Creek Road (1.14 miles from 7th Street). *From the west:* at 0.82 mile from 7th Street (1.09 miles from Cave Creek Road).

Read Down	Detailed Trail Description	Read Up
0.00	Leave CMC, heading S on wide, rocky track (1,520').	0.62
0.16	**Junction (4-way):** Sunnyside Access 40' to L (off 16th St.). Sharp R is poor track back to CMC. Bear slightly R.	0.46
0.19	**Junction:** ahead, track leads 160' to side-trail L to Sierra St. (poor parking) and further S as poor, rough track to private land and poor connection to legal access at Cortez St. Cross 2 washes; track improves.	0.43
0.30	**Junction:** track L to private land; turn R, uphill (rocky, steady ascent).	0.32
0.34	**Junction (4-way):** ahead, very poor rocky pipeline track reaches CMC in 0.10 mi. Half-L, road leads around to W & junction with this trail in 0.17 mi. Go L, on straight track, descending, then ascend.	0.28
0.46	**Junction:** track on L leads to private land and 12th St. in about 0.25 mi. Turn R here, uphill.	0.16
0.49	**Junction:** track bearing R is road from 0.34 mi. Bear L, ascending.	0.13
0.53	**Junction:** poor track bears R. Go straight on, then bear R.	0.09
0.60	**Junction:** rocky track R to CMC in 300'. Continue straight.	0.02
0.62	**Junction (5-way):** this trail ends at CMC 0.82 mi from 7th St., 1.09 mi from Cave Creek Road. Sharp L is [U]. Elevation 1,580'.	0.00

[T] Valley Trail EAST to WEST

General Description. From the Christiansen Trail and back to it. Distance is shorter, but it is less scenic. Descent is 60'.

Access. *From the east:* at the Christiansen Trail, 0.80 mile from Cave Creek Road. *From the west:* at the Christiansen Trail, 0.50 mile from 7th Street.

Read Down	Detailed Trail Description	Read Up
0.00	Leave CMC where it ascends L, 0.80 mi W of Cave Creek. Descend gradually.	0.47
0.01	**Junction:** short-cut trail L, uphill to CMC in 75'.	0.46

0.11	**Junction (4-way):** on R, trail descends to cross wash in 270', ascends, crosses other washes at 0.09 and 0.15 mi, reaching junction with this trail ahead in 0.28 mi (no saving of distance). Sharp L is rocky track ascending 300; to CMC.	0.36
0.15	**Junction:** uphill on L is poor, rocky track leading in 380' to CMC on ridge. Ignore trail descending on R.	0.32
0.24	**Junction:** rough track L into wash (poor way to CMC).	0.23
0.29	In open area, bear R (NE).	0.19
0.32	Open area narrows, this track heads W. Picnic area on L.	0.15
0.35	**Junction:** trail L ascends 0.14 mi to CMC (is good after first 40'. Continue. In 30' pass crossover on R to other picnic area.	0.12
0.39	**Junction:** track on R rejoins (from 0.11 mi). Pass near picnic area.	0.08
0.45	**Junction (4-way):** trail sharp L to CMC in 170'; trail R passes picnic area in 315' on way to junction.	0.02
0.47	**Junction:** CMC sharp L, uphill. This trail ends.	0.00

[U] EAST to WEST

General Description. A looping route from the Christiansen Trail over minor humps gives good views and returns to that trail in 0.23 mile.

Access. *At the eastern end:* at 1.09 miles from of Cave Creek Road (0.84 mile from 7th Street). *At the western end:* at 0.73 miles from 7th Street (1.19 miles from Cave Creek Road).

Read Down	Detailed Trail Description	Read Up
0.00	Leave CMC at 5-way junction, head SW.	0.23
0.07	**Junction:** top of rise (1,680'), VP. Trail ahead splits, rejoins.	0.16
0.10	**Junction (4-way):** sharp R is short-cut 105' back to this trail ahead at 0.16 mi. Straight ahead is another short-cut. For best views, keep L, rising briefly.	0.13
0.12	**Junction:** VP (1,670'). Turn R, descend.	0.11
0.13	**Junction (5-way):** sharp R is short-cut. To L is trail ascending, then descending toward 12th St. (messy area, private land). Straight ahead is 65' side-trail up bump on ridge. Go half-R, with easy descent.	0.10
0.16	**Junction:** short-cut sharp R back to this trail at 0.10 mi. Descend steadily on rocky trail.	0.07
0.22	**Junction:** trail L 75' to CMC W-bound. Go straight.	0.01
0.23	**Junction:** CMC L & R. Trail ahead half-R descends to valley and [T].	0.00

Charles M. Christiansen Trail Summary

[100] Eastbound

Read Down	Description of Major Points
0.00	Mountain View Park. Trail heads north, past Charles M. Christiansen Monument.
1.08	**Junction:** trail [F] on right (east) to North Mountain.
1.67	**Junction:** trail [306] ahead leads to Shaw Butte and Central Ave. Turn right.
2.15	Parking area east of 7th St., on south side (Pointe at Tapatio Cliffs).
4.07	Cortez east of Cave Creek Road.
5.00	**Junction:** Shea Access 335' to east.
5.43	**Junction:** trail [C] on left (east) to 24th St.
6.36	**Junction:** Hatcher Access [A] on right (west).
7.04	**Junction:** spur trail right 100' to Dreamy Draw parking.
7.65	**Junction:** Nature Trail [220] straight ahead. Go left.
7.86	**Junction:** Perl Charles Trail [1A] on right.
8.03	**Junction:** Perl Charles Trail [1A] on right.
9.89	**Junction:** Quartz Ridge Trail [8] on right (south).
9.96	**Junction:** choice of routes: north to 40th St., or straight ahead to Tatum.
10.33	40th Street *(Tatum Boulevard is 11.04 miles from start)*.

[100] Westbound

Read Down	Description of Major Points
0.00	40th Street; head south.
0.37	**Junction:** entrance spurs join here; *access from Tatum is 0.71 mile longer.* Turn west.
0.44	**Junction:** Quartz Ridge Trail [8] on left (south).
2.30	**Junction:** Perl Charles Trail [1A] on left.
2.47	**Junction:** Perl Charles Trail on left.
2.68	**Junction:** Nature Trail [220] left; go right.
3.29	**Junction:** spur trail on left 100' to Dreamy Draw parking area.
3.97	**Junction:** Hatcher Access [A] to the west.
4.90	**Junction:** short trail [C] on right leads to 24th St.
5.33	**Junction:** Shea Access 335' to right (east).
6.26	Cortez just east of Cave Creek Road.
8.18	Parking area on left (Pointe at Tapatio Cliffs) just east of tunnel under 7th St.
8.66	**Junction:** trail [306] on right leads to Shaw Butte and Central Ave. Turn left.
9.25	**Junction:** trail on left (east) is [F] to North Mountain.
10.33	Mountain View Park, just past Charles M. Christiansen Monument.

City of Phoenix

South Mountain Park

Introduction. South Mountain is the world's largest municipal park. There is no doubt that it is an impressive and popular area, with much variety for the recreationist. A Master Plan for the park will be implemented over the next few years, leading to some significant changes in the area.

History. The park area is alleged to have been claimed for Spain by Father Marcos de Niza, travelling through the area in 1539. (His inscription[1] is to be seen on the short trail south of the ramadas off the Pima Canyon Road.) The area to the east was the Yaqui Indian village of Guadalupe. In 1694 Father Kino passed through the area, but the first Americans did not arrive until about 1838. Charles Holbert became first custodian of the new park in 1929 and dedicated himself to the development of a largely inaccessible area. Starting in 1933, this task was eased by the efforts of the Civilian Conservation Corps.

Geology. The South Mountain area actually consists of three parallel ranges trending northeast-southwest like the White Tank Mountains. They represent a "metamorphic core complex" of intrusive and metamorphic rock that upwelled and extended in the northeast-southwest direction. Rocks to be seen today in the western part of the park are mostly granitic *gneiss* (coarse-grained rock with alternating light and dark minerals) and *schist* (better-defined planes of minerals result in easy cleavage), both of Precambrian age. In the eastern part of the park the rocks are intrusive granite, much younger than those in the western end. In some places *petroglyphs* have been carved or pecked into the rock surfaces; these are usually 500-1500 years old.

Maps. *Our maps 9-13, "South Mountain A" through "South Mountain E."* The USGS 1:24,000 topo maps Laveen (1952, photorevised 1973), Lone Butte (1952, photorevised 1973) and Guadalupe (1952, photorevised 1982) show the topography and some of the trails, but there have been many changes since these were published.

Access. There are several main access points within the park itself, which is entered from the south end of Central Avenue. The Pima Canyon Road leads to the eastern end of the National Trail [162]. From the north there are separate access points for the Mormon, Kiwanis, Ranger, and Holbert Trails.

Facilities. Picnic ramadas serve up to 3100, with electricity, drinking water, toilets and firepits (250 first-come, the remainder reservable).

Recommended Hikes and Trail Rides. Numbers used are either official City of Phoenix numbers or our own arbitrary letters for non-designated trails. Almost all of the trails are highly recommended. The western and eastern sections of the National Trail are especially scenic and provide almost continuous distant views.

Cautions. In some areas there are many trails of use that can be confusing, especially in bad weather. Some trails are very long and traverse rugged terrain.

---

[1]There is some doubt as to its authenticity.

[62] Kiwanis Trail

General Description. Built by members of the Kiwanis Club, opened in 1926, and improved by the Phoenix chain gang, this trail can be confusing because of many side-trails and minor trails of use. From Las Lomitas it ascends a valley past several rock dams (built for water storage and erosion control but unsuccessful) and then runs between the bends of the highway to reach it at 1.04 miles near the National Trail. Ascent is 400'.

Access. From the Las Lomitas area, at the bend in the road. *(Map 11 -- South Mountain C)*

Read Down	Detailed Trail Description	Read Up
0.00	Leave road bend in wide, open area, ascending (1,590'). To R, alternate trails lead 0.25 and 0.34 mi W to parking area with washrooms.	1.04
0.04	Pass picnic tables, go up wide trail at end of open area.	1.00
0.07	**Junction:** trail of use on L (alternate route).	0.97
0.10	**Junction:** alternate rejoins.	0.94
0.18	**Junction:** 50' to R is rock wall and grassy area. Go straight.	0.86
0.23	Start steady, rocky ascent.	0.81
0.30	Level area, stone dam.	0.74
0.36	Dam. Start steady ascent in 150'.	0.68
0.40	**Junction:** alternate trail on L; go straight.	0.64
0.42	Cross under power line. Trail goes up and down.	0.62
0.53	Trail runs alongside wash.	0.51
0.54	Ascend in wash for 45', leave it to R.	0.50
0.56	Switchback to R, then 3 more.	0.48
0.58	**Junction:** trail of use on R; big dam on L.	0.46
0.64	**Junction:** trail [E] on L; just beyond, on R, trail leads 325' onto ridge and 4-way junction: 175' R to VP, 0.19 mi ahead, across wash, to highway; to L, 0.13 mi to highway.	0.40
0.75	Ascend rocky trail between bends of Summit Road.	0.29
0.88	Ascend to R, then switchback to L.	0.16
1.02	Cross wash, ascend steadily, then steeply.	0.02
1.04	**Junction:** highway, signpost (1,990') in Telegraph Pass. National Trail W-bound is 120' E of here.	0.00

Kiwanis Trail Alternates

There are several additional trails from the Las Lomitas area to the Summit Road, other than trail [E]. They ascend up ridges or valleys to different points on the highway. *These are described here for the descent.* West of Telegraph Pass there are 3 trails leaving the highway to the north. *The first,* at an overlook, leads 625' past views to a junction with a trail right to the Kiwanis Trail in 325', or left back to the highway in 0.19 mile. *The second,* from a smaller overlook, has a junction in 30': straight ahead is the trail along the ridge top to a view-point in 0.15 mile. To the right is a trail to the ridge west of the Kiwanis Trail. To the left it is 0.19 or 0.25 mile to the ramadas. *The third* is 400' further west than the second. Its trail descends steadily, with alternates, to a junction at 0.21 mile. Turn right here, descending to meet a trail from the right (2nd overlook) and reaches the ramadas at 0.41 mile (310' of descent).

[64] Holbert Trail

General Description. The trail first leads from the locked Activity Complex gate to the trail-head at 0.44 mile, then over rolling terrain near the base of the mountain to briefly join a road past a water tank and ascends by a scenic route up the side of a major valley past unusual rock formations to a junction with the 0.21 mile side-trail to Dobbins Lookout (and road) at 2.29 miles. Beyond, it continues up for another 0.26 mile to the Summit Road at 2.55 miles. Ascent is 950'.

Access. From the Activity Complex gate, follow the road for 0.44 mile to the actual trail-head on the south side; at the top, from Summit Road *(see Map 11 -- South Mountain C)*.

Read Down	Detailed Trail Description	Read Up
0.00	Leave Activity Complex gate (1,350').	2.55
0.44	Leave parking area at sign-post.	2.11
0.51	**Junction:** bear L, go over hill.	2.04
0.55	**Junction:** with cookout area on R, cross road, head E, following posts near base of mountain slopes.	2.00
0.67	Pass petroglyphs on rock on L.	1.88
0.86	Bottom of deep wash; ascend.	1.69
0.96	**Junction:** join paved road, go R on it.	1.59
1.02	**Junction:** leave road on R, at angle; in 200' pass along fence for 80'.	1.53
1.13	Bear R.	1.42
1.20	Top of rise. Side-hill, ascend valley side. Apparently dry waterfall on R.	1.36
1.57	Turn L.	0.98
1.64	Switchback to R.	0.91
1.74	Cross wash.	0.81
1.79	Turn L, then to R in 0.05 mi.	0.76
1.85	**Junction:** 90' to R is fine VP. Pass rock cave on L in 0.18 mi.	0.70
2.12	Switchback to L.	0.43
2.16	Switchback to R, then to L in 55', just above wash.	0.39
2.22	Switchback to R at unusual rock formation, then switchback to L in 95'.	0.33
2.29	**Junction:** to R, side trail ascends 300' to Dobbins Lookout (2,350'). *[details: at 90' go straight; switchback to L at 265', R at 0.13 mi, where spur trail R leads 60' to VP; Dobbins Lookout at 0.21 mi, 2.50 mi from start.]*	0.26
2.31	Switchback to L, then pass trail of use.	0.24
2.37	Enter moderate wash, leave it in 60'.	0.18
2.43	**Junction:** switchback to L, then to R.	0.12
2.55	Summit Road (2,255').	0.00

Rock dam on the Kiwanis Trail

Petroglyphs near the Holbert Trail

[162] National (Sun Circle) Trail EAST to WEST

> This trail is described in 4 sections, a total of 12.74 miles

PIMA CANYON to BUENA VISTA LOOKOUT

General Description. This popular trail segment leads from the Pima Canyon road along a very scenic section, past the Hidden Valley loop trail at 1.35 and 1.92 miles, then on to Buena Vista Lookout on Summit Road, a distance of 3.59 miles. Ascent is 890'.

Access. *At the eastern end,* the trail leaves the dirt road at 1.1 miles from the gate at the end of paving at the Marcos de Niza ramadas, 0.6 mile west of the park entrance at 48th Street. **Note: the road must now be walked.** *At the western end* it departs from Buena Vista Lookout. *(Maps 12, 13 -- South Mountain D, E)*

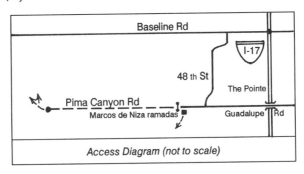

Access Diagram (not to scale)

Read Down	Detailed Trail Description	Read Up
0.00	Leave Pima Canyon road loop (1,580') after 1.1 mile road walk. Head <u>NW</u>.	3.59
0.03	Cross major wash and ascend.	3.56
0.05	Trail post; turn L.	3.54
0.06	**Junction:** slightly R is [G], alternate route to Mormon Trail (1.34 mi). To continue, turn L here. Turn R in 60', then L in 40' more and ascend.	3.53
0.09	Ascend more steadily, then turn L.	3.50
0.12	Switchback to R.	3.47
0.16	Switchback to L where trail ahead has been closed.	3.43
0.20	Turn R along hillside.	3.39
0.23	Switchback to R.	3.36
0.25	Top of rise (closed trail on R). Bear L, ease grade of ascent.	3.34
0.34	Reach crest of ridge.	3.25
0.43	Bear R and side-hill to E.	3.16
0.47	Switchback to L.	3.12
0.52	Trail post. Old trail on L is closed.	3.07
0.53	**Junction:** on crest is VP to R.	3.06
0.58	**Junction:** ignore track on L.	3.01

0.64	Go steeply up to L.	2.95
0.65	Cross over crest of ridge, then take narrow trail to L of hump.	2.94
0.68	**Junction:** on crest, 50' to R is VP.	2.91
0.72	Pass through area of huge rocks.	2.87
0.83	Turn sharp R.	2.76
0.85	Go L.	2.74
0.88	Switchback to R.	2.71
1.00	Go through area of huge rocks.	2.59
1.05	Jog L, then sharp R. Ahead, there are several rocky areas that provide natural shelters.	2.54
1.29	Old metal sign on L (ignore).	2.30
1.35	**Junction:** Hidden Valley Trail [F] on L. Keep R for main trail.	2.24
1.48	**Junction:** sharp R is Mormon Trail [264].	2.11
1.53	**Junction:** trail of use on L. Leave wash, bear R.	2.06
1.56	**Junction:** trail of use on L.	2.03
1.58	Switchback to L.	2.01
1.68	Go L, ascending, then to R.	1.91
1.69	Rop of rise (VP). Turn L.	1.90
1.76	Switchback to R, up to top of rise. In 200', turn R, then L.	1.83
1.87	Top of rise.	1.72
1.90	**Junction:** trail of use on L by-passes Fat Man's Pass.	1.69
1.92	**Important junction:** Hidden Valley Trail [F] on L.	1.68
1.95	Enter wash, then stay in it for 325'.	1.64
2.13	Turn R, then L.	1.46
2.19	Jog R, then to L.	1.40
2.29	Cross wash and ascend through rocky area.	1.30
2.39	**Junction:** trail of use on L.	1.20
2.45	**Junction:** trail of use sharp L.	1.14
2.50	Cross 3 washes in next 0.13 mi, the last near rock shelter on R.	1.09
2.67	Cross wash, then another in 0.06 mi.	0.92
2.77	Bear L.	0.82
2.83	Cross wash.	0.76
2.88	**Junction:** trail of use on L.	0.71
2.93	Level area.	0.66
3.01	Shelter in rocks on L.	0.58
3.02	National Trail sign on L.	0.57
3.03	**Junction:** trail of use on R.	0.56
3.06	**Junction:** trail on R rejoining.	0.53
3.20	**Junction:** trail of use on R.	0.39
3.22	**Junction (4-way):** on N, trail descends 250' in elevation to valley, then ascends steadily for 220' to Geronimo Trail (now closed at bottom). To the S, trail ascends 0.17 mi (145') to ridge, 0.26 mi to end of ridge (2,555'); both have fine views.	0.35
3.59	Buena Vista Lookout (2,360'). To N, Geronimo Trail descends toward valley, and side-trail from it leads along ridge to Peak 2380, and beyond.	0.00

[162] National (Sun Circle) Trail EAST to WEST

BUENA VISTA LOOKOUT to TELEGRAPH PASS

General Description. This trail segment leads from Buena Vista Lookout to a long descent of the ridge north of South Mountain's highest peak (Mt. Suppoa, 2,690'), closed to the public because of the presence of dozens of transmission towers. After passing the summit, the trail takes a very scenic route to Telegraph Pass at 3.01 miles. Ascent is 320', descent is 440'.

Access. *At the eastern end,* the trail leaves Buena Vista Lookout. *At the western end* it departs from the Summit Road in Telegraph Pass. *(Maps 11, 12 -- South Mountain C, D.)*

Read Down	Detailed Trail Description	Read Up
0.00	Leave Buena Vista Lookout (2,360'). Follow highway W.	3.01
0.08	Leave road just past small parking area on L.	2.93
0.09	**Junction:** trail L to hump. Ascend gradually, parallelling highway.	2.92
0.16	**Junction:** cross dirt road, continue on level trail. "Chinese Wall" of rocks can be seen ahead.	2.86
0.27	Top of rise. Bear L and descend.	2.74
0.32	Level out, then reach top of rise in 0.12 mi.	2.69
0.59	Bend of highway below.	2.41
0.63	Top of rise.	2.38
0.72	**Junction:** reach dirt road at highway (across highway, just to R of dirt road, is old section of Holbert Trail, now overgrown). Cross highway, follow it to L.	2.29
0.77	**Junction:** leave road on R (sign).	2.24
0.95	Pass to R of rocky hump.	2.06
1.06	Top of rise.	1.95
1.10	Start descending past towers on summit.	1.90
1.11	Turn sharp L.	1.89
1.16	**Junction:** trail L to highway in 235'; another in 40'.	1.85
1.27	Turn L. Route goes up and down, bypassing summit.	1.73
1.68	Cross moderate wash.	1.32
1.92	Go onto side-ridge. In 45', start descent.	1.09
2.11	**Junction:** cross dirt road (R to highway).	0.90
2.25	Bear L on scenic route with good views. In 45' pass under phone line.	0.76
2.51	Cross wash.	0.50
2.63	**Junction:** old trail descends R to highway in 50'. New trail continues along hillside.	0.38
2.76	Switchback to R, then to L.	0.25
2.79	Turn R onto crest (shortly thereafter there is a 100' spur to hump on L).	0.22
2.86	Turn sharp L, off crest. Turn sharp L in 150'.	0.15
2.90	Switchback to R and down.	0.11
2.91	**Junction:** old trail L descends to cross private land. Keep R.	0.10
2.92	Join highway, go L.	0.09
3.01	Road in Telegraph Pass (1,990').	0.00

[162] National (Sun Circle) Trail EAST to WEST

TELEGRAPH PASS to SAN JUAN ROAD

General Description. This trail segment leads from Telegraph Pass up a high ridge and generally keeps on or near the crest for 1.38 miles where it passes the Ranger Trail [C] and then the side-trail to Goat Hill at 1.72 miles. There is then a long, sometimes steep descent of 1,000' to the San Juan Road at 4.64 miles. Ascent is 850', descent is 1,630'.

Access. *At the eastern end,* the trail leaves Telegraph Pass at a signpost. *At the western end* from the San Juan Road opposite the section to the San Juan Ramada. *(Maps 9-11 -- South Mountain A-C).*

Read Down	Detailed Trail Description	Read Up
0.00	Leave Telegraph Pass (1,990'), ascending W at signpost.	4.64
0.04	Turn R, then switchback to L in 195'.	4.60
0.12	**Junction:** trail of use on L (avoid -- cuts switchback).	4.52
0.13	**Junction:** switchback to R (spur trail ahead leads 65' and a further 135' to VP).	4.51
0.16	VP on L. Bear R, ease grade of ascent.	4.48
0.21	Reach crest again; turn R, avoiding poor trails of use.	4.43
0.25	Ascend into side-valley.	4.39
0.28	**Junction:** trail of use on L ascends. Go straight.	4.36
0.30	Switchback to L, then in 200' switchback to R (old stone ramada on L).	4.34
0.37	**Junction:** trail of use ascends straight ahead. Bear R here.	4.27
0.38	**Junction:** trail of use on L. Ascend rocky area.	4.26
0.39	**Junction:** trail of use rejoins on L.	4.25
0.48	**Important junction:** trail on L [D] crosses crest, leads along parallel ridge.	4.16
0.54	Reach crest, bear slightly R with easy walking.	4.10
0.63	**Junction:** poorly-defined trail of use sharp L to hump on ridge in 0.12 mi.	4.01
0.65	Reach top of rise; descend from hump.	3.99
0.77	Switchback to L, then turn R in 50'.	3.87
0.84	Start steady ascent.	3.80
0.88	Top of rise. Return to crest in 110'.	3.76
0.97	Top of small summit. Pass another hump on crest.	3.67
1.10	Top of major summit with excellent views. Descend.	3.54
1.16	Bottom; ascend gradually.	3.48
1.21	Top of rise on crest.	3.43
1.26	Hump on R, just off trail.	3.38
1.28	**Junction:** trail R to top of hump.	3.36
1.35	**Junction:** good side-trail straight ahead ascends ridge to top of hump in 275', meets short-cut at 305', passes rock knob at 0.27 mi, and ends at flat area on ridge at 0.33 mi. There are fine views from it. Descend to R.	3.29
1.38	**Important junction:** Ranger Trail [C] descends on R to road in 0.74 mi.	3.26
1.43	**Junction:** trail on L returns from 1.35 mi. Continue up crest.	3.21
1.50	Cross wash, bear slightly L with easy ascent.	3.14
1.67	**Junction:** poor trail of use sharp R.	2.97
1.72	**Important junction:** trail on R to Goat Hill *[7 switchbacks start in 145'. Ascend stone steps at 0.12 mi to top (2,526') and fine views at 0.14 mi].*	2.92
1.89	Ridge broadens.	2.75

2.00	Flat area on L; ascend.	2.64
2.06	Turn L; reach top of rise in 150', then descend.	2.58
2.31	Switchback to R, ascend.	2.33
2.33	Top of rise. Bear L and descend gradually.	2.31
2.40	**Junction:** trail of use on L.	2.24
2.45	**Junction:** trail sharp L (overgrown) leads S to private land. Continue side-hilling.	2.19
2.55	Reach crest. Descend in 200'.	2.09
2.63	Bottom. Ascend to L of peak ahead.	2.01
2.71	Top of rise (excellent VP in attractive area).	1.93
2.83	Reach crest; descend, reaching bottom in 65', another sag in 200'.	1.81
2.94	**Junction:** 100' R to hump. Descend easily to bottom in 400'.	1.70
3.07	Reach crest, descend to L, reaching bottom in 255'.	1.57
3.17	Reach crest, ascend to top of rise (cairn) in 0.05 mi; descend.	1.47
3.32	Turn R, level off.	1.32
3.33	Switchback down to L.	1.31
3.39	Bottom. Ascend gradually.	1.25
3.42	Pass white rocks.	1.22
3.47	Reach crest again.	1.17
3.52	Last hump on ridge (it is all down from here).	1.12
3.70	Switchback to R, then to L in 65'.	0.94
3.84	Descend loose rock.	0.80
3.86	Switchback to R, then to L in 50'.	0.78
3.89	CAUTION: switchback R & L, *do not go straight here.* Descend steeply down N side of ridge.	0.75
3.98	**Junction:** on L, trail of use is blocked. Descend with care.	0.66
4.04	**Junction:** other route (obscure) joins on L. Go R of rocks and descend. Pass trail of use on R. In 200' ease grade of descent.	0.60
4.11	Level, rocky area. Descend.	0.53
4.13	Switchback to R, then turn L in 20'. Cross very rocky wash in 150'.	0.51
4.17	Level area. Trail improves, then becomes rocky as it descends.	0.47
4.20	Cross wash, bear R. In 200', ease grade on flat area.	0.44
4.29	**Junction (4-way):** cross alternate trail.	0.35
4.51	Cross wide wash. In 150' switchback to R, then cross major wash in 45'. ...	0.13
4.64	San Juan Road (1,300').	0.00

[162] National (Sun Circle) Trail EAST to WEST

SAN JUAN ROAD to SAN JUAN RAMADA

General Description. This trail segment leads from the San Juan Road to the pass and ramada at the road end. It leads over a mostly flat slope toward the pass in the range. Crossing several washes, it heads northwest to 0.83 mile, then north to parallel the road, ascending to end at the Alta Trail next to the road end at 1.50 miles. Ascent is 50'.

Access. *At the eastern end,* the trail leaves the road at 4.3 miles from the entrance gate at a small sign. This is 1.90 miles west of the Alta Trail. *At the western end* it departs from the Alta Trail just a few feet east of the stone wall at the ramada. *(Map 9 -- South Mountain A.)*

Read Down	Detailed Trail Description	Read Up
0.00	Leave San Juan Road, heading NW at signpost (1,310').	1.50
0.10	Head slightly R, cross small wash onto flat plain.	1.40
0.12	Cross old road, turn L (W).	1.38
0.16	Cross major wash.	1.34
0.23	Survey marker on R (General Land Survey).	1.27
0.36	Cross major wash; head toward mountain slopes.	1.14
0.42	Cross major wash, head W.	1.08
0.83	Cross small wash, then swing around to N, descending gradually.	0.67
0.96	Road parallels trail below on L. Ascend gradually.	0.64
1.50	**Junction:** Alta Trail on R in pass. San Juan Ramada on L at road end (1,320').	0.00

[262] Geronimo (Hieroglyphic) Trail

This renamed, formerly popular trail from the Boy Scout Heard Pueblo to the National Trail at Buena Vista Lookout is *closed* due to the need for re-routing.

[264] Mormon Trail

General Description. This trail ascends by a circuitous route and switch-backs to a pass at 1.16 miles, then descends briefly to the National Trail at 1.39 miles. Ascent is 730'.

Access. From Euclid at 24th Street. *(Map 12 -- South Mountain D.)*

Read Down	Detailed Trail Description	Read Up
0.00	Leave road at dirt barrier on rocky, wide trail (1,290'). In 200', bear L on rocks.	1.39
0.06	**Junction:** trail R ascends for 210' to poor VP.	1.33
0.10	**Junction:** trail on L rejoins. Bear R, up rocks for 100', then level off.	1.29
0.14	Overhanging rock on R.	1.25
0.31	**Junction:** trail to R descends, ends at poor VP.	1.08
0.34	**Junction:** trail L to hump in 135'.	1.05
0.36	Bottom of descent. Ascend; turn L in 150' and ascend again.	1.03
0.41	**Junction:** cut-off on L.	0.98
0.44	**Junction:** cut-off trail on L (blocked); switchback to L.	0.95
0.51	Switchback to L, then again in 0.06 mi.	0.88
0.63	Switchback to R, then to L in 130'.	0.76
0.71	Switchback to R.	0.68
0.75	**Junction:** 40' L is VP near hump.	0.64
0.85	USCGS marker on L.	0.54
0.93	Cross wash.	0.46
0.98	Reach bottom of descent. Turn L in 200'.	0.41
1.16	**Junction:** in pass, trail L [G] leads to hump in 325'; just a few feet up this trail is **junction** where trail [G] leads R to National Trail [162] in Pima Canyon in 1.34 mi.	0.23
1.25	**Junction:** trail of use on L.	0.14

1.33   **Junction:** this trail splits, reaching National Trail either way (L is 340'; go R). 0.06
1.39   **Junction:** National Trail (1,960'). 1.48 mi L to Pima Canyon; 2.11 mi R to
       Buena Vista Lookout. 0.00

---

[362] **Alta Trail** WEST to EAST

General Description. Travelling east, the trail starts from the San Juan Ramada at the road end in a pass. This section is moderately strenuous on a well-built trail with very good views. It ascends steadily up a valley to 1.13 miles, then circles around the valley's head to a pass at 1.52 miles where short side-trails lead to fine views. From there it switchbacks down and contours around Maricopa Peak, reaching the ridge crest at 2.71 miles and passing or going over several peaks with the last summit at 3.07 miles. The trail then makes a long, switchbacking descent to reach the park drive at 4.46 miles. Total ascent is 1,300'; descent is 1,100'.

Access. *At the western end,* from San Juan ramada; *at the eastern end* from the road at 2.4 miles west of the park entrance. *(Maps 9, 10 -- South Mountain A, B.)*

Read Down	Detailed Trail Description	·Read Up
0.00	Leave ramada at sign, heading E. There is a junction (to the R) at the start (National Trail heading SE). Elevation here is 1,320'.	4.46
0.41	Switchback to R, then to L, ignoring short-cut trail.	4.05
0.44	End of ridge and VP. View of peak ahead. Continue ascent.	4.42
0.70	Cross wash. Bear L around end of valley, ascending; in 100' switchbacks start. ...	3.76
0.80	Go around end of subsidiary ridge. Ascent continues.	3.65
0.98	Switchback to R, up open rock. Use care.	3.48
1.09	Top of rise, VP. Ease grade.	3.37
1.13	**Junction:** spur trail R 45' to VP. Ascend.	3.33
1.17	Switchback to R, level off along ridge. 110' beyond switchback is VP just off trail to R. Contour around N side of head of valley.	3.29
1.38	Trail switchbacks again, on ascent.	3.08
1.43	Cross ridge crest; switchbacks follow.	3.03
1.52	Pass; turn L and follow ridge just N of crest.	2.94
1.54	**Junction:** spur trail to L leads 190' onto hump with good VP of main ridge and Maricopa Peak; spur trail R, up minor crest, leads onto main ridge in 0.10 mi. (There, at junction, spur R leads 190' to hump; spur L leads 110' to another rise and route [no trail] to Maricopa Peak.) Descend switchbacks.	2.92
1.72	Ridge crest (2,325'). Head into larger valley. Trail soon ascends again.	2.74
1.82	Base of cliffs on R. Ascend gradually.	2.64
1.89	Top of rise; descend gradually.	2.57
2.01	End of ridge; switchback to R, around it.	2.45
2.13	Top of rise; switchback down to R, then turn R in 0.05 mi.	2.33
2.20	Landmark: big rock on R.	2.26
2.41	Bear R into valley, up and down, gradually ascending.	2.05
2.50	Trail passes just below ridge crest on R. Continue just below crest.	1.95

2.71	Cross over crest to S side of ridge.	1.75
2.77	Reach crest again; follow it, then contour along N side of next summit on ridge. ...	1.69
2.87	Crest again. Follow S side, ascending gradually.	1.59
2.92	Ascend. Subsidiary ridge on R.	1.54
3.00	Crest again. Ascend, heading toward last summit.	1.46
3.07	Last summit of ridge.	1.39
3.09	Switchback to L, then trail levels off.	1.37
3.12	Turn L into valley, then follow circuitous route.	1.34
3.37	Switchback to R, off crest, then to L.	1.09
3.48	Top of rise. Descend gradually.	0.98
3.53	Switchback to L; other turns and switchbacks follow.	0.93
3.66	Turn to R; trail makes long traverse.	0.80
3.71	Cross ridge crest, descending steadily.	0.75
3.78	Landmark: pass stone bench on L.	0.68
4.15	Cross wash, switchback to L, and descend steadily over loose rock. Beyond, trail is almost level and not well defined.	0.31
4.46	**Junction:** road (1,570'). *For National Trail, and return to start, turn R on road for 1.90 mi, then take trail for 1.50 mi: total to return is 3.40 mi.*	0.00

[A] Peak 1600 FROM SAN JUAN RAMADA

General Description. For a relatively short trip with fine views of South Mountain and the Sierra Estrella as well as Phoenix, this trail is perfect. It leaves the San Juan road end, and ascends steadily up the crest, past several bumps, to one of the last peaks on the ridge at 0.63 mile. Ascent is 300'.

Access. From the end of the San Juan Ramada parking lot, head northwest. *(Map 9 -- South Mountain A.)*

Read Down	*Detailed Trail Description*	*Read Up*
0.00	Leave parking area at N end (1,320'), heading NW up ridge, passing several trails of use on R.	0.63
0.12	**Junction:** trail sharp R drops off crest, intersects [B] in pass at 385' (back to ramada in another 475'). Ascend.	0.51
0.14	**Junction:** poor alternate trail on R ascends very steeply onto crest over loose rock (rejoins ahead at 0.22 mile - is 20' longer than main trail).	0.48
0.19	Bear R.	0.44
0.22	**Junction:** on crest, alternate trail rejoins on R.	0.40
0.30	Leave crest; follow ridge along its N side, ascending gradually.	0.32
0.37	Cross over crest to S side.	0.26
0.40	Crest again: stay on it or close to it from here. Start final ascent in 0.08 mi.	0.22
0.53	Switchback to R, then to L in only 15'.	0.09
0.54	**Junction:** at L switchback, trail of use R leads onto crest in 125'.	0.09
0.55	Top of rise, almost on crest. Descend, reach bottom in 100'.	0.07
0.58	**Junction:** trail of use R onto crest.	0.04
0.63	Top of Peak 1600. Fine views.	0.00

Old stone ramada above Telegraph Pass

Goat Hill on National Trail

[B] Peak 1400   FROM SAN JUAN RAMADA

For a very short hike with good views (ascent of only 100'), take this trail north at the parking area *(see Map 9 -- South Mountain A)*. In 335' there is a trail of use on the left and the pass is reached at 475' (a side-trail ascends left to [A] on the ridge in 385'). Here turn right. At 0.13 mile another trail of use joins on the right (back to ramada in 0.10 mile). Ascend, passing a 4-way junction at 0.14 mile where a poor track crosses. Here the trail side-hills along the west side of the ridge, reaching the crest again at 0.17 mile. Shortly thereafter it turns left and ascends more steadily to 0.23 mile where it levels out. A hump on the ridge is passed at 0.28. From here there is a short descent before the final peak is attained at 0.34 mile. (Beyond, the trail deteriorates.)

[C] Ranger Trail

General Description. This old trail leads from some ramadas up to the Summit Road at 0.74 mile and then ascends to the National Trail at 1.41 miles, an ascent of 300' to the road and 800' to the National Trail.

Access. 0.5 mile from the second gate and park administration office, turn left on a paved road. Take the first right turn (dirt) across an open area to the farthest ramada ("Five Tables" area) next to the major wash (there is a drinking fountain here). Park here. The trail post can barely be seen looking west along the wash. *(Map 10 -- South Mountain B.)*

Read Down	Detailed Trail Description	Read Up
0.00	Leave ramada area (1,460'), heading W on track.	0.68
0.06	**Junction:** where trail continues ahead, turn L and descend to wash.	0.62
0.08	Cross major wash, bearing slightly R, then ascend along side-wash.	0.59
0.12	Top of rise out of wash and ravine.	0.57
0.20	**Junction:** trail of use on L.	0.49
0.22	**Junction (4-way):** trail of use crosses.	0.46
0.55	**Junction:** on L, trail is closed.	0.13
0.63	Switchback to L, then to R in 165'.	0.05
0.68	Summit Road (1,760').	0.00
0.00	Leave road 180' below small parking area on S side.	0.74
0.09	Switchback to L.	0.65
0.27	**Junction:** on L is closed trail. In 15' reach switchback to R, where trail of use continues into ravine ahead.	0.48
0.65	Switchback L, above valley.	0.10
0.74	**Junction:** National Trail L & R (2,260'). (180' L, 240' R to crest.)	0.00

[D]

General Description. A fine side-trip to a parallel ridge, giving good views of the main ridge and valley between. There are several humps on the ridge as it leads to the end at 1.07 miles. Ascent is 150', descent is 250'.

Access. From the National Trail [162] at 0.48 mile west of Telegraph Pass. *(Maps 10, 11 -- South Mountain B, C.)*

Read Down	Detailed Trail Description	Read Up
0.00	Leave National Trail, cross crest to S (2,360'). Return to crest at 0.07 mi.	1.07
0.14	Ascend rocks. Trail leads through pleasant rocky area.	0.93
0.24	Start descent (fine views of valley to N). Pass rock hump on L in 150'.	0.83
0.32	Bottom, ascend. Pass small knob on L.	0.74
0.36	Return to crest. Start ascent in 55'.	0.70
0.49	Go to R of crest.	0.58
0.51	**Junction:** poor trail ahead. Switchback to L, then to R near crest in 60'. Keep S of crest.	0.56
0.55	**Junction:** short-cut straight ahead. Constructed trail turns R.	0.52
0.58	Switchback to R, descend.	0.48
0.65	**Junction:** L on crest is spur rejoining.	0.42
0.67	Top of hump, excellent walking.	0.40
0.75	Switchback to R, then go W onto crest and follow it.	0.32
0.82	Head R of hump.	0.25
0.89	Bottom of descent; go to R of large peak.	0.17
0.93	Switchback to L.	0.14
0.97	Switchback to R, then to L in 210'.	0.09
1.04	Top of rise. Descend to sag in 50'.	0.03
1.07	Summit cairn (2,241'), VP.	0.00

[E] Kiwanis Alternate

At 0.64 mile on the Kiwanis Trail, turn left and descend to cross a wash in 145', then reach a junction at 210'. (On the left, a poorer alternate ascends for 250' and meets this trail at 0.10 mile. The area can be confusing.) Ascend, reaching junction with trail of use on the left at 320'. Then swing up and to the left to a junction with the alternate at 0.10 mile. From there the trail ascends, then parallels the highway to join it at 0.28 mile, just 170' west of where the National Trail spur leaves the highway (0.26 mile from Telegraph Pass).

[F] Hidden Valley WEST to EAST

General Description. One of the most spectacular and varied trips in the park, this trail is also an alternate to the main National Trail route. It includes the very narrow Fat Man's Pass [shown in color picture #13], petroglyphs, and a tunnel through the huge rocks. Allow much more time than the distance of only a bit over one half mile indicates. (There is a bypass of Fat Man's Pass from the National Trail just east of the junction.)

Access. On the National Trail, the *western end* is 1.35 miles, and the *eastern end* 1.92 miles, from Pima Canyon Road. *(Map 12 -- South Mountain D.)*

Read Down	Detailed Trail Description	Read Up
0.00	Leave National Trail. In 85' turn L through Fat Man's Pass (or one can bypass it by going over the rocks). Use care.	0.53
0.03	Emerge from rocks, then follow wash.	0.50
0.06	Leave wash on L.	0.47
0.10	Cross wash.	0.43
0.14	Descend rocks, go under low rock (caution), then over and under rocks.	0.39
0.24	Cross brushy wash. Trail of use to L, to cave. Turn R.	0.33
0.25	**Junction:** keep L (trail braids). In 60' turn L.	0.32
0.32	Join wash.	0.21
0.38	Valley turns L. Petroglyphs on R. Descend rocks.	0.15
0.43	**Junction:** trail of use on R, past shelter rock.	0.10
0.46	Go through rocks, then through spectacular tunnel in 50'.	0.07
0.51	**Junction:** trail of use on R.	0.02
0.53	**Junction:** National Trail (0.13 mi to L is Mormon Trail junction).	0.00

[G] Alternate Ridge Trail

General Description. This is a pleasant 1.34-mile alternate for the National Trail out of Pima Canyon, and can be combined with the Mormon Trail.

Access. *At the western end:* from the Mormon Trail at 1.16 miles or 0.23 mile from the National Trail. *At the eastern end:* at Pima Canyon Road. *(Maps 12, 13 -- South Mountain D, E.)*

Read Down	Detailed Trail Description	Read Up
0.00	Leave junction with Mormon Trail, heading E. In 40' at **junction** head around S side of hump (side-trail straight ahead leads up hump in 285').	1.34
0.56	Top of minor summit; descend.	0.78
0.68	**Junction:** sharp L is horse trail to private property.	0.66
0.70	**Junction:** in pass, trail ahead to hump in 445'; descend to S, then turn E.	0.64
0.90	Cross moderate wash, then side-hill above it.	0.44
1.17	**Junction:** poor track crosses; another is in 70'.	0.17
1.27	**Junction:** track descends on L. Continue straight.	0.07
1.28	**Junction:** cross poor track, then in 25' turn L, descend. Cross wash, then in 35' go L on trail where old trail ascends on R.	0.06
1.34	**Junction:** at triangle is National Trail [162]. To L on it, Pima Canyon Road is 330' away.	0.00

City of Glendale

Thunderbird Recreation Area

Introduction. Thunderbird Recreation Area consists of 1,082 acres located in the Hedgpeth Hills north of Glendale. Hiking trails climb to 1800' and 1682' on two summits. More are planned.

History. The park name derives from the air force's large primary training facility south of the park (Thunderbird Field No. 1) in World War II. Use of the area for picnicking by Glendale residents predated the park's establishment and the area was also used for hunting cottontails and quail. Lack of water in the area and rugged terrain made the land unsuitable for homesteading and at best marginal as rangeland. Significant mineralization is absent. In 1951-52 the City of Glendale acquired the land from the federal government.

The Hedgpeth Hills are named after a family that homesteaded in the region and pioneered the northwest part of the Salt River Valley in the later years of the last century.

Geology. The Hedgpeth Hills jut upward from the alluvial plain of Deer Valley, a northward extension of the Salt River Valley. They consist largely of igneous and metamorphic rocks, with the eastern part a tilted fault block consisting of basaltic lavas. Rock units in the western part contain some rocks of Precambrian age (1-1.5 billion years old). Schist and quartzite are the oldest rocks, originally shale and sandstone that were later subjected to intense heat and pressure. Lava flows occurred during Tertiary and Quaternary time. Current topography is probably less than one million years old. The dominant wash trending southeasterly through the area past the amphitheater and picnic area is along a concealed fault.

Maps. *Our map 14.* The USGS Hedgpeth Hills 1:24,000 topo (1971) shows the Recreation Area but no trails. There is a small map put out by the Glendale Recreation Department showing facilities and most of the trails.

Access. From the Black Canyon Freeway (I-17) take the Deer Valley Drive exit and drive west for 1.6 miles to 35th Avenue. Turn right for 1 mile to Pinnacle Peak Road and head west on it for 2 miles to the park boundary. The entrance to the spur road to Loop Trail [3] is 1 mile further on, on the left, and the main picnic area entrance is a further 0.3 mile on the right. Alternatively, take 59th Avenue north from Bell Road for 3.6 miles past the Arrow Lakes Ranch to the picnic area entrance.

[Previous page: View north from Loop Trail [3]

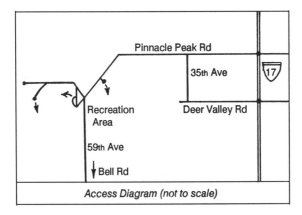

Access Diagram (not to scale)

Facilities. There are several picnic ramadas with covered tables, cooking grilles and fire-pits, and there is drinking water and a comfort station. The horse staging area (ramadas 2 & 3) also has hitching posts and troughs. The gate is closed from sunset to 7 a.m. There is no camping and the area is closed to off-road travel and unlicensed vehicles. Ground fires and amplified music are prohibited, as is horseback riding in the picnic loop. There is no electricity available.

Recommended Hikes. Numbers used are our own (the City of Glendale has not yet assigned official numbers or letters to these trails). The best is the constructed Main Trail [1] and the Thunderbird Trail [2] to Peak 1682, which has a fine view. The trail loop up to 1,800' on Hedgpeth Ridge [3] is much rougher.

Cautions. *These are arid hills with rough terrain. Carry enough water. Rattle-snakes are said to frequent the area.*

[1] Main Trail

General Description. From the top of the dirt road above the amphitheater (west of the picnic loop) the wide, well-defined trail leads northwest at a sign, gradually ascending along the base of the mountain to a major junction at 0.30 mile. Here the Thunderbird Trail [2] diverges. Continuing, the trail almost immediately reaches another junction with a spur trail to Lookout Point (and down to the park drive). Here the Main Trail descends to ramadas 9-11 near the covered reservoir at 0.39 mile. Ascent is 80'; descent is 50'.

Access. Park either along the dirt road near the trail-head or below at the picnic area.

Read Down	Detailed Trail Description	Read Up
0.00	Leave road near amphitheater, at a sign (elevation 1,370'). Head NW.	0.39
0.21	Cross wash.	0.18
0.27	**Junction:** steep track ascends L onto crest of ridge in 170'.	0.13
0.30	**Junction:** trail sharp L is Thunderbird Trail [2] to summit of Peak 1682. Go R.	0.09
0.31	**Junction:** trail R 150' is to Lookout Point (1,450') and down to park drive. Bear L (W), then R, and descend.	0.08
0.37	**Junction:** narrow trail of use ahead (160') to road. Bear slightly L and descend rocky trail.	0.03
0.39	Gate and paved road (elevation 1,400').	0.00

To the right along the road, a trail of use joins in 70' and another in 145' (leading back up to Lookout Point in 350'). Toilets and ramadas 9-11 are reached in 160' at the end of the park drive. The road leads back to the trailhead.

[2] Thunderbird Trail

General Description. This well-kept trail ascends the side of the ridge by switchbacks to the top at 0.37 mile, or a total of 0.67 from the start of the Main Trail [1]. There are good views in all directions. Side-trails to a subsidiary bump and a trail directly down the ridge crest are also described. (There are many trails of use to be ignored, especially near the top.). Total ascent is 230'.

Access. From 0.30 mile on the Main Trail from its south end, or 0.12 mile from the north end (ramadas 9-11).

Read Down	Detailed Trail Description	Read Up
0.00	Take trail W from **junction** with Main Trail. Elevation here is 1,450'. By-pass a knob.	0.37
0.05	**Junction:** trail of use on L. 40' beyond is **junction:** good trail sharp L leads onto ridge crest in 130' and junction there with poorer trail up crest.	0.33
0.11	Switchback to L at **junction:** trail to R drops along a side ridge through an area with many "jumping" chollas to a sag in 175', then continues onto a hump at 500' and ends at elevation 1,500'. To continue, ascend to N.	0.26
0.17	**Junction:** on R, trail cuts across switchback. Go slightly L, on level grade.	0.20
0.18	**Junction:** trail on ridge descends 210' to a pass and rejoins this trail at 0.05 mi (or to Main Trail in 170' more). Switchback to R here.	0.19
0.19	**Junction:** on R is trail cutting off switchback. Head SW, ascending.	0.18
0.25	VP on crest (1,620'). Ascend N slope, passing trails of use on R. (Circle around summit.)	0.13
0.35	**Junction:** trail on L leads 0.28 mi SE, down to road. Turn R (N) onto crest.	0.02
0.37	*Summit of Peak 1682.*	0.00

[3] Loop

General Description. This trail leads from ramadas on the south side of Pinnacle Peak Road directly up the ridge toward Peak 1862. There are several alternate routes. The crest is reached at 0.21 mile and the first summit at 0.25 mile, with fine views. The extension of the trail leads another 0.23 mile east to Peak 1862, with even better views. From the first summit an obvious path switchbacks down to the north, then east, and north again, reaching the ascending arm of the loop at 0.36 mile and the ramadas at 0.41 mile, or a total of 0.62 mile. Ascent is 380'. It is 35' more to Peak 1862.

Access. Off the spur road from Pinnacle Peak Road, at the ramadas (#15 and an unnumbered one).

Read Down	Detailed Trail Description	Read Up
0.00	Leave ramadas (elevation 1,450'), heading toward knob.	0.48
0.05	**Junction:** trails diverge and rejoin. Trail joining ahead on L is returning Loop.	0.43
0.11	**Junction:** trail braids; go R.	0.37
0.14	Turn R.	0.34
0.15	Route diverges.	0.33
0.16	**Junction:** trail of use descends L.	0.32
0.18	Route rejoins. (Just beyond this is trail of use on R.)	0.30
0.21	Crest, VP (1780'). Head up narrow ridge crest; just before first summit there is a **junction** to the L (see Continuation, below).	0.27
0.25	*First summit (1,830'),* with "#7" painted on it. Take trail E along crest (last part of trail is faint).	0.23
0.48	*Main summit (1,862').* Fine VP.	0.00

- CONTINUATION -

0.00	To descend, head N at tree on first summit, then turn E, descending.	0.41
0.03	Trail of use joins (descends from crest), and another in 20'.	0.36
0.13	Switchback to L (NW). Elevation 1,710'.	0.26
0.36	**Junction:** trails intersect; descend one of them.	0.05
0.41	Ramadas; trail ends. *You are now back at the start.*	0.00

Maricopa County

An Introduction

Maricopa County is recognized as having the largest county parks system in the United States. Currently the system consists of slightly over one hundred thousand acres and, with the planned acquisition program, should increase to nearly one hundred and forty thousand acres in 1988. Much of the credit for this distinction must be given to the earlier leaders of the County who had the courage and foresight to acquire the majority of the park land to preserve for future generations.

Our parks system was created as major desert-mountain sites encircling metropolitan Phoenix. This "necklace" was made complete with the acquisition of the San Tan parcel in 1987. The primary function of the parks system is to set aside major parcels of prime desert terrain and to concentrate development in specified areas of these parcels. Development would be centered around camping, picnicking, and trails.

The bond programs in 1972 and 1986 provided a funding source for development and also to complete acquisitions of private and state land holdings. Of special importance in the development area was the creation of hiking/riding trails both within the respective parks and as inter-connecting links between parks and points of interest throughout the County.

Of priority importance is the establishment, continuation, and expansion of a comprehensive hiking trail system. It would be a credit to the County if we could be recognized not only for having the largest parks system, but also the most complete and comprehensive trail system in the country.

Bill Richwine, Director
Parks and Recreation Department

Maricopa County

Estrella Mountain Regional Park

Introduction. The Sierra Estrellas ("star of the desert") are a range of mountains that are quite prominent when viewed from Phoenix (to the south-west, beyond South Mountain). They extend from the northwest tip of Pinal County northwesterly to the Gila River near its junction with the Salt. On the southwest they are bordered by Rainbow Valley (Waterman Wash), an area now the site of a large residential development.

The park occupies about one-third of the Estrellas (18,592 acres) in the foothills of the higher ranges. The highest elevation in the park is 3,650'. (No trail presently ascends from the park to the high peaks.)

Extensive residential development of the area west of the park (Estrella Ranch), and trails leading into it, were planned. The developer's nationally-publicized financial difficulties have postponed that plan for now.

History. The Park area had religious significance for the Pima Indians who lived at their feet along the fertile Gila River lowlands. Twelve archeological sites are located within the park, mostly representing temporary camps (one was permanent). Nine of the sites were occupied by the Hohokam peoples who were in the area between A.D. 500 and 1450. During the historic period the area was controlled by the Pima and Maricopa Indians and was used as a hunting and gathering range.

The park area was also along the route of the California-bound trappers and drovers, perhaps including Kit Carson. To the south of the range was the Gila Route of Kearny's Army of the West, the Mormon Battalion, and thousands of Argonauts.

Geology. Geologically they are similar to the White Tank Mountains although there are no "tanks" or tinajas.

Maps. *Our map 15.* The USGS 1:24,000 topos Avondale SE and Avondale SW (both 1957, photorevised 1978) show the general topography and some of the old roads, but no trails.

Access. From Phoenix, take Interstate 10 west to Exit 126, Estrella Parkway, at sign "Estrella Park." (This is 2 miles west of Litchfield Road Exit 128.) Head south for 3.6 miles to State Route 85. Here you continue to West Vineyard Avenue, and turn left to the park entrance. Turn left on Casey Abbott Drive North for 1.6 miles to 143rd Drive and Arena Drive, at which point the 143rd Drive trail-head is straight ahead, and the Rodeo Arena another 0.3 mile to the right. Alternatively, you can go south from Exit 128 on Litchfield Road through Goodyear. After 2.3 miles take State Route 85 to the right for 1.2 miles, then turn left on Bullard, 5.7 miles total to park entrance. [See access diagram.]

[Previous page: Rock Knob]

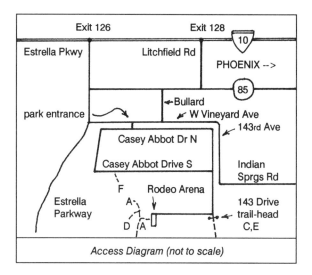

Access Diagram (not to scale)

Facilities. The park has 56 acres of grass, with 7 ramadas (with electricity and lights), comfort stations and picnic tables. There is a group campground (no hook-ups) and golf course. *Phone: 932-3811; P.O. Box 252, Goodyear 85338.*

Recommended Hikes and Trail Rides. The trail designations used are either official Maricopa County letters or (in one case) our own number. There are 6 designated trails and their branches. The shortest is the Gold Fever Interpretive Trail [F]; another short trail is the Ridge Trail [G] (neither of these is for horse use). Of the other trails, there are two that are quite long (Rainbow Valley [A] and Gadsden [C]). Most have been recently re-marked. The best for a one-day hike are: the northern and western sections of the Rainbow Valley Trail [A] using a number of alternatives on the return; the Spur [D], Rock Knob Buggy [E], or eastern section of the Rainbow Valley Trail with any of these for the return from the Pack Saddle Trail [B], and the Gadsden Trail [C]. Any combination is good on horseback.

Cautions. *Note that this park's terrain is very arid and is broken and dissected by washes. Cross-country travel can be arduous if you are lost. Use care.*

[A] Rainbow Valley Trail COUNTERCLOCKWISE

General Description. A long, 18.68-mile trail loop leads over scenic hills, mountain-sides, through passes and over flat desert. There are excellent views. *Since not many will take the full loop, the detailed description that follows is divided into 8 segments. At the end of each segment the total distance from the start is indicated.*

Access. From the trail-head sign at the west side of the Rodeo Arena (heading counter-clockwise) or 0.20 mile south of the 143rd Drive trail-head (clockwise). There are many other points at which this trail can be intersected by other trails.

Read Down	*Detailed Trail Description*	*Read Up*

SEGMENT 1
Rodeo Arena to Rainbow Valley Connector [A-1]

0.00	Leave Rodeo Arena (1,015'), heading straight W at sign.	1.75
0.02	**Junction:** join [A] running N-S here; go R, uphill.	1.73
0.04	**Junction:** Spur Trail [D] goes L [connects with Rainbow Valley Trail via Spur Trail North Connector [D-1] in 1.94 mi]. Continue uphill.	1.71
0.07	**Junction:** where old track continues straight, bear R.	1.68
0.09	Top of rise. Beyond is view of valley and downtown Phoenix. Cross several small washes.	1.66
0.27	**Junction:** Connector Trail [A-1] leads sharp L (not very well defined here) for 0.23 mi to rejoin Rainbow Valley Trail at 1.75 mi. Continue up and down.	1.48
0.52	Top of rise.	1.23
0.59	Pass (1,040'). Descend on very rocky trail, then level out.	1.16
0.67	Descend very steadily to L.	1.08
0.70	Cross moderate wash, ascend; level out in 0.05 mi.	1.05
0.79	**Junction:** steep, rocky track [G] descends R for 165' to Amphitheater Drive. On L, this track is the Ridge Trail [G]. Continue level.	0.96
0.86	**Junction:** another steep, rocky track descends R for 190' to Amphitheater Drive; on L it joins Ridge Trail [G] in 220'.	0.89
0.97	Cross small wash, ascend, switchback to R in 100', then level out in 80'.	0.78
1.02	Ignore trail of use descending on R. Go L, ascending.	0.73
1.16	Pass old mine site on L, ease ascent, then pass another.	0.59
1.23	**Junction:** connecting spur descends R to Gold Fever Interpretive Trail [F] in 225'. On L, Ridge Trail [G] enters (and ends).	0.52
1.29	**Junction:** trail of use ascends very steeply L to ridge *[avoid this approach]*.	0.46
1.31	Turn around end of ridge.	0.44
1.33	**Junction:** to L is faint trail of use up ridge crest (joins Ridge Trail [G] in 500'). Descend steadily on rocky trail, then ease in 150'.	0.42
1.40	Pass. Avoid trails of use on R and up crest on L.	0.35
1.54	Cross small wash; reach top of rise in 150' and descend.	0.21
1.64	Cross small wash.	0.09
1.66	Cross very small but deep wash, ascending steadily on opposite side.	0.11
1.68	**Junction:** trail to R ends at fence; go L.	0.07
1.75	**Junction:** Connector Trail [A-1] leads L 0.23 mi back to Rainbow Valley Trail (0.50 mi to Rodeo Arena trail-head) [saves 1.25 mi]. (elevation 1,070')	0.00

SEGMENT 2
Connector [A-1] to Spur Trail North Connector [D-1]

0.00	Leave Connector [A-1], ascend.	2.16
0.08	Top of rise. In 0.07 mi descend more steadily and bear R.	2.08
0.29	Top of ridge. Side-hill on R (W) side of it.	1.87
0.37	Ascend to R of crest.	1.79

0.47	Turn R and descend, crossing small wash in 110'.	1.68
0.52	Descend. In 0.05 mi reach top of rise with fence on R.	1.64
0.66	Pass (1,160') with fence on R. Descend.	1.50
0.96	Cross moderate wash, then turn sharp L, parallelling wash.	1.20
1.00	Start ascending at very small wash.	1.16
1.11	Switchback to R, then to L in 100', then to R in 35'.	1.05
1.20	Reach crest of subsidiary ridge; level out (1,280').	0.96
1.25	Top of high point with good VP (1,380'). Descend steadily.	0.91
1.28	Turn R, descend off crest.	0.88
1.33	Turn L, continue descent.	0.83
1.52	Edge of major wash, trail forks: take either branch.	0.64
1.54	Enter wash, turn L in it, then take minor branch to R.	0.62
1.67	Turn sharp R, up-hill (use care here).	0.49
1.69	Cross old faint vehicle tracks. Head SW.	0.47
1.76	Cross moderate wash.	0.40
2.07	Turn R, then L in 100', descending toward W.	0.09
2.16	**Junction:** sharp L is Spur Trail North Connector [D-1] (leads to Spur Trail [D] to Rodeo Arena). Elevation 1,150'. *[3.91 mi from start at Rodeo Arena.]*	0.00

SEGMENT 3
Spur Trail North Connector [D-1] to Spur Trail [D]

0.00	Leave junction with Spur Trail North Connector [D-1], ascending.	1.03
0.32	Ascend more easily.	0.71
0.40	Pass (1,290'). Descend gradually.	0.63
0.53	Level out briefly.	0.50
0.64	Top of rise with rock hump on L; reach pass (1,330') in 100'.	0.39
0.73	Pass (1,370'). Descend steeply on eroded trail.	0.30
1.03	**Junction:** To L is Spur Trail [D] (elevation 1,200'). *[4.94 mi from start at Rodeo Arena.]*	0.00

SEGMENT 4
Spur Trail to Pack Saddle Connector [B-1]

0.00	Leave junction with Spur Trail [D] (1,200'); cross large wash in 100'.	1.28
0.23	Cross very small wash; ascend high above major wash with views.	1.06
0.31	Ease ascent for 0.13 mi.	0.98
0.43	Level out beside deep wash.	0.85
0.61	Pass (1,370'). Descend gradually.	0.67
0.68	Begin steady descent.	0.60
0.79	Swing around to N, then to R (SE).	0.49
0.84	Parallel major wash on R.	0.44
0.88	Cross moderate wash.	0.40
1.00	Follow along ridge and almost reach its summit; then side-hill gradually down.	0.28
1.14	Bear R, descend more steadily.	0.14
1.22	Cross moderate wash. Head S.	0.06
1.28	**Junction:** red arrow on R. To continue on Rainbow Valley Trail, turn R, up-hill here. Downhill 75' on Connector [B-1] are other junctions [see inset map], with trails to Pack Saddle Trail [B] in 0.35 mi and across to Rock Knob Buggy Trail [E] in 0.62 mi. (Elevation 1,260'). *[6.22 mi from start at Rodeo Arena.]*	0.00

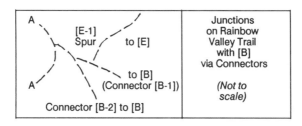

SEGMENT 5
Pack Saddle Connector [B-1] to Pack Saddle Trail

0.00	Leave junction with Connector [B-1], ascending rocky trail.	1.17
0.04	Top of rise (another at 0.13 mi).	1.13
0.14	Pass through dramatic quartz outcroppings.	0.84
0.33	Cross 4 moderate washes in next 0.06 mi.	0.82
0.40	Cross wash, ascend bank.	0.77
0.45	Descend between two washes, then cross one.	0.72
0.50	Cross small rocky side-wash, then head S on level trail.	0.67
0.63	**Junction:** ignore trail of use branching R. Bear L, cross small wash in 40'.	0.54
0.72	Cross flat plain heading S.	0.45
0.93	Cross major wash. Bear R, ascending.	0.24
0.94	**Junction:** alternate cross-trail. Use care to follow tapes through open area, heading SSW.	0.23
1.04	Bear R (S), using care to follow trail.	0.13
1.17	**Junction:** Pack Saddle Trail [B] (jeep road) L & R. Rainbow Valley Trail joins road, heads S [across road is minor trail used by horses to reach jeep road in Corgett Wash in 0.10 mi]. (elev. 1,160'). *[7.39 mi from start at Rodeo Arena.]*	0.00

SEGMENT 6
Pack Saddle Trail back to Pack Saddle Trail

0.00	Leave junction on jeep road, heading W.	7.79
0.29	Turn L in sandy level area.	7.50
0.32	**Junction:** cross broad Corgett Wash. (Road goes L in it; in 0.38 mi trail L leads back to junction at start of this segment.)	7.47
0.57	**Junction:** jeep road.	7.22
0.62	**Junction:** road R is Pack Saddle Historical Trail [B] to park boundary in 0.45 mi. *[8.01 mi from start at Rodeo Arena.]*	7.17
0.92	Ruins on R (W).	6.87
1.52	**Junction:** jeep road R to boundary fence in 0.5 mi.	6.27
2.47	**Junction:** roads R & L.	5.32
2.92	Road bends to R, then to L, becomes a bit steeper, rockier.	4.87
3.32	**Junction:** road on L.	4.47
3.67	**Junction:** road splits. Go L, descending gradually, parallel to major wash on R.	4.12
4.07	**Junction:** where road continues ahead, take trail to R.	3.72
4.14	**Junction:** go R, descending toward wash.	3.65
4.26	**Junction:** trail R ascends steeply back to jeep road. Continue.	3.53
4.38	Take trail R, ascending out of wash, at arrow.	3.41
4.40	Bear L on trail.	3.39

4.43	Top of rise. Descend gradually.	3.36
4.66	Cross moderate wash.	3.13
4.82	Top of rise.	2.97
4.97	Top of rise.	2.82
5.24	Moderate wash. Follow it up for 90', leave it on L, head N.	2.65
5.28	Bear R (NE), parallelling wash.	2.51
5.34	Bear L, ascending away from wash.	2.45
5.56	Descend into major wash.	2.23
5.59	Ascend to L out of wash, then switchback up.	2.20
5.61	Top of rise. Turn R, parallel wash.	2.18
5.78	Top of rise.	2.01
6.34	Descend into wash, follow it to R.	1.45
6.36	Switchback L out of wash. *USE CARE*, this turn is obscure.	1.43
6.41	Descend L into deep wash.	1.38
6.43	Bottom. Follow it down.	1.36
6.44	Ascend steeply to R, out of wash.	1.24
6.55	Cross moderate wash.	1.24
6.72	Descend into major wash; head L down it, then in 90' ascend R out of it.	1.07
6.76	Brink of wash. Descend.	1.03
7.08	Cross moderate wash.	0.71
7.16	Cross moderate wash.	0.63
7.79	**Junction:** Pack Saddle Historical Trail [B] L & R. Rainbow Valley Trail continues across jeep road. (1,245'.) *[15.18 mi from start at Rodeo Arena.]*	0.00

SEGMENT 7
Pack Saddle Trail to Gadsden Loop Trail [C-1]

0.00	Leave Pack Saddle Trail [B] (old jeep road), on red markers. Ascend N, then NW, toward Rock Knob.	2.15
0.21	Top of rise (1,330'). Descend briefly, then head W.	1.94
0.24	Cross small wash, ascend, then go up and down.	1.91
0.31	**Junction:** trail of use heads S at cairn. Go straight, ascending.	1.84
0.43	Top of rise at minor pass (1,360').	1.72
0.61	Cross small wash, turn R (E).	1.54
0.68	Swing L (N). Ascend, crossing several small washes.	1.47
1.08	Major pass (1,480'). Descend steadily N (over very loose rock at first).	1.07
1.57	Level out (1,230').	0.58
1.64	Parallel wash on L, then ascend gradually.	0.52
1.74	Top of rise.	0.41
1.77	**Junction:** trail of use. Bear R. Trail improves.	0.38
1.90	Cross moderate wash.	0.24
2.04	Top of rise.	0.11
2.15	**Junction:** On R is Gadsden Loop Trail [C-1] [to Gadsden Connector [C-2] in 0.94 mi]. (Elevation 1,100'.) To continue, descend. *[17.33 mi from start at Rodeo Arena.]*	0.00

SEGMENT 8
Gadsden Loop Trail [C-1] to Rodeo Arena

0.00	Leave Gadsden Loop Trail [C-1] junction, descending.	1.57
0.01	Cross moderate wash; ascend.	1.56
0.05	Top of rise; others at 0.11 and 0.15 mi.	1.52
0.37	Top of rise.	1.20

0.99	Cross branch of wash.	0.36
1.02	**Junction:** road (Rock Knob Buggy Trail [E] sharp L). Go R, down road.	0.33
1.04	**Junction:** on R is Gadsden Trail [C] ascending out of wash. Cross wash to L, ascend out of it. (Ahead, road leads to 143rd Drive in 0.20 mi.)	0.31
1.27	Switchback down into wash, then out of it.	0.08
1.33	**Junction:** straight ahead, [A] continues, shortly meeting [D]. Go R.	0.02
1.35	This trail ends at Rodeo Arena parking lot (elev. 1,015'). *[18.68 mi total from start.]*.	0.00

[A-1] Rainbow Valley Connector

A short (0.23-mile) segment connects the two sides of the Rainbow Valley Trail, avoiding the trip around the ridge just south of the entrance area. The trail makes an easy descent from west to east.

[B] Pack Saddle Historical Trail NORTH to SOUTH

General Description. At present this 5.15 mile-long trail consists of a jeep trail that leads in and out of washes. Parts of it are slow and sometimes very hot going for those on their own feet. It provides connections with the Gadsden [C], Rock Knob Buggy [E] and Rainbow Valley [A] trails and therefore makes possible several short or moderate loop trips. It partly overlaps sections of the Rainbow Valley and Gadsden Trails. It is not practical to take it as a full trip in its own right, since it runs from boundary fence to boundary fence. Total ascent is about 330', descent about 140'.

Access. Reach the northern park boundary by way of the Gadsden Trail [C]. Reach the southwestern end via the Rainbow Valley Trail [A].

Read Down	Detailed Road Description	Read Up
0.00	Park boundary. Head S (elevation 1,075').	5.15
0.05	**Junction:** Gadsden Trail [C] (E-bound) on L.	5.10
0.09	**Junction:** trail angling off to R is Gadsden Trail W-bound.	5.06
0.33	**Junction:** trail L is Gadsden Spur [C-3] to Gadsden Trail [C] E-bound.	4.82
0.36	**Junction:** road sharp R [C-3] leads to Gadsden Trail [C] W-bound.	4.79
0.44	**Junction:** sketchy road angling L, up-hill.	4.71
0.59	**Junction:** to L is obscure track leading 225' up to ridge. Trail half-L is horse trail 370' to top of same small ridge.	4.56
0.63	4WD track up opposite bank.	4.52
0.76	**Junction:** to L is Gadsden Trail [C] climbing out of wash.	4.39
0.85	Switchback to R.	4.30
0.86	Bend in road ahead to R; instead, short-cut to L across & over bend in road.	4.29
0.87	Rejoin road in wash. Follow wash.	4.28
1.01	Where wash turns L, ascend to R, out of wash.	4.14
1.16	**Junction:** 4-wheel-drive track ascends very steeply to R where wash heads L.	3.99
1.22	Go into wash again, follow it.	3.93
1.42	Leave wash on R, up-hill, where it bends to L.	3.73

1.45	Cross level benchland, then 3 very small washes.	3.70
1.70	Ignore old tracks off to R. Bear L, descend.	3.45
1.73	On bench, steep scar of 4WD track leads up knob on R & another on L.	3.42
1.76	**Junction:** 4WD tracks L & R.	3.39
1.78	Where wash splits, ascend between two branches.	3.37
1.93	Ease grade of ascent.	3.22
2.08	**Junction:** 4WD track on R. Keep L. Top of rise.	3.07
2.13	**Junction:** turn L.	3.02
2.26	Top of rise (USGS Bench Mark on L, 1,256').	2.89
2.44	**Junction:** Rainbow Valley Trail [A] crosses here (1,240').	2.61
2.68	**Junction:** Rock Knob Buggy Trail [E] ascends on R (1,220'). Bear L, back into wash. Pass several washes, entering main wash.	2.47
2.90	**Junction:** up-hill on R is Connector [B-1] (to Rainbow Valley Trail in 0.35 mi).	2.25
2.91	Enter wash; keep R up it.	2.24
2.97	Bear L where wash splits.	2.18
2.98	Leave wash on R.	2.17
3.02	Rejoin wash.	2.13
3.06	**Junction:** on R is Connector [B-2] to Rainbow Valley Trail in 0.38 mi. Continuing, pass toe of ridge on R; way becomes rockier.	2.09
3.24	Top of rise.	1.91
3.35	Track enters on L, then another in 70'.	1.80
3.43	**Junction:** 4WD road ascends on R.	1.72
4.08	**Junction:** Rainbow Valley Trail [A] to R (back to Rodeo Arena in 7.79 mi).	1.07
4.36	Road corner. Road turns L on sandy flats.	0.79
4.40	**Junction:** in very broad Corgett Wash, road goes L. Continue.	0.75
4.70	**Junction:** Pack Saddle Trail goes R here at junction of roads, where Rainbow Valley Trail continues ahead.	0.45
5.15	Boundary fence, private land beyond. Pack Saddle Trail ends (1,120').	0.00

[C] Gadsden Trail

General Description. For a moderately long, varied trip not too far from civilization, the Gadsden Trail is ideal. It is a long trail with several alternative routes. It intersects the Pack Saddle Trail [B] at two points.

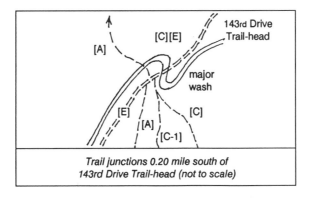

*Trail junctions 0.20 mile south of
143rd Drive Trail-head (not to scale)*

Access. From the 143rd Drive trail-head. Follow the trail (road) south for 0.20 mile, turning left at the first junction beyond, at 0.22 mile. *The area is complex - - see diagram above.*

Read Down	Detailed Trail Description	Read Up
0.00	Leave trail-head at end of 143rd Drive on wide, sandy road, coinciding with Rock Knob Buggy Trail [E] (elevation 990').	6.76
0.20	**Junction:** in wash, bear slightly L, crossing a subsidiary wash, where jeep road [E] continues ahead. Rainbow Valley Trail [A] goes R.	6.56
0.22	**Junction:** on R is Gadsden Loop Trail [C-1]. Bear L here.	6.54
0.27	Ascend.	6.49
0.57	Overturned metal bin on other side of boundary fence.	6.15
0.58	**Junction:** short-cut trail to R to Gadsden Connector Trail [C-2].	6.16
0.59	**Junction:** trail descending R is Gadsden Connector [C-2] back to this trail at 0.22 mi via [C-1]. Go R, ascending along fence (park boundary).	6.17
0.66	Park corner. Turn L here and descend gradually SE.	6.10
0.81	Top of rise. Descend, then steeply over loose rock.	5.95
1.00	Cross moderate wash.	5.76
1.09	Cross major wash; ascend out of it for 100'.	5.65
1.28	Cross 4WD road.	5.48
1.31	Cross moderate wash, then switchback out of it.	5.45
1.64	Cross small, deep wash.	5.12
2.16	Pass (1,120').	4.60
2.41	Enter wash, follow it to L, then over into smaller branch wash.	4.35
2.54	Go L in large wash, then climb out of it.	4.22
2.59	**Junction:** at road, go L *(R is Gadsden Connector [C-3]).*	4.17
2.68	**Junction:** leave road on trail on R (ahead 800' to park boundary).	4.08
2.85	**Junction:** Pack Saddle Historical Trail [B] (jeep road). Go L.	3.91
2.89	**Junction:** where Pack Saddle Trail leads 280' to park boundary, take trail R.	3.87
2.98	Cross moderate wash, ascend hillside, parallel fence line on L.	3.78
3.07	Top of rise, VP.	3.69
3.26	Cross moderate wash.	3.50
3.28	**Junction:** 4WD road on R. Go straight ahead.	3.48
3.48	**Junction:** 4WD roads L & R. [L to park fence. On R, road leads 325' up to first of two summits; higher one, just beyond, is 1,213', good VP on both.]	3.28
3.49	Go R on road, then in 85' bear L at small cairn.	3.27
3.51	Descend to cross moderate wash.	3.25
3.62	**Junction:** 4WD road crosses. Bear slightly L (E).	3.14
3.69	Descend into very large wash and follow it to R (S).	3.07
3.86	**Junction:** 4WD road out of wash on L.	2.90
4.16	**Junction:** messy 4WD roads L & R.	2.60
4.19	**Important turn:** where wash continues and branches ahead, take trail L at tree, cross over little divide between branches of wash. Go E in wash, *not south,* follow wash around major bends.	2.57
4.70	Take R-hand branch of wash; avoid going straight ahead.	2.06
4.73	Ascend out of wash, to R.	2.03
4.77	**Junction:** 4WD road descends L back into wash. Ascend steadily.	1.99
5.45	Rejoin wash at cairn.	1.31
5.48	Go up moderate wash, leave it on R in 65' ascending steadily.	1.28
5.96	Pass (1,360'). Descend brushy trail for 0.14 mi, where it improves.	0.81

6.22	**Important junction:** here there are two routes. Keep L here on better trail, ascending. (On R is [C-3], 0.66 mi to Pack Saddle Trail [B].)	0.54
6.59	**Junction:** where road descends to R, cross it and descend on trail.	0.17
6.76	**Junction:** Pack Saddle Historical Trail [B] in wash. (To L, Rainbow Valley Trail is 1.68 mi; to R, Gadsden Spur [C-3] is 0.41 mi.)	0.00

[C-1] Gadsden Loop Trail

General Description. This short trail is an alternate to the northeastern section of the Rainbow Valley Trail and also provides an alternate to the west end of the Gadsden Trail itself. It can be used to connect between the Rainbow Valley and Gadsden Trails.

Access. From the Rainbow Valley Trail [A] at 1.16 miles south of 143rd Drive Trail-head, or from the Gadsden Trail [C] 0.22 mile south of the same point.

Read Down	Detailed Trail Description	Read Up
0.00	Leave Rainbow Valley Trail [A]. This trail heads E (1,100').	1.03
0.08	Cross small, deep wash.	0.95
0.18	Top of rise.	0.85
0.21	Bear L, ascend.	0.82
0.25	Top of rise. Head NW.	0.78
0.40	Top of rise.	0.62
0.57	Cross two small washes.	0.45
0.78	Trail leads along rim of large wash.	0.24
0.94	**Junction:** on R is Gadsden Connector [C-2] to Gadsden Trail [C] in 0.28 mi. (elevation here is 1,030').	0.09
1.03	**Junction:** Gadsden Trail [C], 0.02 mi from [A] & [E], 0.22 mi from trail-head.	0.00

[C-2] Gadsden Connector Trail

General Description. A shorter alternate to the Gadsden Trail, it ascends the end of a small ridge to 0.28 mile where it meets the main Gadsden Trail [C].

Access. Where the main Gadsden Trail leaves the other trails in the major wash 0.20 mile south of the 143rd Drive trail-head *(see diagram for details)*, continue for another 0.02 mile on [C] to a junction. Go right on the Gadsden Loop Trail [C-1] for 0.09 mile. The Connector turns left here.

Read Down	Detailed Trail Description	Read Up
0.00	Leave Gadsden Loop Trail [C-1] 0.31 mi S of trail-head. Ascend L.	0.28
0.15	VP at end of ridge.	0.13

0.26	**Junction:** straight ahead is short-cut to [C]. Go R, ascending along fence (park boundary).	0.02
0.28	**Junction:** main Gadsden Trail [C] L & R. This trail ends. L to trail-head in 0.59 mi. To R, it is 2.26 mi to Pack Saddle Trail [B].	0.00

[C-3] Gadsden Spur

A short trail from the Gadsden Trail [C] (at 6.22 miles) descends down a valley, then meets the Pack Saddle Trail [B] in 0.66 mile. It jogs left on it to 0.70 mile, then sharp right onto another road for 0.14 mile (to 0.84 mile) to rejoin the Gadsden Trail [C] at 2.59 miles in that description.

[D] Spur Trail

General Description. From the trail-head several washes are crossed on the way to a junction at 1.10 miles where the Spur Trail North Connector [D-1] leads west to the Rainbow Valley Trail. The trail then ascends somewhat more steadily to end at the Rainbow Valley Trail at 1.97 miles. As a way into the center of the Park, it is somewhat more difficult (and more scenic) than the Rock Knob Buggy Trail [E]. Total ascent is about 210'.

Access. From the Rodeo Arena trail-head, head west for 90' to intersect the trail (also the Rainbow Valley Trail). Take it to the right. At 0.04 mile go sharp left from the Rainbow Valley Trail [A] onto the Spur Trail.

Read Down	*Detailed Trail Description*	*Read Up*
0.00	The trail leaves the Rodeo Arena Trail-head (1,015').	1.97
0.02	**Junction:** take Rainbow Valley Trail [A] R (L is also [A]).	1.95
0.04	**Junction:** Spur Trail goes sharp L where Rainbow Valley Trail [A] goes straight ahead. Cross moderate wash.	1.93
0.11	Top of rise. Head S toward Rock Knob.	1.86
0.26	Cross moderate wash, ascend out of it.	1.71
0.32	**Junction:** obscure old road angles to R.	1.65
0.38	Ascend.	1.59
0.42	Top of rise.	1.55
0.47	**Junction:** old road re-enters on R.	1.50
0.51	Top of rise.	1.46
0.63	Cross small rocky wash. (In next 0.24 mi cross 5 more washes.)	1.34
0.93	Top of rise (1,100').	1.04
0.98	Top of rise.	0.99
1.01	Cross toe of ridge on R.	0.96
1.08	**Junction:** ignore short-cut angling L.	0.89
1.10	**Junction:** Spur Trail North Connector [D-1] on R to Rainbow Valley Trail [A]). (Elevation 1,100'.)	0.87
1.17	Descend.	0.81
1.18	Switchback to L.	0.80

1.20	Cross major wash.	0.79
1.21	Level out, parallel wash (4WD roads on side of wash).	0.78
1.68	Cross moderate wash (branch of main wash).	0.30
1.97	**Junction:** Rainbow Valley Trail [A] on R on sandy flat (1,210').	
	This trail ends.	0.00

[D-1] Spur Trail North Connector EAST to WEST

General Description. The connection between this trail and the Rainbow Valley Trail was re-worked in late 1987 and colored tapes were placed on it. Ascent is insignificant except for washes.

Access. From Rodeo Arena Trail-head take the Spur Trail [D] for 1.10 miles.

Read Down	*Detailed Trail Description*	*Read Up*
0.00	Leave main Spur Trail 1.10 mi from Rodeo Arena by angling to R (1,100').	0.84
0.09	Turn R, descend into wash.	0.75
0.11	Turn L into moderate wash and follow it. In 35' ascend out of it to R.	0.73
0.14	Reach brink of wash, level out.	0.70
0.17	Turn L into moderate wash.	0.67
0.18	Leave wash on R.	0.66
0.27	Cross moderate, deep wash.	0.57
0.84	**Junction:** at Rainbow Valley Trail [A] this trail ends. [To R it is 2.66 mi back to Rodeo Arena via shortest route, or 3.91 mi via full route. To L, Rainbow Valley Trail meets Spur Trail [D] in 1.03 mi and Pack Saddle Historical Trail [B] in 3.48 mi.]	0.00

[E] Rock Knob Buggy Trail NORTH to SOUTH

General Description. The Rock Knob Buggy Trail is the easiest and shortest way into the center of the park (it is an old vehicle way). It leaves the 143rd Drive trail-head, runs past a junction at a wash, then gradually ascends and leads into the pass between Rock Knob (1,801') on the east and the unnamed peak (1,781') to its west. It then crosses a major washout on the road and descends gradually to the Pack Saddle Trail [B] at 2.86 miles. Ascent is 230'.

Access. From the gate at the 143rd Drive Trail-head.

Read Down	*Detailed Road Description*	*Read Up*
0.00	The trail leaves the 143rd Drive trail-head at a gate, coinciding with the Gadsden Trail [C] (Elevation 990').	2.86
0.20	**Junction:** continue ahead on jeep road where Gadsden Trail [C] diverges in wash to L and [A] leads R to Rodeo Arena.	2.66

0.22	**Junction:** on ascent out of major wash, trail to L is Rainbow Valley Trail [A]. Ascend gradually on wide road.	2.64
0.80	Top of rise.	2.07
0.82	Cross moderate wash, then turn L in 100'.	2.05
1.03	**Junction:** turn L where branch road on R leads to Girl Scout area.	1.83
1.26	Turn L.	1.61
1.49	**Junction:** road branch on R rejoins later on.	1.38
1.60	**Junction:** road branch rejoins on R.	1.27
1.86	Turn L, then R.	1.00
2.01	**Junction:** on L trail leads up around small knob for 360', then peters out. Turn R here; use care with route.	0.85
2.03	**Junction:** just before descending into steep, washed-out area, poor trail leads L. Descend into eroded wash in 30', then steeply out of it.	0.83
2.05	Rim of washed-out area. Ascend gradually.	0.82
2.15	Height of land (1,310'); descend gradually.	0.71
2.20	**Junction:** on R, Rock Knob Buggy Spur [E-1] (cairn) leads 0.62 mi to Connector [B-1] just below its junction with Rainbow Valley Trail [A] (1,320'). Beyond, road descends gradually.	0.67
2.86	**Junction:** Pack Saddle Trail [B] (jeep road) L & R. This trail ends (1,210'). [To the L, Rainbow Valley Trail [A] is 0.24 mi away. To the R, Connector [B-1] to Rainbow Valley Trail is 0.22 mi away.]	0.00

Sierra Estrella Mountains from park

[E-1] Rock Knob Buggy Spur

A narrow trail leads from 2.20 miles on the Rock Knob Buggy Trail [E] southwest across several washes for 0.62 mile to connect with Pack Saddle Connector [B-1] just below the Rainbow Valley Trail [A].

[F] Gold Fever Interpretive Trail

General Description. This is a new, self-guiding *hiker-only* trail (1988). An interpretive flyer is available that explains in greater detail the features at, or visible from, the 18 stops shown below.

Access. From Casey Abbott Drive South, 0.6 mile west of 143rd Drive and 0.3 mile east of Golf Course Drive.

Read Down	Detailed Trail Description	Read Up
0.00	Leave Casey Abbot Drive South at the sign, immediately ascending.	0.70
0.05	Stop 1: general observation of Estrella Mountains.	0.65
0.09	Stop 2: palo verde tree. In 45' start very steady ascent.	0.61
0.13	Stop 3: Monument Hill (about 4 miles due E) is point of origin for all land surveying in Arizona. **Junction:** 25' L up to ridge crest and another **junction** [to R is this trail returning; to L is spur to bump on ridge; track descending to Casey Abbot Drive South ahead]. Continue, almost level.	0.57
0.17	Stop 4: pegmatite (quartz) dike across ravine.	0.53
0.19	Stop 5: pack rat midden (nest) on R.	0.51
0.25	Stop 6: fissure vein of "rusty quartz."	0.45
0.28	Reach crest.	0.42
0.29	Stop 7: Gila River. **Important junction on crest:** where this trail turns L and descends on other side of ridge, spur trail leads up crest, splits in 180', rejoins at **junction** in 225' at Rainbow Valley Trail [A].	0.41
0.32	Stop 8: look back, up the trail to see gneiss banding (black and white).	0.38
0.33	Stop 9: barrel cactus on L.	0.37
0.38	Stop 10: vandalized saguaro.	0.32
0.39	Level out.	0.31
0.42	**Important junction:** leave wider track (descends to Casey Abbot Drive South in 0.14 mi), ascending sharp L on less worn trail. In 40' is Stop 11: pincushion or fishhook cactus on L.	0.28
0.43	Stop 12: bursage (10-30' to R).	0.27
0.44	Stop 13: saguaro skeleton with wood-like ribs.	0.26
0.46	Bear R; stop 14 on R in 20' (desert varnish from intense sun).	0.24
0.48	Level out, bear R. Stop 15 (range rattany) in 20'.	0.22
0.50	Stop 16: hedgehog cactus on L.	0.20
0.51	**Junction:** spur L to bump on ridge. Go R, descending track.	0.19
0.54	Stop 17: brittlebush.	0.16
0.55	Stop 18: creosote bush on R.	0.15
0.57	**Junction:** trail ahead leads to hump on ridge. Descend L 25' to **important junction:** you are now back on the original route. Turn R and descend steadily.	0.13
0.70	Casey Abbott Drive South (start).	0.00

[G] Ridge Trail EAST to WEST

General Description. Although a popular trail because of its views and easy access from the developed park area, this is not a worked, designated route and sections are quite steep. It can be approached from a number of locations (see map). The description begins at the eastern end above the Amphitheater. Ascent is 440'.

Access. From the junction of 143rd Drive and Casey Abbot Drive South, follow the latter 0.1 mile to gated Amphitheater Drive East. Walk up it for 0.19 mile to the trail. It can also be reached from Amphitheater Drive West (0.16 mile walk), 0.35 mile west of the road junction, and from above the Gold Fever Interpretive Trail [F] and sections of the Rainbow Valley Trail [A].

Read Down	Detailed Trail Description	Read Up
0.00	Leave Amphitheater Drive East, ascending steep track (880').	0.69
0.03	**Junction (4-way):** Rainbow Valley Trail [A] crosses. Continue ascent.	0.65
0.09	**Junction:** branch on R descends to Amphitheater Drive West. Head up crest.	0.59
0.19	Track ends at concrete ruin. Trail ascends just R of crest.	0.50
0.31	Trail steepens, with loose rock; use care.	0.38
0.35	**Junction:** summit (1,320') is 110' up-hill to L, excellent VP. Head W, pass N of rocks.	0.34
0.38	Next summit on ridge (slightly lower). Use care heading W; 25' beyond, drop off crest to R; reach crest again in another 160'.	0.31
0.43	**Junction:** where poorer trail continues, descend to R of crest.	0.26
0.45	Reach crest again; trail improves.	0.23
0.49	Head R of crest, ascending with bump on ridge ahead.	0.20
0.51	Summit (1,250').	0.17
0.54	Go to R of small, sharp peak; reach top again in 35'; use care on R.	0.14
0.56	Bottom; ascend.	0.13
0.57	Top of bump; descend to R of it; ignore trail of use dropping to R.	0.11
0.62	**Junction:** at top of rise (1,200'), trail drops R off ridge, descending N. Poorer trail continues along crest to Rainbow Valley Trail in 500'.	0.07
0.69	**Junction:** trail ends at Rainbow Valley Trail (L & R) (1,125'). Straight ahead is trail 225' to Gold Fever Trail [F], leading 0.29 mi to Casey Abbot Drive South.	0.00

Maricopa County

McDowell Mountain Regional Park

Introduction. The 21,099-acre McDowell Mountain Regional Park is located 15 miles northeast of Scottsdale on the eastern slope of the McDowells, an impressive group of mountains rising to 4,002'. They separate Paradise Valley from the Verde Valley and are prominently visible from Phoenix. The park area itself slopes between the high ranges on the west and the Verde River to the east from elevations of 3,100' to 1,550'. It is known for its abundant Sonoran desert vegetation and has several excellent trails.

History. Five archeological sites within the park area include sherd areas and small villages along arroyos, probably representing temporary camps. During the historic period the area was within the range of the Southeastern Yavapai Indians.

Mining has never been of importance though prospectors swarmed over the area after the discovery of gold in the Prescott area in 1853. There are only traces of minerals and consequently no mining towns sprang up.

The main historic significance of the area is centered on nearby Fort McDowell, established by five companies of California volunteers in 1865. The fort's location was determined by King Woolsey's expedition against the Tonto Apaches in 1864. In 1890 the troops were withdrawn and the military reservation was transferred to the Bureau of Indian Affairs. The fort provided several services to settlers (mail, constable, and marriage) before such officials were available in Phoenix. The remains of the fort are on what is now the Fort McDowell Mohave-Apache Indian Reservation southeast of the park boundary near the Verde River.

The park area itself is desert cattle range. There is no available water except in cattle tanks. The rainfall supports attractive desert vegetation but is insufficient for crops. There was one stockraising homestead (Whitehead, 1919-1926) and the Pemberton Ranch. Stock grazing has been continuous, but as a supplement to other neighboring areas. (In fact, grazing leases in the park will not be extinguished until 1992 and at certain times of year stock do graze the area.).

Geology. The west side of the park contains some rocky hills of Precambrian igneous and metamorphic rocks. From the east the area slopes gently toward the Verde River due to the common level of surfaces between arroyos. There is, however, a steep escarpment along the eastern side of the park, of which Lousley Hill and the Asher Hills (just to the north of the boundary) are one part. Washes and arroyos are steep-sided with a depth of 20-100 feet.

After a lake was formed in the area in Tertiary time, vulcanism started in the late Tertiary Period: volcanic ash covered especially the northern and eastern parts of the park, falling on top of lacustrine clay deposits and forming beds of tuff. The Asher and Lousley Hills are remnants of the erosion of Tertiary lacustrine and alluvial deposits in the Pleistocene Epoch. Predominant rock types are granite and schist, with some gneiss and quartzite in the western part. The best granite exposure (massive and coarse-grained with large talus blocks) is at Rock Knob, which is probably a disintegrated fault block. Huge granite erosion remnants and outcrops (some looking like druid stones) are present [see picture]. Deposits of sand, gravel, and boulders have resulted from erosion from the McDowell Mountains to the west, transport through the canyons formed by block faulting, and spreading out in fan shape. In the eastern section the land appears to be a largely featureless plain dissected by washes trending southeast.

Maps. *Our maps 17-18.* The USGS 1;24,000 McDowell topo (1974) shows the area but not the trails. A small park map is available at the park.

Access. The park's main entrance is reached from Phoenix via Shea Boulevard to the Fountain Hills turn-off, thence north 4.2 miles through Fountain Hills to the park entrance on the left. The alternate approach from the north is via Pinnacle Peak Road to Rio Verde Drive, 10.3 miles to Forest Road, where you turn right for 4.5 miles to the entrance on the right.

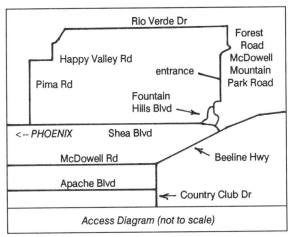

Access Diagram (not to scale)

Facilities. The park has two large family picnic areas with 88 picnic tables, grills, and comfort stations; 80 family campsites and a Group Campground with ramada and sani-station (advance reservations required), large Horse Staging Area and Scout Field Camp. *Phone: 471-0173 or 272-8871.*

Recommended Hikes and Trail Rides. The trail letters used are those of Maricopa County. Please note that several trails are *hiker only:* [A], [F], [G], [H], [I], [J], [N]. Of the short trails, probably the most scenic is the Lousley Hill Trail [A]. The Scout Trail [H] is an easy short loop through typical desert, and the Eagle Trail [I] leads up a rocky knob with a good view. The Gordon Wagner [F] and Cornell Club [G] Trails provide easy walks near the Family and Group Campgrounds. The North Trail Loop [N] is moderately long and includes one view-point on the Asher Hills. The Wilderness Campground Trail [J] is an easy walk into very different terrain with opportunities for further exploration. Best for a full day's hike or a trail ride are the Pemberton Trail [B], Goldfield Trail [C], and Scenic Trail [D]. (The Stoneman Historical Trail, shown on old park maps, has a reserved designation [E], but is not presently restored for travel.)

NOTE: *Descriptions of the longer circuit trails [B], [C], and [D] have been divided into segments.* This will assist those who are not starting from the centrally-located Horse Staging Area or who are combining segments of different circuit trails. Total distances to main points of interest from the Horse Staging Area *[HSA]* are given in *italics* in the tabular descriptions.

Cautions. The distances on the Pemberton Trail [B] are quite long and the terrain broken and confusing if the trail is lost. Sections of the Goldfield [C] and Scenic [D] Trails follow washes. Prolonged walking in washes can be quite hard on hikers' feet. Several of the trails follow old roads and are subject to erosion. Otherwise, general cautions apply. You may encounter cattle on their winter range from November through April.

[A] Lousley Hill Trail

General Description. For a short climb, this 1.25-mile trail offers wide views of the Verde Valley, the Superstitions, and the Four Peaks. There are extensive fields of teddy bear ("jumping") cholla. Use care. Pieces may be lying on or near the trail and can easily penetrate shoes and clothing. This is a hiker-only trail.

From the picnic area, the trail heads across country, then crosses a wide wash at 0.09 mile, reaching a junction at 0.21 mile. Here take the right fork, ascending the hillside by switchbacks to the summit at 0.53 mile. Heading along the crest, the trail then descends to a cliff-top at 0.78 mile where it switchbacks down the crest and then into a valley at 0.93 mile and the previous junction at 1.03 mile, for a total loop trip of 1.25 miles. Ascent is 270'.

Access. Take McDowell Mountain Park Drive 5 miles to Lousley Drive South and find the trail-head 0.35 mile further along it, in the Ironwood Picnic Area.

Read Down	Detailed Trail Description	Read Up
0.00	Leave road (elevation 1,780'); head S at sign, crossing 2 small washes.	1.25
0.09	Major wash. Rock-bordered trail parallels wash on its L.	1.16
0.20	Cross wash and ascend gradually.	1.05
0.21	**Junction:** two ends of loop. Go R here and ascend.	1.04
0.26	Turn L (steps lead up). In 100' turn R, then L in 35'.	0.99
0.32	Switchback to R onto short level stretch, then to L and ascend.	0.93
0.40	Teddy bear cholla start about here.	0.85
0.44	Turn L and head up crest.	0.81
0.51	**Junction:** level trail turns L here. Spur R leads to summit (2,048', good VP) in 100' (0.53 mi). Spur continues back to this trail in another 65'.	0.74
0.54	**Junction:** spur trail back to summit on R. Head gradually down crest, with good walking.	0.71
0.78	Cliff-top (edge of escarpment, 1,920'). Switchback down to L.	0.47
0.82	Switchback to R.	0.43
0.86	Switchback to L at edge of drop-off, then to R.	0.39

0.90	Switchback to L at cliff's edge, descending.	0.35
0.93	Turn L, descending into valley, then making several turns.	0.32
0.98	Parallel small wash.	0.27
1.03	**Junction:** you have now returned to start of loop section.	0.22
1.25	Road and trail-head.	0.00

[B] Pemberton Trail CLOCKWISE

General Description. This is a 15.32-mile *hiker/horse* trail, longest in the park, described here in a clockwise direction in 5 segments. The first two overlap the Goldfield Trail [C] and the last two segments overlap the Scenic Trail [D], and are described under those trails in the reverse direction. As a hike, this makes a very varied and interesting but long and strenuous day. There are three stock "tanks" on this trail, but there is no drinking water for people; carry enough of your own. The total ascent is 800'.

The trail first crosses the Park Drive, then leads across relatively flat terrain and the old Pemberton Ranch area to the Goldfield Trail at 2.00 miles. Here it turns west and begins a gradual ascent through a scenic area on an old road. At 4.84 miles it leaves the road and crosses broken terrain past Tonto Tank, unusual rock formations, Granite Tank, and the park corner at 9.03 miles. Here it abruptly turns east, gradually descending an old road to Cedar Tank at 12.27 miles. Just beyond it the trail leaves the old road and crosses the Park Drive at 13.81 miles. The last segment is easy, passing the Scenic Trail [D] junction and returning to the Horse Staging Area at 15.32 miles.

There are interesting vegetation changes with elevation; these differ on the two sides of this loop.

Access. There are several access points. The trail description starts at the Horse Staging Area *[HSA]*, but the trail can also be reached at the end of each segment via other trails or the Park Drive.

Read Down	*Detailed Trail Description*	*Read Up*
	SEGMENT 1 - HSA to Park Drive	
0.00	Trail leaves HSA at its SW side (1,960') on old road.	0.26
0.26	*McDowell Mountain Park Drive 2.3 mi from entrance, 0.65 mi from Palisades Way (trail continues across drive). [15.06 mi ahead to HSA.]*	0.00
	SEGMENT 2 - Park Drive to Goldfield Trail	
	[See Goldfield Trail, Segment 5, for reverse description]	
0.00	Leave Park Drive (1,985').	1.74
0.09	Cross moderate wash, then go up and down on wide, sandy old road.	1.65
0.20	Cross wash by going R, then L.	1.54
0.30	Cross moderate wash.	1.44
0.36	**Junction:** ignore road to R; go straight (fine view of Weaver's Needle).	1.38
0.38	Enter wash, turn L to cross it.	1.36

0.54   Cross large wash. 1.20
0.61   Cross 5 washes in next 0.31 mi. 1.20
1.08   Old road angles to R (this is old Pemberton Ranch area). 0.66
1.09   Ruined water tank and foundation on L. 0.65
1.12   Cross wash, then another. 0.62
1.51   Pass dirt piles and tank on L in eroded area, then go R where roads join.
        Road parallels ridge on R briefly. 0.23
1.53   Cross wash. 0.21
1.58   Old road to R (obscure). 0.16
1.62   Cross major wash and bear R, up-hill. 0.12
1.74   **Junction:** to L is Goldfield Trail [C] (3.29 mi to Park Drive near park entrance)
        (1,860'). Go R to continue *[2.00 mi from start at HSA; 13.32 mi ahead to HSA].* 0.00

SEGMENT 3 - Goldfield Trail to Park Corner and Yellow Shed

0.00   Go R from **junction**, on old road. 10.68
0.26   Start gradual ascent away from wash on R. Road diverges, keep R. 10.42
0.31   Road branch rejoins. Way becomes rockier, then eroded. 10.37
0.49   Erosion ends on ridge crest in attractive area. 10.68-0.49.....................................10.19
0.97   Fields of prickly pear, cholla, and staghorn cactus. 9.71
1.11   **Junction:** road on L; bear slightly R on less obvious road. 9.57
1.31   Parallel poorer road that diverges L. 9.37
1.38   Park-like area with fields of prickly pear cactus on both sides. 9.30
1.64   **Junction:** road enters from L. 9.04
1.80   Road less well-defined. Park-like area on L. 8.88
2.19   Top of rise. Descend gradually. 8.49
2.31   Bottom of descent. Wash on L. 8.37
2.52   Road bears R. 8.16
2.55   Bear L, ascend. 8.13
2.67   Bear L, then R. 8.01
2.84   **Important junction:** leave road for trail on R, where road continues
        straight ahead. Elevation 2,285' *[4.84 mi from start at HSA].* 7.84
2.98   Cross first of 3 washes. 7.70
3.13   **Junction:** obscure trail of use on R, then another to L in 70'. 7.55
3.21   Cross valley with several washes, turn up one for 25' (old vehicle way follows
        it), then leave it on R. 7.47
3.30   Cross fence line. 7.38
3.34   Follow fence line on R; trail not well defined here. 7.34
3.38   *Tonto Tank 125' to R* (2,300'). This water-filled depression is for cattle. Use
        care with several trails of use in area. Head N, straight toward Rock Knob
        [5.38 mi from start at HSA; 9.94 mi ahead to HSA]. 7.30
3.56   **Junction:** trails of use L & R; descend. 7.12
3.62   Cross moderate wash. 7.06
3.78   Head up branch of small wash, then cross it. 6.90
3.83   **Junction:** trail of use on L. 6.85
4.19   Ascend. 6.49
4.26   Cross moderate wash, ascending to NE. 6.42
4.30   VP 230' to L toward Superstitions, Four Peaks, Weaver's Needle. 6.38
4.32   Pass large stones on R & L. 6.36
4.46   Top of rise. Descend through very attractive area, crossing several
        washes, heading NW and W. 6.22
4.83   Go up moderate wash for 50', then leave it on R. 5.85
4.85   Join other wash briefly, then leave it on L. 5.83

4.89 Cross wash. Head N, then NW. 5.79
4.94 Join wash briefly. 5.74
5.22 Cross 2 washes. 5.46
5.33 Trail splits, rejoins in 65'. 5.35
5.59 Bear R. 5.09
5.68 **Junction:** trail of use on L. 5.00
6.00 Huge standing pillar of rock 20' to R; VP (trail splits). *[See color picture #18]* 4.68
6.10 Top of rise; drop. Go up & down through rocky area (erosional remnants). 4.58
6.17 Cross broad, flat area, then moderate wash. Ascend. 4.51
6.18 **Junction:** minor trail (alternate route) L leads 100' to VP on top of hump,
       then descends to rejoin main trail at 6.27 mi. 4.50
6.23 Top of rise. 4.45
6.27 **Junction:** at top of rise, minor trail L is alternate rejoining. 4.41
6.42 Descend into valley; use care with many cattle trails, then bear L (E). 4.26
6.46 **Junction:** go L at fork. 4.22
6.53 **Junction:** pass near shed and go R on road. 4.15
6.58 *Granite Tank* on L (2,480'). *[8.58 mi from start at HSA; 6.74 mi ahead to HSA.]* 4.10
6.63 Join fence line and parallel it on L (follow road). 4.05
6.93 Cross moderate wash. 3.75
7.03 *Park Corner.* Turn R (E). *[9.03 mi from start at HSA; 6.29 mi ahead to HSA.]* 3.65
7.09 **Junction:** old road on L. 3.59
7.25 **Junction:** old road L; keep R here, on old road. 3.43
7.40 Turn R (private home in view, across park boundary). 3.28
8.02 Parallel moderate wash on R, then cross it. 2.66
8.14 Cross moderate wash. 2.54
8.30 Turn L (N), then cross moderate wash in 100'. Reach top of rise in 300'. 2.38
8.53 Top of rise, descend. 2.15
8.57 Road bends to L, and again to R in 0.07 mi. 2.11
8.66 **Junction:** trail of use on L. 2.02
8.93 Eroded area of road. 1.75
9.13 **Junction:** trail of use on L. (Yuccas and crucifixion thorn bushes in next mile). ... 1.55
10.25 Fence ends at corner. 0.43
10.26 Old rusting water tower on L. 0.42
10.27 *Cedar Tank* on L (2,090'). *[12.27 mi from start at HSA; 3.05 mi ahead to HSA.]* 0.41
10.32 Fence corner (barbed-wire). 0.36
10.68 **Junction:** service road straight ahead, 1.10 mi to Park Drive. Elevation 2,020'.
        "Yellow Shed" (maintenance building) is on L here. On L is Scenic Trail [D].
        To continue, go R on trail *[12.68 mi from start at HSA; 2.64 mi ahead to HSA.]* 0.00

SEGMENT 4 - Yellow Shed to Park Drive
[See Scenic Trail, Segment 2, for reverse description]

0.00 Leave Yellow Shed and **junction**, by going R on trail. 1.13
0.03 Cross wash area for 30'. 1.10
0.11 Head along side of moderate wash. 1.02
0.19 Enter braided wash area; follow it for 85'. 0.94
0.33 Enter moderate wash; leave it in 150'. 0.80
0.47 **Junction:** avoid trail of use on L. 0.66
0.67 Turn L into moderate wash for 35.' 0.46
1.01 Enter wash area, then turn R, out of it, in 0.06 mi. 0.12
1.13 *McDowell Mountain Park Drive* (1,920'). *[13.81 mi from start at HSA;*
       1.51 mi ahead to HSA.] 0.00

SEGMENT 5 - Park Drive to HSA
[See Scenic Trail, Segment 1, for reverse description]

0.00	Leave Park Drive.	1.51
0.22	Cross deep, small wash.	1.29
0.31	Enter wash, turn L in it.	1.20
0.32	Turn R, out of wash.	1.19
0.80	Cross wash and barbed-wire fence, use care. Way follows old road.	0.71
0.90	**Junction:** road enters from R; turn L on it.	0.61
1.07	Road turns R.	0.43
1.15	Cross broad, flat wash.	0.36
1.24	**Junction:** leave old road to L.	0.27
1.27	Jog R, then L, then cross 3 small washes in next 0.13 mi.	0.24
1.44	Bear R.	0.07
1.50	**Junction:** minor trail R to road.	0.01
1.51	*Horse Staging Area*, elevation 1,960'. Goldfield [C] and Scenic [D] Trails to L. *[This is 15.32 mi from start of circuit.]*	0.00

[C] Goldfield Trail CLOCKWISE

General Description. This is an 8.11-mile *hiker/horse* trail, two segments of which (5 & 6) overlap the Pemberton Trail [B]. It leaves the Horse Staging Area and descends washes to a junction with the Scenic Trail [D] at 1.84 miles. It then joins an old road, turning southwest to reach the Park Drive at 2.25 miles. The Park Drive is crossed twice, then finally left at 2.82 miles. From here the old road parallels the highway (McDowell Mountain Road) and then turns north, ascending gradually to a junction with the Pemberton Trail [B] at 6.11 miles, which it joins past the site of the "Pemberton Ranch," crossing the Park Drive at 7.85 miles. The Horse Staging Area is reached at 7.81 miles. Total ascent is about 320'.

Access. From the Horse Staging Area, here abbreviated as *HSA,* and from the Park Drive at the end of Segments 2 and 5.

Read Down	*Detailed Trail Description*	*Read Up*

SEGMENT 1 - HSA to Scenic Trail [D] Junction
[See Scenic Trail, Segment 5, for reverse description]

0.00	The trail leaves HSA at 1,960' elevation at its NE end.	1.84
0.02	Bear L at corral. Descend obvious trail.	1.82
0.17	**Junction:** trail of use on R. Trail less obvious from here.	1.67
0.29	Turn L out of wash, then R.	1.55
0.26	Cross two washes (avoid trail of use in first), then turn R into wash. ..	1.58
0.34	**Junction:** trail of use on L.	1.50
0.40	**Junction:** trail of use on L.	1.44
0.50	Turn L out of wash.	1.34
0.52	Turn R into wash for 35', then go L, out of it.	1.33
0.53	Turn R into wash.	1.32

0.59	**Junction:** trail of use on R.	1.26
0.66	Turn R out of wash.	1.18
0.67	**Junction:** trail of use on R. Keep L.	1.17
0.78	Turn R down wash for 80', then pass through pleasant, meadow-like area.	1.06
0.84	Turn L in wash.	1.00
1.33	Go between 2 washes, then descend wash.	0.51
1.84	**Junction:** Scenic Trail [D] continues E, then N to Lousley Hill Trail [A] (2.98 mi) or Park Drive near Asher Circle (3.41 mi). Turn sharp R here to continue on Goldfield Trail. *[6.27 mi ahead to HSA.]*	0.00

SEGMENT 2 - Scenic Trail to Park Drive

0.00	Leave junction with Scenic Trail.	0.41
0.03	Cross major wash. Start ascent in 100'.	0.38
0.30	Top of rise.	0.11
0.33	Cross major wash, then ascend eroded road.	0.07
0.38	**Junction:** go L (ignore road branch to R). Reach gate in 100'.	0.03
0.41	*Park Drive (1,700'). Cross it to continue, or follow road (see next segment). [2.25 mi from start at HSA; 5.86 mi ahead to HSA.]*	0.00

SEGMENT 3 - Parallel to Park Drive

0.00	From Park Drive, cross it, following old road *[the Park Drive can be followed instead, for 0.45 mi].*	0.57
0.13	**Junction:** cross Park Drive again, continuing on road.	0.44
0.57	**Junction:** Park Drive (1,650'). *[2.82 mi from start; 5.29 mi ahead to HSA.]*	0.00

SEGMENT 4 - Park Drive to Pemberton Trail [B]

0.00	Leave Park Drive, heading S. Pass gate in 60'.	3.29
0.06	**Junction:** go straight where road branch leads L.	3.23
0.11	Turn L.	3.19
0.31	Descend and reach sandy bottom in 200', then bear L.	2.98
0.42	Cross major wash (highway nearby on L).	2.87
0.95	Cross broad valley bottom.	2.34
1.01	Cross moderate wash; ascend.	2.29
1.05	Top of rise (highway close by on L).	2.25
1.09	Cross major wash with highway on L, then cross a smaller, partially revegetated wash in 80'. Cross 3 more washes in next 0.1 mi.	2.20
1.25	Top of rise.	2.04
1.34	**Junction:** L leads toward highway, ends. Go R, ascending to W. Parallel wash on R.	1.96
2.24	Deep wash on L in attractive area.	1.05
2.38	Level area with fire ring on L.	0.91
2.73	Eroded section of old road.	0.56
3.29	**Junction:** Pemberton Trail continues ahead (1,860'). To continue on Goldfield Trail, turn R. here. *[6.11 mi from start at HSA; 2.00 mi ahead to HSA.]*	0.00

SEGMENT 5 - Pemberton Trail to Park Drive
[See Pemberton Trail, Segment 2, for reverse description]

0.00	Leave Pemberton Trail.	1.74
0.12	Cross major wash.	1.62
0.16	Old road to L.	1.58
0.21	Cross wash; parallel ridge on L.	1.53

0.23	Go L where roads join; pass dirt piles on R in eroded area.	1.51
0.62	Cross 2 washes.	1.12
0.65	Ruined water tank and foundation on L.	1.09
0.66	Old road joins from L (this is old Pemberton Ranch area). Beyond, cross 5 washes.	1.08
1.20	Cross large wash.	0.54
1.36	Cross wash.	0.38
1.38	**Junction:** ignore road to L.	0.35
1.44	Cross moderate wash.	0.30
1.54	Cross wash.	0.20
1.65	Cross moderate wash.	0.09
1.74	*McDowell Mountain Park Drive* 2.3 mi from park entrance (1,985'). Cross it. *[7.85 mi from start at HSA; 0.26 mi ahead to HSA.]*	0.00

SEGMENT 6 - Park Drive to HSA

0.00	Leave Park Drive on dirt road, heading NE.	0.26
0.26	*Horse Staging Area,* SW side (1,960') *[8.11 mi from start].*	0.00

[D] Scenic Trail CLOCKWISE

General Description. This is an 11.62-mile long *hiker/horse* trail. In a clockwise direction it leaves the Horse Staging Area and heads north, mostly level, to the Park Drive, which it crosses at 1.51 miles. It then reaches the Yellow Shed at 2.64 miles, where it leaves the Pemberton Trail and heads northwest, reaching the park boundary at 3.28 miles, turning right and following the fence line east to the top of a hill at 4.50 miles, then descending to cross the North Trail [N] twice at 4.83 and 4.97 miles. The old park entrance road is reached at 5.50 miles, and followed south to the gate, where this trail heads east to cross the Scout Camp Road and the spur to the Park Drive at 6.41 miles. This road is followed south all the way to 9.78 miles, where it joins the Goldfield Trail [C] and heads north to reach the Horse Staging Area at 11.62 miles. Total ascent is 500'.

Access. From the Horse Staging Area at its northern side; from the Park Drive just south of Scout Camp Drive; and from the Park Drive 0.75 mile from the entrance, via Segment 2 of the Goldfield Trail [C].

Read Down	*Detailed Trail Description*	*Read Up*

SEGMENT 1 - HSA to McDowell Mountain Park Drive
[See Pemberton Trail, Segment 5, for reverse description]

0.00	The trail leaves HSA (1,960') at its NE end. Pass minor trail L to road in 60'.	1.51
0.07	Bear L, then cross several small washes.	1.44
0.24	Jog R, then L.	1.27
0.27	**Junction:** turn R on old road, crossing wash in 100'.	1.24
0.36	Cross broad, flat wash. In 0.07 mi road turns L.	1.15
0.61	**Junction:** turn R where road goes L.	0.90

0.71	Barbed-wire fence; cross wash.	0.80
1.51	Cross the Park Drive (elevation 1,920') *[10.11 mi ahead to HSA]*.	0.00

SEGMENT 2 - Park Drive to Yellow Shed
[See Pemberton Trail, Segment 4, for reverse description]

0.00	Leave Park Drive.	1.13
0.06	Enter wash area for 0.06 mi.	1.07
0.46	Enter moderate wash for 35'.	0.67
0.66	**Junction:** avoid trail of use on R.	0.47
0.77	Enter moderate wash for 150'.	0.36
0.93	Go through braided wash area for 85'.	0.20
1.02	Go along side of moderate wash.	0.11
1.10	Cross wash area.	0.03
1.13	**Junction:** service road crosses; to R it is 1.10 mi back to Park Drive; to L Pemberton Trail [B] follows road. Across road and to R is Yellow Shed. To continue, cross road and continue on trail. Elevation 2,020'. *[2.64 mi from start at HSA; 8.98 mi ahead to HSA].*	0.00

SEGMENT 3 - Yellow Shed to Old Park Entrance Road

0.00	Leave **junction** near Yellow Shed, heading N, then NW.	3.01
0.64	Turn sharp R on section of old trail with fence line ahead.	2.37
1.26	Gate in fence on L.	1.75
1.85	Ascend hill next to fence.	1.16
1.88	Top of hill (1,910') with VP, flat area.	1.13
1.94	Turn R, away from fence line.	1.07
2.03	Turn L into moderate wash, then L out of it in 50'.	0.98
2.08	Enter large wash and follow it below ridge on L.	0.93
2.19	**Junction:** North Trail [N] crosses.	0.82
2.33	**Junction:** North Trail [N] crosses.	0.68
2.86	**Junction:** go R on old park entrance road.	0.15
3.01	**Junction:** leave road 20' before gate; go L (elevation 1,740'). *[5.65 mi from start, 5.97 ahead to HSA].*	0.00

SEGMENT 4 - Old Park Entrance Road to Park Drive Spur

0.00	Leave old park entrance road just N of gate.	0.82
0.07	Turn L onto old vehicle way.	0.78
0.17	Leave it, go R.	0.74
0.44	**Junction:** cross Scout Loop Road, parallel that road on far side.	0.71
0.49	Join water line on R.	0.40
0.76	**Junction:** old road, Scenic Trail goes L on it. To R, gate is 165', Park Drive is 215'. *[6.41 mi from start at HSA; 5.21 mi ahead to HSA].*	0.00

SEGMENT 5 - Park Drive Spur to Goldfield Trail [C]

0.00	Leave road junction with trail.	3.37
0.25	Cross moderate wash.	3.12
0.29	**Junction:** just before top of rise, rock-bordered trail goes L, peters out in 0.1 mi. .	3.08
0.36	Cross moderate wash.	3.01
0.67	Top of rise; descend.	2.70
0.70	Cross very large, broad wash.	2.67
0.74	Cross major wash.	2.63
0.84	Top of rise.	2.53

0.88	Road eroded beyond.	2.50
0.97	Cross valley bottom, then ascend.	2.40
1.06	Top of rise (1,690').	2.31
1.20	Briefly parallel highway on L, then ascend.	2.18
1.22	Top of rise at telephone line (1,695'). Descend eroded road into valley.	2.14
1.36	Cross wash. Road improves.	2.01
1.47	Top of rise, bear R.	1.90
1.54	Post with "8" on it. Bear L.	1.83
1.61	Cross moderate wash, then ascend.	1.77
1.87	Cross flats to top of rise in 200'.	1.51
1.99	**Junction:** road to L (toward highway). Bear R, ascending gradually.	1.38
2.32	**Junction:** go R on narrow trail where road ahead leads 125' to fence near highway culverts.	1.05
2.36	Bear R, away from road.	1.02
2.47	Top of rise.	0.90
2.60	Cross moderate wash, bear L.	0.77
2.64	**Junction:** go R, joining road from L (fence visible).	0.73
2.69	**Junction:** road L to gate; keep R.	0.68
2.86	Cross moderate wash.	0.51
2.90	Top of rise. Parallel highway.	0.47
3.22	Ascend branch of moderate wash.	0.15
3.36	**Junction:** cut-off trail to R. Continue straight.	0.01
3.37	**Junction:** Goldfield Trail [C] continues straight ahead. Go R for Scenic Trail up wash (1,680') *[9.78 mi from start at HSA; 1.84 mi ahead to HSA]*.	0.00

SEGMENT 6 - Goldfield Trail to HSA
[See Goldfield Trail, Segment 1, for reverse description]

0.00	Leave junction with Goldfield Trail, ascending wash (poor footway for hikers).	1.84
0.51	Take L fork of wash, then bear R between 2 washes.	1.33
0.54	Bear L, to same wash as before.	1.30
1.00	Leave wash on R.	0.84
1.04	Rejoin wash for 80', then leave on L. Pleasant trail leads through meadow-like area.	0.80
1.17	**Junction:** trail of use on L. Bear R, then turn L into wash.	0.67
1.26	**Junction:** trail of use on L.	0.59
1.32	Turn L out of wash.	0.53
1.33	Go R up smaller wash for 35', then turn L out of it.	0.52
1.34	Turn R up wash (trail of use joins from L).	0.50
1.44	**Junction:** trail of use on L.	0.40
1.48	Head R, out of wash, with fence ahead across wash, then swing to L.	0.36
1.50	**Junction:** trail of use on R.	0.34
1.55	Turn L, then R in wash.	0.29
1.58	Leave wash on L, cross two washes (avoid trail of use in second).	0.26
1.67	**Junction:** trail of use on L. Ascend on obvious trail.	0.17
1.82	Bear R at corral.	0.02
1.84	*Horse Staging Area* (1,960'). *[total = 11.62 mi]*.	0.00

Rock Knob on the Pemberton Trail [B]

A stock tank on the Pemberton Trail

[F] Gordon Wagner Trail COUNTERCLOCKWISE

General Description. A short, self-guided trail through easy terrain for 0.58 mile, *hiker-only.* At 0.48 mile it intersects the Cornell Club Trail [G] before reaching Palisades Circle North. Ascent is 40'.

Access. *For eastern end,* leave Group Campground parking area opposite entrance off of Palisades Way from Palisades Drive, at sign. *For western end,* leave Palisades Circle North between campsites 10 and 13.

Read Down	Detailed Trail Description	Read Up
0.00	Leave Group Campground parking area (1,990').	0.58
0.04	Cross moderate wash, then another in 300'.	0.54
0.19	Bear L.	0.39
0.20	**Junction:** go L on old road that becomes trail, ascending gradually.	0.38
0.32	Go diagonally across moderate wash.	0.26
0.48	**Junction:** Cornell Club Trail [G] to L.	0.10
0.58	This trail ends at Palisades Circle North (2,030').	0.00

[G] Cornell Club Trail CLOCKWISE

General Description. A self-guided, *hiker-only* trail, 1.18 miles in length, or a total of 1.28 miles as a circuit, with a segment of the Gordon Wagner Trail [F]. Ascent is 60'.

Access. From three points: (a) at campsite #22 on Palisades Circle South; (b) from 0.48 mile on the Gordon Wagner Trail [F], 0.10 mile from its western end; or (c) in the southern Family Campground area from Comfort Station #9 on Palisades Way North at Whitehead Way.

Read Down	Detailed Trail Description	Read Up
0.00	Trail leaves campsite #22 (2,020'), parallels road.	1.18
0.30	**Junction:** spur trail L 0.12 mi to Comfort Station #9.	0.88
0.34	**Junction:** sharp L is dirt road; turn R on it.	0.84
0.47	**Junction:** ahead old road [J] descends toward Wilderness Campground; *keep R to stay on [G] here.*	0.71
0.65	Where road continues, turn sharp R.	0.53
0.73	Go R on paved road, then L (not well defined) in 100'. Go sharp R in 0.07 mi.	0.45
0.88	Go down moderate wash; leave it in 100'.	0.30
0.95	Join wash again.	0.23
0.97	Two washes join, descend wash.	0.21
1.18	**Junction:** *this trail ends* at trail [F]. To R it is 0.10 mi to Palisades Circle North (2,020').	0.00

[H] Scout Trail CLOCKWISE

General Description. An 0.80-mile *hiker-only* trail from the Scout Loop. It leads around through typical Sonoran desert. Ascent and descent are 35'.

Access. Take McDowell Mountain Park Drive for 5.8 miles to Asher Circle and Scout Camp Drive on the right. This is usually gated. Park here and walk 0.34 mile on the dirt road to the Loop in the Scout Field Camp area. Walk 300' further around the circle to the northeast side of the Loop next to two privies.

Read Down	Detailed Trail Description	Read Up
0.00	Leave road loop next to 2 privies at sign (1,700').	0.80
0.06	Top of rise, descend gradually.	0.74
0.17	Bear L (E).	0.63
0.22	Cross moderate wash. Head S.	0.58
0.29	Turn R.	0.51
0.49	Head W up open area (becomes road); grade gradually increases.	0.31
0.57	Leave road to N; way levels in 120'.	0.23
0.70	Bear L.	0.10
0.80	Road loop (no sign) just W of water tap.	0.00

[I] Eagle Trail CLOCKWISE

General Description. From the Scout (road) Loop this 0.40-mile *hiker-only* trail leads up and over a small knob with good views, then returns to the Loop. Ascent is 85'.

Access. Start on the west side of the Scout Loop, 85' from where the stem of Loop enters.

Read Down	Detailed Trail Description	Read Up
0.00	Trail leaves road loop at W side (1,700').	0.40
0.07	Switchback to R.	0.33
0.08	Switchback to L (trail of use descends to R).	0.32
0.13	Top of hill (1,785'). Views of Superstitions, Four Peaks, etc.	0.27
0.15	Turn R (E).	0.25
0.17	Switchback to L, then to W.	0.23
0.23	Cross small wash. In 25' turn R *(use care)*, parallel wash on R.	0.17
0.25	Bear L away from wash at big sag.	0.15
0.26	Enter moderate wash and go down it.	0.14
0.27	Turn R.	0.13
0.30	Edge of wash: veer R, along it.	0.10
0.31	Cross small wash, ascend steps.	0.09
0.32	Top of rise, descend gradually.	0.08
0.40	This trail ends at road loop near N end.	0.00

[J] Wilderness Campground Trail

General Description. This fine *hiker-only* trail is 1.36 miles long. It leaves the Cornell Club Trail [G], descends to a valley, and ascends gradually through very attractive easy country to a totally wild area near a rocky draw where there are no facilities other than flat areas for camping. The draw can be ascended further for some views. Ascent is 150'.

Access. From the Cornell Club Trail at 0.47 mile from the road at the northern Family Campground at Palisades Circle South.

Read Down	Detailed Trail Description	Read Up
0.00	The trail leaves the Cornell Club Trail [G] at 0.47 mi (2,050'). Descend here from road, crossing flats.	1.36
0.09	Cross broad wash after road ends.	1.27
0.15	Go up large wash.	1.21
0.17	Leave wash on R.	1.19
0.77	Cross moderate wash.	0.58
0.81	Cross small wash, parallelling larger one, then cross it.	0.54
1.15	Cross small wash.	0.19
1.22	**Junction:** trail of use sharp L [to broken tank, fire ring, small rock shelter].	0.13
1.28	Cross major wash.	0.07
1.30	Cross moderate wash to attractive rocky area (2,200').	0.05
1.36	Valley ends in rocky draw [one can continue up draw by taking short steep trail up, then descending R into draw again. Rocks ahead can be climbed for wider views].	0.00

[N] North Trail Loop COUNTERCLOCKWISE

General Description. This is a *hiker-only* loop trail (with a short "stem") into fine desert terrain with one view-point on the south slope of the Asher Hills. The "stem" of the loop is 0.29 mile, then the loop leads north, crossing the Scenic Trail [D] to the view-point at 1.05 miles. It then drops off the hill and crosses the Scenic Trail and many washes, mostly on a level, and then turns east, descending gradually to reach the "stem" again at 3.13 miles. The total round-trip distance from the road is 3.42 miles. Circuit traips may be made with the Scenic Trail [D]. Total ascent is 200'.

Access. Take McDowell Mountain Park Drive to Asher Drive South at 5.6 miles from the park entrance and drive 0.4 mile along it to a parking area on the right; the trail is on the left at a sign near some picnic tables.

Read Down	Detailed Trail Description	Read Up
0.00	Trail leaves Asher Drive South at a sign (elevation 1,750').	3.13
0.29	**Junction:** actual loop starts here. For view-point, go R (counter-clockwise), *as does this description.* Trail meanders NE and N, crossing some very small washes.	2.84
0.80	Cross moderate shallow wash, then head L along washes.	2.33
0.92	Cross moderate wash, heading directly NW toward Asher Hills.	2.21
0.93	**Junction:** cross moderate wash and Scenic Trail [D]. Start ascent.	2.20
1.00	Go up a little valley on L.	2.13
1.02	Switchback to L, then across slope.	2.11
1.03	Apparent junction here on L is water diversion channel; go up to R.	2.10
1.05	View-point area (1,920'); descend gradually to L, off ridge.	2.08
1.07	Switchback to L and down.	2.06
1.12	Bottom of descent; bear R (SW), then cross 4 branches of major wash.	2.01
1.22	**Junction:** near where Scenic Trail [D] crosses, turn R into moderate flat wash, then L (SW) out of it in 50'.	1.91
1.31	Head W, parallelling wash on L.	1.82
1.35	Cross small wash, parallel wash on R.	1.78
1.52	Cross large shallow wash.	1.61
1.54	Cross moderate wash, then 7 very small ones in next 0.5 mi.	1.59
2.02	Cross small wash.	1.11
2.06	Turn L (E). Trail winds around, gradually descending.	1.06
2.24	Turn L, head toward hill on S (no trail leads up it).	0.88
2.68	Turn L, away from hill. Cross moderate wash.	0.44
2.79	Cross moderate wash.	0.34
3.10	Cross moderate wash.	0.02
3.13	**Junction:** back at "stem" of loop. Asher Drive is 0.29 mi to R.	0.00

Maricopa County

Usery Mountain Recreation Area

Introduction. Usery Mountain Recreation Area is in an unusual administrative situation: the lower area is in Maricopa County, but the main mountain trails are in the Tonto National Forest, which borders the Park. It consists of 3,324 acres, 12 miles northeast of Mesa. The Superstitions are to the east, the Goldfield Mountains on the north and northwest, immediately northwest are the Usery Mountains, and the McDowells are easily visible across the Salt River valley, also to the northwest. Two of the 8 dams of the Salt River Project are within 7 miles of Usery Mountain: Granite Reef Dam (4 miles) and Stewart Mountain Dam (7 miles), forming Saguaro Lake.

History. Between what is now the recreation area and the Salt River there was an Indian village and the ruins of the old Hohokam canals.

The mountain itself was named for King Usery, a cattleman in the area between 1878 and 1880. It was not an easy way of life in this arid area, and in 1891 he and Bill Blevins (after whom the Blevins Trail was named) held up the Globe-Florence stagecoach and stole two bars of silver bullion. Usery was surrounded at his ranch and was later sentenced to 7 years in the Territorial Prison at Yuma. He was pardoned after only two years, but later was convicted of horse-stealing for which he received a light sentence. Later he disappeared.

The desert plain around the Recreation Area has had some limited grazing use since the 1890s. There were several homesteads in the area, two of which have given names to trails described here. One was Chester McGill's (outside the present recreation area but inside the Tonto National Forest on the old road along the major wash near the Pass Mountain Trail) who held it only from 1932-34; it changed hands many times thereafter. The Coleman homestead existed from 1931-1937, inside the present recreation area, to the east of the junction of the Blevins Trail and the Superstition View Loops. Lack of dependable water was the reason the area was not more attractive to settlers. An old wagon road crossed the area near the present Bush Highway, which was constructed early in the century and later improved.

Usery Mountain itself is not mineralized. Eight miles to the east, in the Goldfield Mountains, low-grade gold ores were extensively worked in the 1890s. After World War II open-pit mining was attempted but failed. Many mining claims were filed, but none have become producing mines.

Pass Mountain is connected to the Goldfield Mountains to its east and forms the eastern flank of the pass between it and Usery Mountain to the west.

Geology. There are no significant mineral resources. The Recreation Area is part of a granite pediment -- a broad, plain-like surface sloping away from the higher mountains with occasional small granite hills and Pass Mountain standing upon it. Most of the nearby washes are shallow and poorly developed. The saddle between the two peaks of Headquarters Hill contains a shear zone marking a fault line (in the wash to the northwest is a prospect pit).

[Opposite page: Pass Mountain from Wind Cave Trail-head]

The hills are caused by tilted fault-blocks. Bedrock is thought to be Pre-cambrian granite (one to one and one-half billion years old). Volcanic rocks capping Pass Mountain are of Tertiary age. Pass Mountain has a prominent "tuff" layer[1] that turns greenish after a period of rain. Wind Cave is a hollowed-out portion of this layer that is softer than granite. The region's common northwest trend is evident in parts of this area and its geological faults.

Maps. *Our maps 19-21 (map 21 for Headquarters Hill).* The area is shown on the 1:24,000 USGS Apache Junction topo, but the trails are not shown.

Access. The park's main entrance is reached from Usery Pass Road. Turn east onto Usery Park Road. From Phoenix, take the Superstition Freeway (State #360) to its present end at Power Road, head north (it becomes Bush Highway), and turn east on either Apache Trail (U.S. 60/89) or McKellips Road to 92nd Street (Ellsworth Road) which leads north into Usery Pass Road.

From the Recreation Area's entrance, the first road on the right is Buckhorn Camp Drive to the Group Campground and the McKeighan, Camp-ground, and Coleman Trails. From Wind Cave Drive there is access to the Wind Cave, Pass Mountain, and Coleman Trails. The Horse Staging Area (soon to be renamed the Multi-Use Area) is access point for the Pass Mountain and Blevins Trails, while the Merkle Memorial parking area and picnic area #6 give access to the Merkle Trails.

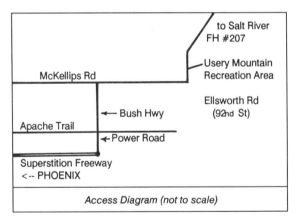

Access Diagram (not to scale)

Facilities. There are more than 50 picnic sites, a 75-unit Family Campground, a Group Campground (advance reservations required), archery range, Group Picnic Area, and Horse Staging Area (reservations required). Water is available. Picnic areas and the archery range close at sunset. *Make sure your vehicle is outside the gate by that time.* No off-road travel or unlicensed vehicles are permitted. Horseback riding is restricted to existing designated trails. *(Phone 834-3669.)*

---

[1] A solidified layer of volcanic ash or other ejected material.

Recommended Hikes and Trail Rides. The trail designations used here are those on the official Maricopa County park map. Of the hiker-only trails, the most popular is the Wind Cave Trail [G] which leads up to a break in the tuff layer below the summit ridge. It has good views to the west. Simplest are the Merkle Memorial Trail [D] and Merkle Vista Trail [E], which circle and climb Headquarters Hill, with good all-around views. The McKeighan [A] and Campground [C] Trails are very short, essentially flat, self-guided nature trails.

Of the hiker/horse trails, the best wilderness experience is the Pass Mountain Trail [F], which takes the better part of a day for hikers. *Be absolutely sure to carry enough water on this long trip!* The Blevins Trail [I] and Superstition Loops [J] are shorter and have varied terrain, but no significant climbs. *(NOTE: parts of the Blevins Trail and Superstition Loops were being re-routed in 1990-91. Be sure to inquire at the Park Ranger station about the status of the relocation if you intend to take one of these trails.)*

[A] McKeighan Trail

General Description. This is an 0.49 mile long *hiker-only* loop through almost flat desert, crossing a moderate-sized wash twice before returning to the start.

Access. From Buckhorn Camp Drive (across from campsite #4, just past the first bend in the road) across from the host site.

Read Down	Detailed Trail Description	Read Up
0.00	From Buckhorn Camp Drive opposite campsite #4, head W at sign (2,000').	0.49
0.01	**Junction:** trail L is loop headed clockwise. Go R (counter-clockwise), parallelling road in distance.	0.48
0.05	Bear L, then R, parallelling road.	0.44
0.08	Cross moderate wash; bear R on far side.	0.41
0.12	Cross major wash. Go L, despite arrow heading down wash, then head W.	0.37
0.15	Cross small wash.	0.34
0.19	Head S, then W.	0.30
0.28	Head SE, then in 55' turn L (around to N), past ironwood and palo verde trees.	0.22
0.32	Cross moderate wash and head E.	0.17
0.35	Turn R (S), then L in 100'.	0.14
0.38	Cross small wash.	0.11
0.41	Pass huge boulder. Cross moderate wash; turn R, parallel road and wash.	0.08
0.45	Turn L.	0.04
0.48	**Junction:** back to start of loop; go R for road and trail-head.	0.01
0.49	Trail-head at road.	0.00

[B] Coleman Trail

General Description. An easy *hiker only* trail, crossing several washes and displaying a wide variety of flora.

Usery Mountain

Leave the Group Campground and cross Usery Park Road at 0.16 mile, then cross 8 washes to reach the Pass Mountain Trail [F] at 0.86 mile, just 0.07 mile north of the parking area at Wind Cave Drive. Total ascent is 125'.

Access. From the east side of the Group Campground parking area, at a sign; or from Wind Cave Drive where the Wind Cave Trail leads north 100' to the Pass Mountain Trail, then left 0.05 mile on the latter.

Read Down	Detailed Trail Description	Read Up
0.00	Leave Group Campground parking area at center of east side, at sign (1,990').	0.86
0.16	Cross Usery Park Road.	0.70
0.19	Descend into broad wash.	0.67
0.29	Cross deep wash.	0.57
0.37	Cross moderate, shallow wash.	0.49
0.39	**Junction:** join level old road ascending from sharp R; bear L on it.	0.47
0.44	**Junction:** where old road ascends to L, go straight (E).	0.42
0.46	Cross small wash; bear R.	0.40
0.56	Cross moderate wash.	0.30
0.77	Cross major wash.	0.09
0.86	**Junction:** Pass Mountain Trail [F], 0.07 mi N of Wind Cave Drive trail-head. (Elevation 2,045'.)	0.00

Approaching the pass on Pass Mountain Trail

[C] Campground Trail

General Description. A short, 0.39-mile self-guided nature loop, *hiker-only*. There is no significant ascent.

Access. From south end of the Family Campground (between campsites #35-37).

Read Down	Detailed Trail Description	Read Up
0.00	From road in Family Campground area, head S, cross small wash.	0.39
0.04	**Junction:** take trail L (loop headed clockwise).	0.38
0.14	Turn R (W), cross small wash, then turn R, and then L.	0.25
0.16	Bear R.	0.23
0.17	Bench on L.	0.21
0.19	Bear W.	0.20
0.21	Cross small wash; head N.	0.18
0.26	Head NE.	0.13
0.27	**Junction:** 50' R is bench; spur leads back to this trail.	0.12
0.28	**Junction:** spur R to bench.	0.11
0.32	Turn L (N) up small wash for 30'; leave it on R.	0.07
0.34	Cross moderate wash, then parallel it.	0.05
0.35	**Junction:** back to start of loop; go L for road and trail-head.	0.04
0.39	Trail-head at road; back at start.	0.00

[D] Merkle Memorial Trail

General Description. The Memorial Trail circles Headquarters Hill and can be reached from the south at the memorial plaque parking and picnic area, or at the northeast picnic area (6). It is a *hiker-only* trail with moderate ascent and descent along and across minor washes with some views of desert vegetation. It intersects the Merkle Vista Trail [E] at the north and south end, and a side-trail to the Merkle Vista Trail connects on the southeast corner of the circle. Ascent is 100'.

Access. *From the north:* at Area 6 ramada. Walk southwest between the comfort station and a ramada to ramada 6C. The spur trail leaves from the far side and crosses a wash. This trail starts at 0.09 mile. *From the south:* park at the memorial area and find the spur trail at a sign directly across the road.

Read Down	Detailed Trail Description	Read Up
0.00	From the Merkle Memorial parking area and plaque at 1,890', find the trail at sign on opposite side of road.	0.94
0.01	Triangular **junction** in only 25': *go L* for the clockwise direction of the Merkle Memorial Trail (and for S end of Merkle Vista Trail). (Go R for counterclockwise direction.) *This description is for clockwise (L).*	0.93

0.04	Turn R and ascend.	0.90
0.05	Turn sharp R.	0.89
0.06	Switchback to L on ascent.	0.88
0.07	**Junction:** Merkle Vista Trail [E] sharp R leads to S Peak in 0.22 mi; to N Peak in 0.40 mi; back to Merkle Memorial Trail in 0.50 mi. Continue straight ahead, ascending gradually.	0.87
0.12	Top of rise. Bear slightly R, descend gradually to N. Cross 3 small washes en route.	0.82
0.40	**Junction:** trail sharp R at top of rise is Merkle Vista Trail [E] to N Peak in 0.18 mi. Descend.	0.54
0.48	**Junction:** trail R is continuation of this trail. *(Straight ahead, on spur, large wash is crossed in 45', a smaller one in 110', and just beyond is ramada 6C. The road is 460' or 0.09 mi away.)* Parallel wash, heading S.	0.46
0.51	**Junction:** trail sharp L leads around far side of tree to nature sign "desert hackberry."	0.43
0.52	Trail turns L.	0.42
0.54	Descend.	0.40
0.57	Level out.	0.37
0.61	Bench on R.	0.33
0.70	**Junction:** side-trail R climbs 60' to pass between peaks and to Merkle Vista Trail [E] in 0.14 mi, crossing a small wash in 230' and making two switchbacks. Elevation here is 1,940'. Continue S, passing a number of picnic tables, then parallelling road.	0.23
0.93	**Junction:** back at triangle just 65' from road and memorial plaque.	0.01
0.94	Trail-head at road opposite memorial picnic area.	0.00

[E] Merkle Vista Trail

General Description. From the Merkle Memorial Trail [D] on the north side of Headquarters Hill, this spur ascends steadily up the ridge with three switch-backs. It reaches a fine view-point at North Peak (2,078') at 0.18 mile, then drops to a pass. (From here a side-trail descends east to the Merkle Memorial Trail [D].) The main trail skirts the South Peak (2,052') to a junction with the side-trail to that peak at 0.33 mile. The Merkle Memorial Trail is reached again at 0.50 mile, where this trail ends. Ascent is only 90' to the North Peak.

Access. *From the north (ramada 6C):* take spur to Merkle Memorial Trail [D] for 0.09 mile, go right on it for 0.08 mile to junction; turn sharp left, up-hill. *From the south (Merkle Memorial Parking Area):* take the short spur trail to the Merkle Memorial Trail [D], then left on it for 0.07 mile, where the Merkle Vista Trail turns sharp right.

Read Down	*Detailed Trail Description*	*Read Up*
0.00	From the Merkle Memorial Trail [D] 0.15 mi from ramada 6C, head sharp L (SE) up the ridge.	0.50
0.03	Trail switchbacks to R, levels briefly, then ascends toward pass.	0.47
0.11	Turn sharp L just before a minor summit.	0.39

0.16	**Junction:** switchback up to R where spur trail L leads to VP in 30'. 0.34
0.18	*Summit of North Peak (2,078').* Descend gradually S. 0.40
0.22	**Junction:** on R 100' is spur to minor summit. Just L of that faint trail is
	main trail, descending; take it. (Trail straight ahead along main ridge ends
	in 120'; poor trail leads down 160' to connect with main trail.) 0.36
0.26	Turn L and descend, with minor summit just above on R. Pass rock
	formations on R just before pass. 0.32
0.30	*Pass* (2,000'). **Junction:** trail descending L is spur to Merkle Memorial
	Trail in 0.15 mi. Main trail continues straight, mostly level. 0.20
0.33	**Junction:** trail sharp R is spur to South Peak in 0.05 mi. Descend. 0.17
0.40	**Junction:** poor trail R ascends to South Peak in 0.07 mi. 0.09
0.47	Switchback to L. 0.03
0.48	Switchback to R. 0.02
0.50	**Junction:** back at Merkle Memorial Trail (turn L for 345' to road). 0.00

[F] Pass Mountain Trail

General Description.   This is a 6.92 mile-long *hiker and horse* trail, long and strenuous, with much up and down. It well repays the effort.   Heading east from the Wind Cave Trail [G], it meanders along the flat slopes of Pass Mountain and skirts private property.   After about 2 miles it heads north, crosses a wide valley and climbs the valley's eastern side by switchbacks. Skirting a rocky pinnacle, it enters the pass at 3.45 miles where there are dramatic views, an ascent of 600'. There is then a gradual descent (with many washes to be crossed) around the eastern slopes, swinging around to the west side at about 5 miles.   The section heading south along the fence line back to the start is inside the park (about 4-1/2 hours total, on foot).   Most of this trail is in the Tonto National Forest. *[On the northeastern section there are areas where horses should be walked, and the counter-clockwise direction is strongly recommended.]*

 Note: In using the mileages below, if you start from the Horse Staging Area, *subtract* 0.61 mile for counterclockwise travel; *add* the same for clockwise travel.

Access. (1) From the south picnic loop at the Horse Staging Area (east end), or (2) at the start of the Wind Cave Trail [G], from Wind Cave Drive West (north picnic loop at Area #8), off the park road, near a washroom.   The start is marked with a prominent sign. *Distances here are from the latter.*   (It may also be reached via the Coleman [B] or Blevins [I] Trails.)

Read Down	*Detailed Trail Description*	*Read Up*
0.00	From **junction** on Wind Cave Trail [G] 100' beyond trail-head (elev. 2,030'),	
	turn R (S) and cross a wash in 180'. 6.92
0.05	Cross fence. Descend gradually S. 6.87
0.22	**Junction:** trail-of-use on R. 6.70
0.26	Cross wash, bear R and parallel it. 6.66

0.61	**Junction:** trail to Horse Staging Area on R. Turn L here (elev. 1,880').	6.31
0.65	Cross major wash. Head straight toward the Superstition Mountains.	6.27
0.72	Cross moderate wash; ascend out of it.	6.20
0.88	Cross wash, then head into low pass.	6.04
1.01	Cross large wash.	5.90
1.26	Cross small wash and descend toward private homes in view ahead.	5.67
1.41	Fence alongside on R. Switchback to L and cross wash.	5.52
1.46	Join fence line and parallel it.	5.46
1.56	Leave fence line.	5.36
1.60	Cross major wash; ascend briefly on rocky trail.	5.32
1.72	Cross major wash.	5.20
1.75	Bear R, toward Superstitions, ascending gradually. Road below on R near homes.	5.17
1.92	Top of rise; descend.	5.00
1.97	Cross small wash; major wash is some distance away on R; parallel it.	4.95
2.15	Swing NW into side canyon, then turn R to cross two washes.	4.77
2.27	Top of rise.	4.65
2.33	Cross small rocky wash.	4.59
2.48	Major wash; follow it for 50', then ascend to L.	4.44
2.53	Large wash on R; parallel it, ascending and meandering. Pass Mountain in view ahead.	4.39
2.81	Bottom of another wash.	4.11
2.90	Switchback down to another wash; ascend out of it and switchback to L.	4.02
2.94	**Junction:** track joins on R (from private property). Continue ascent.	3.98
2.99	Head NE, then N. Ascend steadily with pinnacle visible ahead on ridge.	3.93
3.20	Switchbacks up side of valley start, first one to L.	3.72
3.28	**Junction:** short spur trail L to VP.	3.64
3.36	Route splits and rejoins in 60'.	3.56
3.38	Go to L, below cliff.	3.54
3.44	Rock face on R in level section.	3.48
3.45	*PASS (Elevation 2,590')*; excellent VP with grassy areas. (This point is exactly half-way on the circuit.) From here the terrain changes. Descend gradually.	3.47
3.57	Cross small wash.	3.35
3.64	Cross draw and wash.	3.28
3.86	Cross small wash.	3.06
3.92	Landmark: pass between 2 conglomerate boulders.	3.00
4.03	Brink of canyon; descend beside wash, then ascend.	2.84
4.07	Cross major wash, then a small one in 285'.	2.85
4.16	Top of rise; descend gradually.	2.76
4.22	Cross small wash and ascend.	2.70
4.28	Top of rise; descend briefly, then cross 2 washes.	2.64
4.36	Top of rise (2,480'). Descend and bear L; cross a small wash in 0.09 mi.	2.56
4.47	Ascend a steep pitch.	2.45
4.50	Cross small wash (*Note:* eroding trail here made use unsuitable for horses in early 1989; use care).	2.42
4.53	Top of rise. Descend briefly, ascend, cross small wash in 0.05 mi.	2.39
4.63	Top of rise. Mt. McDowell ("Red Mountain") in view ahead. Cross a wash in 200'.	2.29
4.68	Top of rise; cairn. Switchback down to L and head N, with 2 more switchbacks.	2.24
4.73	Cross a wash.	2.19
4.82	**Junction:** go L where spur R ends. In 220' cross small wash.	2.10
4.97	**Junction:** spur R to VP in 235' (2,510').	1.95
4.99	Descend to W; switchback to R and L, then cross wash in 130'.	1.93

5.05	**Junction:** short spur R to VP near small wash. Go L and ascend.	1.88
5.07	Top of rise, VP on R. Drop to L at cairn. Trail meanders; use care with unclear route.	1.85
5.17	Eroded area.	1.75
5.22	**Junction:** cross dirt road (2,310'). Cross small wash in 280'.	1.70
5.36	Cross large wash. Top of rise is reached in 125', then another deep wash in 75'.	1.56
5.42	Pass through fence (from Tonto National Forest into Recreation Area).	1.50
5.49	Sign post. Parallel fence on L.	1.43
5.63	Top of rise.	1.30
5.73	Descend into wide wash; in 170' switchback out of it.	1.16
5.85	Cross wash, then 3 more small washes in next 0.08 mi; parallel fence.	1.07
5.96	Cross large wash, bear S and ascend.	0.96
6.00	Cross major wash.	0.92
6.02	Top of rise. Trail parallels fence line.	0.90
6.51	Cross small wash, then several more minor ones.	0.41
6.76	Cross major wash and turn R in it, then ascend out of it to L in 120'.	0.16
6.87	**Junction:** Coleman Trail [B] on R (0.70 mi to road, 0.86 mi to Group Campground). Go L, into wash.	0.05
6.92	**Junction:** *back at starting point* -- Wind Cave Trail [G] on L (1.29 mi to Wind Cave on side of Pass Mountain). Road is 100' to R on this trail.	0.00

[G] Wind Cave Trail

General Description. This 1.29-mile *hiker-only* trail involves a steady ascent of the flank of Pass Mountain almost to its south peak.

From the trail-head you quickly cross the Pass Mountain Trail [F], enter the Tonto National Forest, and ascend gradually along a wash. The grade increases beyond 0.65 mile, with many switchbacks. Past the last rest stop (at 0.94 mile) the way meanders along the base of the prominent geological layer ("tuff") to reach Wind Cave at 1.29 miles.

There are some good views, both distant and close-up, of the unusual geological formations on the mountain. Though the maintained trail ends at Wind Cave, a poor and very steep route continues onto the ridge and peak.

Access. From Wind Cave Drive West (north picnic loop at Area #8), off the park road, near a washroom. The start is marked with a prominent sign.

Read Down	*Detailed Trail Description*	*Read Up*
0.00	From parking area at sign and washrooms (elevation 2,030'), trail ascends gradually.	1.29
0.02	**Junction (4-way):** cross Pass Mountain Trail [F].	1.28
0.08	Cross fence thru gate (Tonto National Forest boundary) from Recreation Area.	1.22
0.18	Cross wash; parallel it on R from 0.25 mi.	1.11
0.27	Turn L (N), then bear R, crossing wash.	1.03
0.29	Switchback to L (NW); ascend, then switchback to R (E).	1.01
0.39	**Junction:** "rest area" on R (2,140'). Turn R (E) in 50'.	0.91
0.49	Ascend steadily, still parallelling wash on R.	0.81

0.58	Switchback to L.	0.71
0.62	Turn L, then R.	0.67
0.65	Rest area on L, sign: "grade steepens beyond." Turn R, toward summit, in 50'.	0.65
0.70	Turn L, toward E.	0.59
0.71	Switchback to L, then 2 more.	0.59
0.75	Switchback to R, around boulders.	0.55
0.77	Turn L.	0.52
0.79	Switchback to R, level briefly, then to L and ascend.	0.51
0.83	Level briefly on traverse.	0.46
0.87	Switchback to R, ascend; then 3 more switchbacks.	0.43
0.94	Rest area. Switchback to R, toward cliffs.	0.36
0.99	Bear R, then S, on easy grade.	0.31
1.03	Go up rocks, level out in 150'.	0.27
1.07	Reach base of cliff.	0.22
1.09	Swing L toward cleft in rock. Drop briefly, then follow path beneath cliffs, ascending gradually.	0.21
1.16	Level out.	0.13
1.20	Start ascent.	0.10
1.21	Switchback to L, then to R. *(Avoid cutting across switchbacks here.)*	0.08
1.24	Switchback to L, then to R.	0.06
1.28	**Junction:** sign indicates "Trail Ends Here - Not Maintained Beyond". [Beyond this point, route deteriorates and becomes steep and obscure. It reaches a VP on end of ridge in 760'. Summit 3127 is about 0.4 mi -- not recommended for ordinary hikers.] *Turn L here.*	0.01
1.29	*Wind Cave (elevation 2,850').* Beware of bee hives here, above among rocks.	0.00

[H] McGill Trail (Discontinued – 1990)

This trail has been discontinued because of its proximity to the Archery Range.

[I] Blevins Trail

General Description.   This *hiker/horse* trail previously formed a 3.84-mile loop, with a subsidiary Superstition Loop [J]. The eastern portion was being re-routed in 1990-91, and the Superstition Loop divided into two overlapping loops, the North Superstition Loop and the South Superstition Loop. (Examine Map 20 to see the general route planned.)

Although we cannot describe the details of the new sections with the usual accuracy, since the trail work had not yet been completed at time of publication, we have described the sections that will follow the original route, and have added the new sections as approximations.

There are many washes to cross and several sections along dirt roads. Total ascent is about 220'. *The description here is in a counterclockwise direction.*

Access. From the south picnic loop (southwest end of Horse Staging Area).

Read Down	Detailed Trail Description	Read Up
0.00	Leave Horse Staging Area parking area near its SW end (elevation 1,910').	2.80
0.06	Road is close on R, along broad wash.	2.74
0.14	Cross minor wash.	2.66
0.19	Cross flat wash; head R in it, past picnic table. **Junction:** where this trail heads L out of wash, short spur trail R passes picnic table into Merkle Memorial Trail parking lot (610' to road).	2.61
0.32	**Junction:** cross old road.	2.48
0.33	Descend toward wash.	2.47
0.38	**Junction:** cross old road.	2.42
0.45	Cross shallow wash.	2.35
0.48	**Important junction:** turn L onto old dirt Cresmon Road (quarter section boundary as well as boundary between recreation area and Tonto National Forest).	2.32
0.61	Road crosses.	2.19
0.70	Road on L.	2.10
0.95	Turnout on L.	1.85
0.98	Section marker.	1.82
1.09	**Important turn**, L off road at arrow.	1.71
1.12	Cross broad wash.	1.68
1.31	Cross small wash, then two more.	1.49
1.43	**Junction:** old road crosses.	1.37
1.44	Cross moderate wash, then another in 0.12 mi.	1.36
1.58	Arrow -- turn L here (1,820').	1.22
1.62	Picnic area and hitching post on R (no camping).	1.18
1.63	Cross major wash.	1.17
1.68	**Junction:** old road L; bear slightly R.	1.12
1.82	Cross moderate wash, ascend.	0.98
1.88	Cross moderate wash.	0.92
1.97	Go R, then L in 40'.	0.83
1.99	**Junction:** go L on old road approximately here.	0.81
	[Distances from here may not be accurate since the trail is being reconstructed.]	

2.09	**Junction:** Superstion Loops [J] on R. Go L with North Superstition Loop coinciding.	0.71
2.20	Cross small wash.	0.60
2.27	Cross small wash. Bear R (NW).	0.53
2.30	**Junction:** bear R where old vehicle ways diverge.	0.50
2.35	Bear R, parallelling wash on L.	0.45
2.39	Bear L, descend slightly.	0.41
2.41	Cross moderate wash, ascend on far side, pass **junction** with old road.	0.39
2.80	Horse Staging Area.	0.00

[J] Superstition View Loops

General Description. *NOTE:* In 1990-91 what was originally a 0.85 mile loop was being redeveloped into two overlapping loops (see map) connecting with the Blevins Trail. Exact distances cannot be provided, as they were not yet measurable, but we have entered an approximation. There is a short 80' climb over a ridge that has a good view at the top. Although used by horses, the ascent is quite steep in places.

Access. From the Blevins Trail [I] (heading counterclockwise) at 2.09 miles.

[J] North Superstition View Loop CLOCKWISE

Read Down	*Detailed Trail Description*	*Read Up*
0.00	Leave Blevins Trail [I] at 2.09 mi. Coincide with Blevins Trail.	1.49
0.11	Cross small wash.	1.38
0.18	Cross small wash, bear R (NW).	1.31
0.21	**Junction:** bear R where old vehicle ways diverge.	1.28
0.26	Bear R, parallel wash on L.	1.23
0.30	Bear L, descend gradually.	1.19
0.32	Cross moderate wash, ascend on far side, then at **junction** with Blevins Trail keep R, up bank of wash.	1.17
0.42	Bank of major wash on R.	1.07
0.57	Turn R and cross wash, then cross 2 more.	0.92
0.77	Parallel Tonto National Forest fence on L.	0.72
0.88	Cross small wash, descend.	0.61
1.19	Cross small wash.	0.30
1.21	**Junction:** on L is South Superstition View Loop (coincide with it here). Go R.	0.28
1.31	Cross small wash.	0.18
1.34	**Junction:** obscure trail on R. Go L, ascending steadily.	0.15
1.38	*Pass* (1,920'), views. Descend.	0.11
1.45	Level out (1,860').	0.04
1.49	**Junction:** Blevins Trail [I], L & R.	0.00

[J] South Superstition View Loop CLOCKWISE

Read Down	Detailed Trail Description	Read Up
0.00	Leave Blevins Trail [I] at 2.09 mi. Coincide with Blevins Trail.	1.04
0.04	Start ascent.	1.00
0.11	*Pass* (1,920'), views. Descend.	0.93
0.15	**Junction:** obscure trail on L.	0.89
0.18	Cross small wash.	0.86
0.28	**Junction:** on L is North Superstition View Loop. Go R. (Elevation 1,840').	0.76
0.45	Bear R.	0.59
0.51	Bear R.	0.53
0.82	Cross moderate, deep wash.	0.22
0.91	Cross broad wash.	0.13
0.94	**Junction:** approximately near here, Blevins Trail [I] and this Loop go R, where Blevins continues for 1.99 mi to the Horse Staging Area.	0.10
1.04	**Junction:** Blevins Trail [I] goes L. You are now back at the start.	0.00

[NOTE:
DURING 1991, NEW HIKER/HORSE and HIKER/MOUNTAIN BIKE
TRAILS WILL BE ESTABLISHED IN THE SOUTHERN PART OF THE
RECREATION AREA, USING EXISTING TRAILS AND ROADS]

Maricopa County

White Tank Mountain Regional Park

Introduction. The rugged 26,337-acre White Tank Mountain Regional Park is located on the eastern slope of the White Tank Mountains (which separate the Phoenix Basin from the Hassayampa Plains) 15 miles west of Glendale. Wilderness and archeological interest are here combined, with excellent hiking and riding opportunities. The story goes that the mountains were named after either the light-colored eroded stoney depressions that collected water ("tinajas" in Spanish), or possibly for a Mr. White who had dug a well near the north end of the mountain for use by the Prescott-to-Phoenix stage. Elevations in the park range from 1,400' to 4,083'. Reached by jeep roads, several microwave relay stations now perch on the main peaks of the range.

History. Early Indian hunting parties frequented the area and harvested the fruit of the prickly pear and saguaro. There are petroglyphs, pictographs, and 11 Hohokam archeological sites (500-1100 A.D.) in the park, mostly where large canyons lead out of the mountains on the east and north. Prospecting yielded nothing of value. The lower slopes were seasonally grazed by small herds as is obvious from the remains of dams and corrals. Homesteading was limited by the quick water run-off and the lack of permanent watercourses.

Geology. The geomorphology of the area is that of a tilted fault block, characteristic of the Basin and Range Province, oriented north-northwest, tilted upward on the northeast side. Internal structure is complex. Topography is steep-sloped and rugged, due to rapid up-lifting above surrounding older rocks and subsequent erosion. There are thought to have been at least two intrusions of granite. In places eroded fault zones have had dikes of resistant igneous rock injected. The rocks are mostly of Precambrian age (one billion to 500 million years ago), the oldest dominant types being granite and gneiss, with many variations and mixtures.

The "tanks" are a series of huge steps in the bottom of steep-walled gorges. Progressive erosion caused sharp vertical drops adjacent to fault zones. Occasional torrents of water carried rock debris, dropping off each step and scouring out "tanks" at the base.

Maps. *Our map 16.* USGS White Tank Mts topo (1:62,500, 1957) is useful only for general topography. Better are the maps in the 1:24,000 series, Waddell and White Tank Mts. SE. None shows the trails, though old roads are indicated.

Access. There is only one access point: from Olive (extension of Dunlap west of 43rd Avenue) to the park entrance at White Tank Mountain Road.

Facilities. There are comfort stations, many covered picnic sites, cooking grills, 4 large group picnic areas with ramadas (reservations required, fee charged), a group campground (advance reservations and fee), 40 family campsites and a tent camping area. (The park area was up-graded in 1987-1988 to provide electricity and water at the ramadas.)

Picnic areas are closed at sunset. No ground fires are allowed and the park is closed to all off-road travel and all unlicensed motor vehicles. Horseback riding is restricted to existing trails.

Recommended Hikes. Only official trails are described here. (Old park maps show a "Slick Rock Trail" as undeveloped. It is not yet in existence.) The best trail (for hikers only) for an easy taste of the park is the Waterfall Trail [B]. The Goat Camp Trail [A] and the Ford Canyon Trail [F] are not very difficult and have excellent views for hikers and horsemen. The Rock Knob Trail [C] and Willow Springs Trail [E] are more difficult but also have fine views into rugged country. The Black Rock Trail [D] is an easy walk in a less well known area.

Cautions. *The terrain in this park is very rugged, with many steep canyons. Be absolutely certain to carry sufficient water for your own needs. Leave word of your plans and remember: it is especially hazardous to travel off trails on your own.* Rattlesnakes are common.

[A] Goat Camp Trail

General Description. This is a pleasant *hiker/horse* trail into wild canyon country. For the first mile and one-half it keeps to the north side of a flat area, just beneath the mountain, then leads into Goat Canyon and becomes increasingly rocky with some steady ascents. The last mile is a spectacular route through the canyon with cliffs and rock spires above. The trail ends at an old corral with some stone work ("Goat Camp") on the valley floor at 2.96 miles. Total ascent is about 1,600'.

Access. Park at the northwest end of picnic loop #1, just off Black Canyon Drive North, 0.2 mile beyond the park entrance. There is a sign at the start.

Read Down	Detailed Trail Description	Read Up
0.00	Leave parking area (elev. 1,500') on a clearly defined trail. The route ascends gradually.	2.96
0.39	Parallel wash on R.	2.57
0.66	Level out at 1,640'. In 135' start brief ascent again.	2.31
0.77	**Junction:** South Loop Trail [G] (built by Eagle Scouts) on L back to road in 1.04 mi. Ascend gradually, in and among rocks.	2.19
1.02	Parallel major wash.	1.95
1.03	Cross wash (1,700') and ascend more steadily to NW.	1.93
1.06	Edge of wash, ease grade of ascent.	1.91
1.20	Footway roughens.	1.77
1.44	Top of rise (1,880'). Wash on L.	1.53
1.51	Ascend more steadily on rocky, rougher trail.	1.46
1.57	Level out (1,970').	1.39
1.62	Turn L to cross bouldery moderate-sized wash.	1.32
1.68	Switchback to L, then to R.	1.29
1.75	Bear R after crossing very small wash. Good views here.	1.22
1.82	Trail follows along ledge (2,160').	1.14
1.87	Pass below rocky knob on L. From here, trail ascends the valley side with pinnacles above, a spectacular route.	1.09
2.06	Level out very briefly, then ascend again.	0.91
2.10	With cliff ahead, canyon narrows (2,470').	0.86

2.18	Climb above dry waterfall.	0.78
2.20	Level out. Looking back, there are several rock "faces" on the cliff.	0.76
2.22	Switchback to L, then to R.	0.75
2.23	Lovely view of upper valley and towers. Ahead, trail passes through a fine stand of prickly pear cactus.	0.73
2.53	Trail post "TR1" on L.	0.43
2.85	Cross rocks of side-canyon (2,970'). Yuccas and agaves beyond here.	0.11
2.89	Rock walls below on R.	0.07
2.93	Descend briefly.	0.02
2.96	Cross small wash. Just beyond, this trail ends at valley bottom (3,020') where there is an old rock corral ("Goat Camp"). Beyond, there are trails of use only. (One ascends to a VP on side of ridge in 340'.)	0.00

Petroglyphs near Waterfall Trail [B]

[B] Waterfall Trail

General Description. This is a short, easy *hiker-only* trail to the most popular area in the park. Total ascent is only 180'.

Access. Leave White Tank Mountain Road at 1.65 miles from the entrance, taking Waterfall Canyon Road to the left, then a very short spur road. The trail leaves this branch road at a sign 2.0 miles from the park entrance near the picnic ramadas and comfort station #6.

Read Down	*Detailed Trail Description*	*Read Up*
0.00	From road at 1,520' elevation, head W on trail.	0.88
0.14	**Junction:** ignore old rocky trail on L (rejoins).	0.74
0.20	**Junction:** old trail rejoins on L.	0.68
0.38	Petroglyphs 160' to R.	0.50
0.39	**Junction:** on L 70' is meadow-like area. In 310' turn R, then R again.	0.49
0.46	Turn sharp R, then keep to L.	0.42
0.49	**Junction:** trail R rejoins. Keep L, then swing around to R, parallelling wash.	0.39
0.58	Ascend rocky area beside wash on L.	0.30
0.61	**Junction:** alternate route goes sharp R here (passes Burke K. Bird Memorial Bench in 60', rejoining main trail at an obscure point in 175').	0.27
0.72	Edge of wash on L.	0.16
0.74	**Junction:** poor trail on R at rock pile is Rock Knob Trail [C]. Elevation 1,660'.	0.14
0.79	Old steel water tank on R (rancher's attempt to provide water for his cattle here). Many petroglyphs near here. Ascend gradually.	0.09
0.81	Petroglyphs on L.	0.07
0.86	Warning sign.	0.02
0.87	Descend.	0.01
0.88	Bottom (elev. 1,700'). Trail ends at rock jumble about 375' downstream from the waterfall, which only runs after a significant rainfall. *NOTE: The rocks above are used by rock-climbers, but this is extremely dangerous -- there have been fatalities here.*	0.00

[C] Rock Knob Trail

General Description. The first section of this trail is steep and not well maintained, but quite scenic. It climbs from the Waterfall Trail [B] to a junction with a short spur to the Willow Springs Trail [E] at 0.74 mile. Return by that trail is quite a feasible circuit, or one can go 1.86 miles on this trail to its end (2.59 miles total). (You may notice the posts marked "4" for the earlier designation of this trail.) Ascent is 600' to the spur, 920' more (1,520' total) to trail's end on the ridge.

Note: this trail is described in two sections because hikers may wish to use either segment and combine it with other trails. The first segment is *hiker-only,* the upper segment is for *hikers and horses* (horse access is via the Willow Springs Trail [E]).

Access. Leave the Waterfall Trail [B] at 0.74 mile at the rock pile. (The Parks and Recreation Department is planning to place a sign here and brush out the lower section.)

Read Down	Detailed Trail Description	Read Up
0.00	From Waterfall Trail [B] at 1,660' elevation, head W.	0.74
0.02	Go R through brushy area.	0.72
0.06	**Junction:** turn R and ascend steadily. Trail L is alternate (rejoins). There are many alternate trails ahead.	0.68
0.09	Switchback R & L, ascending steep, rocky trail.	0.65
0.10	Turn R, use care with braided route.	0.64
0.11	**Junction:** alternate rejoins.	0.63
0.17	Switchback to R, then L.	0.57
0.26	Start level traverse (1,970').	0.48
0.30	Switchback to R, then L, then R again in next 150'.	0.44
0.42	**Junction:** side-trail to R leads up to VP in 165'.	0.32
0.45	Turn R (W) below rock face.	0.29
0.47	Top of rise (2,220'). (Trail of use on rocks here.) Ascend a bit, then side-hill. This is a very scenic area.	0.27
0.52	Top of rise (2,230'). Descend, then go up and down.	0.22
0.58	Final top of rise (2,240').	0.16
0.64	**Junction:** side-trail L to good VP of Waterfall Canyon in 105'. From here, trail is easy and level.	0.10
0.74	**Important junction:** rough road leads R to Willow Springs Trail [E] in only 220'. *[At junction there, road leads back to start of Waterfall Trail in 1.42 mi, or trail leads to Willow Springs in 1.84 mi.]* From this junction, trail L ascends to ridge for an additional 1.86 miles (see below).	0.00
0.00	**From junction** (elev. 2,230') continue L, up road, then up and down.	1.86
0.20	Ascend steadily.	1.66
0.32	Ascend rocks.	1.54
0.40	Top of rise (2,460') at height-of-land; trail sign.	1.46
0.43	Switchback down to R.	1.43
0.45	Road splits.	1.41
0.46	Rejoins (then descend 110').	1.40
0.54	Bottom of descent (2,350'). Ascend gradually.	1.36
0.62	Top of rise. Descend gradually.	1.24
0.66	Top of rise, drop, then rise again.	1.20
0.80	**Junction:** turn L onto trail where road goes R, ascending ridge.	1.06
0.83	**Junction:** rejoin road.	1.03
0.90	Top of rise, drop gradually.	0.96
0.95	Cross pleasant flat area (2,400').	0.91
1.01	Start of ascent that gets progressively steeper and rockier.	0.85
1.13	Top of rise, post "4" (2,600'). Excellent VP 125' to L.	0.73
1.20	Descend to cross flat area, then ascend again in 0.03 mi.	0.66
1.32	Top of rise; trail continues.	0.54
1.35	**Junction:** alternate trail on L, rejoins in 55'.	0.51
1.43	Ease ascent.	0.43
1.45	Ascend more steadily, then in 100', when almost at end of ridge, head up crest.	0.41
1.49	Turn R (W), level out. Ascend again in 100'.	0.37

1.54	Trail post "4" on R. Side-hill from here.	0.32
1.67	Pass (2,900'). Continue W.	0.19
1.74	Reach crest again.	0.12
1.81	Top of rise, post "4" (2,980'). Trail heads W.	0.05
1.86	Crest (2,970'), good VP. (Valley of Willow Springs is directly N.) *[From here, poor trail continues along ridge toward jeep road that leads to microwave towers (continuation not recommended by park authorities).]*	0.00

[D] Black Rock Trail

General Description. This short *hiker-only* loop trail (1.43 miles) was built as an Eagle Scout project by Troop 408. It does not quite reach the Waterfall Trail [B]. There is one short alternate loop near the start (see map). Description is for clockwise direction of travel. Ascent is 90'.

Access. From road junction directly across from group picnic area access road on White Tank Mountain Road.

Read Down	*Detailed Trail Description*	*Read Up*
0.00	Leave White Tank Mountain Road opposite group picnic area (1,470'). Only 20' from road, reach **junction:** subsidiary loop goes R (alternate); go L.	1.43
0.03	Bear L.	1.40
0.08	Bear R (NW).	1.34
0.09	**Junction:** on R is returning main loop; turn L here.	1.34
0.26	Trail zigzags through fields of cholla cactus.	1.17
0.35	Pass hillside on L (petroglyphs among black rocks).	1.08
0.38	Turn L.	1.04
0.58	Zigzags.	0.81
0.62	**Junction:** old road crosses (shown on topo map; it is easily missed). *[Up road 0.10 mi is brink of wash and washed-out crossing; from there, poor trail of use leads through brushy area along bank for 280', then descends into wash; Waterfall Trail is on far bank, with no official connection.]*	
0.63	Turn R (trail meanders here).	0.80
0.67	Turn E.	0.76
0.78	Trail splits, rejoins in 30', descends very gradually.	0.65
1.07	Reach brink of wash, then go sharp R on old road.	0.35
1.14	**Junction:** old road continues ahead *[in 0.13 mi reaches junction: old road continues to highway; go R to reach main trail in 0.18 mi, only 20' from road].* Go R, around small hill.	0.29
1.33	**Junction:** rejoin original route.	0.09
1.43	**Junction:** loop entering L from 1.14 mi. Keep R; reach White Tank Mountain Road in 20', back at start.	0.00

[E] Willow Springs Trail

General Description. The lower section of this *hiker/horse* trail is an eroded steep "cat" road. It is known locally as the "Cat Scratch," built by a bulldozer driven by a rancher coming out of the park interior where he was making water catchment stock ponds. Above the spur connection to the Rock Knob Trail [C] at 1.04 miles, the way improves and leads over a ridge into the very attractive Mesquite Valley at 1.5 miles. It then climbs 240' out of that valley in another 0.34 mile to a pass, where it starts around the ridge into the valley of Willow Springs. There is considerable up and down before the old homestead and the Springs area is reached at 1.84 miles (2.89 miles total). Total ascent is 1,230' (first segment 630', second 600').

Access. Leave road at Ramada Way off Waterfall Canyon Road at picnic area #7. This is 0.34 mile north of start of the Waterfall Trail [B].

Read Down	Detailed Trail Description	Read Up
0.00	From road at picnic area #7 (1,650'), follow cat track.	1.04
0.28	Start ascent on very rough road.	0.77
0.48	Level out briefly (1,840'), then ascend again.	0.56
0.55	Cross small wash, level off briefly.	0.49
0.71	Ascend again (2,040').	0.33
0.85	Steep pitch on badly eroded road.	0.20
0.93	Steady climb again.	0.11
0.99	Ease briefly, then start final ascent.	0.05
1.04	**Junction:** to L 220' is Rock Knob Trail [C].	0.00
0.00	Leave **junction** (2,280'), ascending easily on trail.	1.84
0.07	Ascend with upper part of Waterfall Canyon in view on L.	1.77
0.11	Top of rise (2,430'), excellent VP. Descend.	1.73
0.19	Turn L, reach top of rise (ridge crest) (2,410') with good views over valley. Descend slightly to W on good trail.	1.65
0.26	Level off; trail narrows, descends.	1.59
0.34	Go over rocks, turn L, descend briefly. Note rock wall across valley.	1.51
0.37	Turn L.	1.47
0.41	Parallel wash, then turn L (S).	1.43
0.42	Bear R, descending to SW, level off, then descend again.	1.42
0.46	Reach and enter moderate wash below "Mesquite Springs" (2,270').	1.39
0.48	Leave wash on R, ascending parallel to it.	1.37
0.54	Trail bends to R, ascends steadily (rocky).	1.30
0.58	Reach end of rocky side-ridge; use care here (elev. 2,450'). Way is easy and gradual beyond here.	1.26
0.80	*Pass (2,510').* Descend gradually, then steadily, into Willow Springs valley.	1.04
0.99	Above cliffs: side-hill along ridge beyond, ascending gradually.	0.86
1.06	Top of rise (2,490'). Descend.	0.79
1.10	End of side-ridge (2,460'); old barbed wire here. Descend steadily.	0.74
1.33	Reach wash, follow it to L (2,340'). Use care.	0.52
1.41	Leave wash on R, ascend slope.	0.44
1.57	Top of rise (2,480'). Side-hill down.	0.27

1.63	Reach wash again at yellow-painted sign. Turn R in wash.	0.21
1.70	Ascend out of wash on L; parallel it.	0.14
1.76	Cross wash.	0.08
1.84	*Willow Springs area (2,460')*. Tank on L, wrecked corral. Springs area is a bit further along wash at base of rock "fall". Up path 60' is ruined homestead site. Poor trail can be followed 500' further to top of minor ridge to N of impassable "fall." (There is no trail beyond, but travel is not difficult.)	0.00

[F] Ford Canyon Trail

General Description. This is a good *hiker/horse* trail with fine views. Sections have been rebuilt by the Arizona Boys Ranch Conservation Project. The first 2 miles consists of sections of trail and road, crossing several low hills to reach the mouth of Ford Canyon. From there the trail climbs into the canyon with some very scenic rocky areas to its end at 2.88 miles. Ascent is 700'.

Access. From White Tank Mountain Road, take either Ford Canyon Road (past Willow Canyon Road), or Waterfall Canyon Road past Willow Canyon Road junction, to trail-head between areas 8 and 9 at a sign.

Read Down	Detailed Trail Description	Read Up
0.00	Leave trail-head at Ford Canyon Road (elevation 1,590').	2.88
0.11	**Junction:** turn R (N) where old trail goes L, then to NW.	2.77
0.39	Edge of huge wash. Descend steps, then parallel wash.	2.49
0.47	Cross side-wash, bear R, then L, on good trail heading NW.	2.41
0.60	**Junction:** road on L; go R on it, toward NE.	2.28
0.61	**Junction:** road joins; head E.	2.27
0.67	**Junction:** turn L (N), leaving road.	2.21
0.74	Switchback to L (W), then R and L.	2.14
0.95	Cross small wash.	1.93
0.97	**Junction:** go L on road, ascending to NE, then N.	1.91
0.99	Top of rise (1,790'). Huge cairn here. Descend.	1.89
1.14	**Four-way junction:** turn L at cairn.	1.74
1.17	Ascend steeply to L.	1.71
1.18	**Junction:** bear R.	1.70
1.23	Top of rise; huge cairn (1,810'). 4WD road ascends on L.	1.65
1.28	**Junction:** trail on L.	1.60
1.33	Cross small wash, parallel it on other side.	1.55
1.42	**Junction:** go L on dirt road toward SW.	1.46
1.72	**Junction:** poorer road joins on R.	1.16
1.80	**Junction of roads:** go straight (elev. 1,810').	1.08
2.01	Road loops and ends, excellent trail starts.	0.87
2.05	Descend into wash.	0.83
2.19	Ascend.	0.69
2.22	Level out (elevation 1,930').	0.66
2.24	End of excellent, constructed trail.	0.64

2.26	Come above huge wash on R.	0.62
2.28	Cross moderate, deep wash and ascend.	0.60
2.37	Top of rise (elevation 1,960'). Descend with rocks on R.	0.51
2.42	Head toward rock wall and into a spectacular side-canyon, ascending steadily.	0.46
2.46	Steep ascent to L (S). Level out in 100'.	0.42
2.52	Steep ascent to L, then switchback to R.	0.36
2.55	Cave in rock to L.	0.33
2.56	Top of rise (elevation 2,070') above dry waterfall.	0.32
2.58	Ascend rocks, then level and ascend among rocks.	0.30
2.63	Ease ascent through a very picturesque area.	0.25
2.65	Switchback up to L and continue spectacular route with care. Above are rock spires.	0.23
2.68	Level out with fine views.	0.20
2.73	Ascend steadily; go L, under cliff (note ferns beneath cliff).	0.16
2.74	Switchback to R along cliff base.	0.14
2.76	Top of rise (2,200'). VP to R from rocks. Trail heads into rock bowl, is less well worn.	0.12
2.80	Switchback to L, then to R.	0.08
2.83	Turn R and ascend rocks, then descend.	0.05
2.88	*Trail ends at "tanks" in Ford Canyon Wash where there is a stone masonry dam built by ranchers for their cattle. (Area is likely to be dry except after a rain.) Elevation 2,260'.*	0.00

[G] South Loop Trail

General Description. This is a short alternate to the start of the Goat Camp Trail [A]. It follows an old road for part of its 1.04 miles. Ascent is 160'.

Access. Leave picnic loop #1 (Black Canyon Drive South) at southwest end at a sign ("Scout Loop Trail"). This trail-head is 0.15 mile south of the Goat Camp Trail-head on the same road.

Read Down	*Detailed Trail Description*	*Read Up*
0.00	From picnic loop #1 head S, then W on trail.	1.04
0.05	Cross small wash.	0.99
0.15	**Junction:** join old road from L, bear R.	0.89
1.03	**Junction:** old road on L.	0.01
1.04	**Junction:** Goat Camp Trail [A]. Go R 0.77 mi to return to road. To L, 0.15 mi trail [A] leads to "Goat Camp" in 1.92 mi.	0.00

Arizona State Parks

An Introduction

As the 21st Century nears, the future of Arizona State Parks is one of growth and challenges to meet the demands of an expanding population and increased interest in what Arizona's recreational, historic, and cultural resources have to offer. Arizona has the distinction of being one of the youngest states in the nation, and Arizona's state park system is also among the nation's youngest.

The creation of the Arizona State Parks Board in 1957 was a major victory for conservationists, outdoor interests and civic leaders from around the state, the result of years of dedicated effort. Since its creation, Arizona State Parks has grown from three employees and an appropriation of $ 30,000 to an agency with wide-ranging responsibilities. These include managing 25 historic and recreational parks, statewide planning of Arizona's recreational and natural resources, administering grants for acquisition and development of recreation areas, and coordinating programs to preserve and protect cultural and historic properties.

The Arizona Hiking & Equestrian Trails Committee, set up by the Arizona State Parks Board, advises the Board on all trails matters and has as its mission to study, inventory, and designate a statewide system of trails. AHETC is actively involved in many other trails issues. The State Trails Program and AHETC are striving to see that Arizona's trails continue to be an important part of the state's recreation opportunities.

Recent documents prepared by Arizona State Parks have emphasized the importance of the state's trail resources. The Arizona Outdoor Recreation Participation Survey found that hiking or walking for pleasure is the most popular activity of the state's residents. To assure that enthusiasts have trails to enjoy, the Arizona Trails Plan has identified a vision of the State Trail System in the year 2000 and an action plan that will make that vision a reality.

Arizona State Parks looks forward to its future of change and growth. Take some time to visit Arizona's outstanding state parks or one of the many trails throughout the state.

Ken Mahoney, Trails Coordinator
Statewide Planning Section, Arizona State Parks

Arizona State Parks

Lost Dutchman State Park

Introduction. Lost Dutchman State Park is a 320-acre area located below the precipitous western flank of the Superstition Mountains, 5 miles northeast of Apache Junction. Except for the Siphon Draw Trail, the trails described here were recently constructed. Most are within the adjacent Tonto National Forest, but outside the Superstition Wilderness.

History. The park name derives from the discredited legend of the fabulous Lost Dutchman Gold Mine. It is said that Jacob Walz (a German immigrant and miner known as "the Dutchman") had re-discovered the mine originally developed by the Peralta family of Sonora, Mexico. Most of the family were reputed to have been killed by Apaches at the Massacre Grounds, but one of them helped Walz to the site. Over the next 20 years he supposedly cached gold dust in various places in the Superstitions and killed several partners. That he died of pneumonia before imparting any details (other than that Weaver's Needle pointed in the right direction) made it somewhat understandable that fortunes were spent on the futile search (and the search goes on!). Geological evidence was that the Superstitions themselves had no significant mineralization (short periods of production were, however, successful in the Goldfield Mountains to the west).

The Apache Trail [highway] was built in 1905 as a supply route for the construction of Roosevelt Dam (1905-1911), the first Bureau of Reclamation project in the west and the world's highest masonry dam.

Geology. Very active volcanic lava flows and explosions occurred during the Tertiary Period around 29 million years ago, forming the Superstitions by deposition of dacite tuff and agglomerate on deeply eroded Pre-Cambrian granite. It is thought that about 20 million years ago there was a resurgent dome formed from a "collapse caldera," followed by further explosions and ash deposition up to 15 million years ago. This gave the Superstitions their dramatic form.[1] Mineral exploration was at its peak in the 1870s and 1880s, but no mines in the Superstitions have ever resulted in production.

Maps. *Our map 22.* The USGS Goldfield 1:24,000 topo (1956, photorevised 1981), the Earth Tracks "Superstition Wilderness West Recreation Map" (1985), and the Forest Service's 1986 "Superstition Wilderness, Tonto National Forest" map all show the area but not the recently constructed trails. There is a trail map available from the ranger station and the park brochure shows the roads and trail-heads.

Access. Via the Apache Trail (State Route 88), 5.3 miles from junction with U.S. 60/89 in Apache Junction east of Phoenix. (From Phoenix/Tempe, the Superstition Freeway (Route 360) ends at Power Road (1991); from there head north to U.S. 60/89 (Apache Trail), then east to Route 88.)

[Previous page: Superstition Mountain from Siphon Draw Trail]

---

[1] M. & J. Sheridan (1984). *Recreational Guide to the Superstition Mountains and the Salt River Lakes,* pp. 21-29 (published by authors); and Nations & Stump (1983), pp. 166-8 and 173-4.

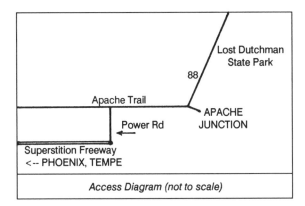

Access Diagram (not to scale)

Facilities. There are 35 undeveloped campsites, rest-rooms, drinking fountains, and picnic facilities including tables, 2 group ramadas and 13 single ramadas. The park's address is 6109 N. Apache Trail, Apache Junction 85219 (Phone: 982-4485).

Recommended Hikes. With the exception of the un-numbered Discovery Trail, the descriptions that follow are referred to by the official numbers of the Tonto National Forest. Hikes with significant but not difficult ascents are [53], [56], and [57]. Jacob's Crosscut [58] has many brief up-and-down stretches. (The Siphon Draw Trail [53] has a much rougher footway than the other trails.) There is also a short self-guiding Native Plant Trail near the park entrance.

Cautions. Beware the temptation to rock-climb on spires and cliffs without adequate equipment and training. Stay out of old mine shafts. Summer heat here can exceed 115° and there is little shade; be sure to bring enough water and appropriate clothing for prolonged exposure to the sun.

Park Regulations. Except for Jacob's Crosscut, these trails are *hiker-only*. Keep pets under control and pack out all garbage. Shooting is forbidden.

[53] Siphon Draw Trail

General Description. From the Campground trail-head, an old road crosses into the Tonto National Forest and ascends gradually for 0.77 mile to a junction. (Here the road turns north and ends at the old Palmer Mine site, first claim near the Superstitions, 1886.) The trail continues and steepens, entering a very scenic area at the western end of the mountains at about 1.1 miles. It then follows a wash and reaches the end of trail at a box canyon at 1.61 miles with views among the cliffs and spires. Ascent is 1,030'. *NOTE:* if there is any possibility of a rain-storm in the vicinity, stay out of washes.

Access. Park at the Siphon Draw Trail-head in the Campground area.

Read Down	Detailed Trail Description	Read Up
0.00	Leave trail-head at sign (elevation 2,080').	1.61
0.05	**Junction:** to L is Discovery Trail to Upper Picnic Area.	1.56
0.20	**Junction:** dirt road to R at Park and National Forest boundary. Continue straight, on dirt road.	1.42
0.21	Pass through gate in fence, ascending gradually on old road.	1.40
0.38	**Junction:** Prospector's View Trail [58] on L (0.59 mi to junction with Treasure Loop [56]; 310' to junction with Jacob's Crosscut [58]).	1.23
0.43	**Junction (4-way):** Jacob's Crosscut Trail [57] on L & R (225' L to Prospector's View Trail [58]; 4.38 mi R to Broadway Road).	1.18
0.63	**Junction:** trail of use sharp R leads back to Jacob's Crosscut in 0.21 mi.	0.98
0.72	Pass foundation of building on L; way steepens.	0.89
0.77	**Junction:** road turns L to Palmer Mine; elevation 2,420'. (Spur road ascends to covered shaft at 0.11 mi and beyond to another at 0.17 mi; ends at 0.21 mi; poor trail of use can be taken N across several washes to [57], but this is not recommended.) Continue ascent; road narrows to trail.	0.84
0.87	**Junction:** trail of use R, to rock.	0.75
0.95	**Junction:** trail braids, keep L.	0.67
0.99	This trail leads along edge of wash on R.	0.63
1.01	Cross wash.	0.61
1.02	Way braids again; go L around boulder.	0.59
1.04	Trails rejoin (they braid again ahead).	0.57
1.12	Level out.	0.49
1.13	Cross small wash; enter scenic area with cliffs above on L.	0.48
1.22	**Junction:** short spur trail descends to R to giant boulders. Ascend steadily.	0.39
1.35	Flat area with good views; canyon in view ahead. Bear L.	0.26
1.42	Go along base of sloping rocks, then cross more rocks.	0.19
1.53	Cross below cliff on L.	0.08
1.55	Cross small wash under trees and ascend.	0.06
1.56	Cross wash into very scenic area.	0.05
1.58	Sloping rocks ahead.	0.04
1.61	*Siphon Draw.* Trail ends in box canyon at elevation 3,110'. Trailless route into western Superstitions can commence here, but is definitely not for ordinary hikers.	0.00

[56] Treasure Loop Trail WEST to EAST

General Description. This fine trail is actually a partial loop. The northern half ascends gradually from the Lower Picnic Area, crossing Jacob's Crosscut Trail [58] at 0.36 mile. It then steepens, leading around the Green Boulder, an area of rocky spires just below the cliffs of the Superstitions, to a junction with the Prospector's View Trail [57] at 1.32 miles. Total ascent is 460'. Beyond, the loop descends 0.71 mile to intersect the Jacob's Crosscut Trail and reaches the Upper Picnic Area at 1.10 miles, for a total distance of 2.42 miles. Most of the trail is in the Tonto National Forest. (Two descriptions are given: both are for the ascent via either branch of the Loop.)

Access. From Lower Picnic Area near restrooms, head east through picnic area D. Or if starting on the southern half, leave from the Upper Picnic Area through area E.

Read Down	Detailed Trail Description	Read Up
0.00	Leave road at Lower Picnic Area (elevation here is 2,080').	1.32
0.03	Signpost.	1.29
0.05	Gate and fence line (Tonto National Forest). Beyond, ascend gradually up excellent trail with wash on L.	1.27
0.24	Drop off bench into wash on R.	1.08
0.26	**Junction:** go R (trail straight ahead ends).	1.06
0.36	**Junction (4-way):** trail L is new extension of Jacob's Crosscut [58] to First Water Trail-head Road in 1.12 mi. On R, Jacob's Crosscut [58] leads 0.09 mi to other branch of [56] and another 0.76 mi to Prospector's View Trail [57], then another 0.11 mi to Siphon Draw Trail [53].	0.96
0.38	Bear R. Grade of ascent gradually increases through very attractive area.	0.94
0.91	Trail bears R, then L, and steepens.	0.41
1.00	Ascend among rock pinnacles with Green Boulder ahead.	0.32
1.05	Bear R and ease ascent.	0.27
1.10	Bear L.	0.22
1.13	Trail swings L, then around to R, ascending.	0.19
1.16	**Junction:** trail straight ahead is closed; keep R.	0.16
1.19	Level out.	0.13
1.23	Cross rocky wash.	0.09
1.26	**Junction:** trail L closed, keep R.	0.06
1.27	Cross wash.	0.05
1.29	Swing R.	0.03
1.32	**Junction:** Prospector's View Trail [57] ahead (elev. 2,540'); (straight ahead it is 0.59 mi to Jacob's Crosscut Trail [58]). Turn R and descend 1.10 mi to continue on this trail to Upper Picnic Area [use reverse of description in following section].	0.00

0.00	Leave Upper Picnic Area at sign "Mountain Trails" near water fountain (2,100').	1.10
0.09	Cross through fence line into Tonto National Forest at signboard with map. Beyond, confusing areas are marked with cairns.	1.01
0.11	Turn L along top of hogback.	0.99
0.20	**Junction:** trail of use on L; turn R.	0.90
0.38	**Junction (4-way):** Jacob's Crosscut Trail [58] crosses. (To L it is 0.09 mi to northern half of this trail; to R it is 0.76 mi to Prospector's View Trail [57]).	0.72
0.60	Start ascent, then follow edge of wash on R.	0.50
0.93	**Junction:** short-cut trail on R.	0.17
0.97	Switchback to R, then to L, ascending with Green Boulder on L.	0.13
1.02	**Junction:** short-cut trail re-enters from R; trail of use on L; cairn. Ascend 4 switchbacks.	0.08
1.10	**Junction:** Prospector's View Trail [57] on R (0.59 mi to Jacob's Crosscut Trail [56]). This trail continues to L, passing around Green Boulder and descending back to Lower Picnic Area in 1.32 mi [see description above]. Elevation here is 2,540'.	0.00

[57] Prospector's View Trail

General Description. This trail ascends from a start at the Siphon Draw Trail [53], near Jacob's Crosscut Trail [58], for 0.70 mile to end at the Treasure Loop [56] above the Green Boulder. The trail is in good condition and has fine views. It can be combined with [56] for a circuit trip. Ascent is 360'.

Access. To start at the bottom, take the Siphon Draw Trail [53] for 0.38 mile to the junction. To start at the top, take either branch of the Treasure Loop [56] from the Lower or Upper Picnic Areas.

Read Down	Detailed Trail Description	Read Up
0.00	Leave Siphon Draw Trail [53], 0.38 mi from Campground trail-head (2,180').	0.70
0.06	**Junction:** on R is Jacob's Crosscut Trail [58]. Bear L.	0.64
0.11	**Junction:** Jacob's Crosscut Trail [58] to L (0.76 mi to Treasure Loop [56]). Ascend E with wash on R.	0.59
0.34	Bear L, away from wash.	0.36
0.36	Switchback to R.	0.34
0.38	Edge of wash, bear L; pass trail of use on R.	0.32
0.43	Switchback to R.	0.27
0.46	Switchback to L.	0.24
0.49	Switchback to R, parallel wash on R.	0.21
0.51	**Junction:** trail of use on R. Ascend beside valley, then grade eases.	0.18
0.70	**Junction:** Treasure Loop Trail [56] on L (sharp L descends 1.10 mi to Upper Picnic Area; straight ahead leads to Lower Picnic Area in 1.32 mi).	0.00

[58] Jacob's Crosscut Trail NORTH to SOUTH

General Description. This *hiker/horse* trail leads along the base of the mountain. From First Water Trail-head Road #78 it crosses the northern half of Treasure Loop [56] at 1.12 miles, the second segment of the Loop at 1.21 miles, and the Prospector's View Trail [57] at 1.89 miles. The Siphon Draw Trail is crossed at 1.97 miles, and the end of Broadway Road at 6.35 miles. The trail offers fine views of the Superstitions. It can be combined with the Discovery Trail or [56] or [57] for circuit trips. Elevation change is 400'.

Access. *At the northern end,* from Forest Road #78, 0.6 mile from Route 88 at the first cattle guard. It can also be reached from the Treasure Loop from the Lower Picnic Area at 0.36 mile; or from the Siphon Draw Trail [53] at 0.38 mile. *At the southern end,* at the eastern end of Broadway Road.

Read Down	Detailed Trail Description	Read Up
0.00	Leave Forest Road #78 near first cattle guard (elev. 2,100').	6.35
0.06	Cross major wash and ascend far bank.	6.29
0.23	**Junction (4-way):** cross dirt road, gate on W.	6.12

0.50	**Junction (4-way):** cross faint road.	5.85
0.67	Reach low point between hump on W and ridge on E.	5.68
0.88	Cross moderate wash, then old mine road in 0.06 mi.	5.47
1.12	**Junction (4-way):** Treasure Loop [56] at 0.36 mi from the Lower Picnic Area trail-head. (Elevation 2,120'.) Head S on a level grade.	5.23
1.21	**Junction (4-way):** cross southern half of Treasure Loop [56] (0.47 mi to R is Upper Picnic Area; 0.71 mi to L is junction with [57] above Green Boulder).	5.14
1.28	Turn L and ascend (note parallel trail [56] on next bench to N). This trail zigzags.	5.07
1.42	Head R and level off.	4.89
1.54	Switchback to L, then to R.	4.81
1.55	Turn sharp L, then R.	4.80
1.56	Cross moderate wash and ascend out of it.	4.79
1.77	Reach edge of major wash. Turn L, then cross it.	4.58
1.84	**Junction:** Prospector's View Trail [57] on L. Elevation 2,200'.	4.47
1.89	**Junction:** Prospector's View Trail departs R, to Siphon Draw Trail in 310'.	4.42
1.97	**Junction (4-way):** Siphon Draw Trail [53] L & R.	4.38
2.15	**Junction (4-way):** L 0.21 mi to Siphon Draw Trail; R to private land.	4.20
2.21	**Junction (4-way):** cross old track.	4.14
3.42	**Junction:** on R trail of use descends.	2.93
3.49	Cross large wash. Excellent views open.	2.86
3.84	**Junction (4-way):** cross old track.	2.51
4.28	Bottom of major wash.	2.07
5.15	Turn W and descend steadily.	1.20
6.35	Gate at end of Broadway Road (1,830').	0.00

Discovery Trail SOUTH to NORTH

General Description. This level, un-numbered trail is entirely within the State Park. It connects the Siphon Draw Trail [53] and Campground Area with the Upper Picnic Area and is useful for circuit trips.

Access. *At the south end,* from 270' east of the Siphon Draw Trail-head; or *at the north end,* at the south side of the Upper Picnic Area road loop just west of the restrooms.

Read Down	*Detailed Trail Description*	*Read Up*
0.00	Leave Siphon Draw Trail [53] 0.05 mi (260') E of its trail-head.	0.56
0.02	Swing around to cross small wash, parallelling campground road.	0.54
0.20	Turn R.	0.36
0.23	**Junction:** spur trail L leads to campground road loop in 120'. Continue N.	0.33
0.27	Cross major wash.	0.28
0.41	Cross moderate wash; ascend gradually.	0.15
0.42	**Junction:** go R (straight ahead to road in 320').	0.14
0.53	**Junction:** trail goes R, toward restrooms (L is spur to road).	0.01
0.56	Trail ends at road beside washrooms on R. (Treasure Loop [56] trail-head is just beyond, at other end of parking area.)	0.00

Tonto National Forest

An Introduction

From the desert to the tall timber, the Tonto National Forest contains a spectacular 2,900,000 acres of cactus, chapparral, pine, and even mixed-conifer country just a few miles north and east of Phoenix and the Valley of the Sun.

When visitors first see this National Forest they often ask "Where're the trees?" They soon learn that Theodore Roosevelt was right in 1908 when he established the Tonto National Forest; he recognized there is a lot more to a National Forest than trees. Today recreation, water, wildlife, forage, natural beauty, and wilderness areas are also provided under the Forest Service's multiple-use guidelines and Congressional charter. Of special importance in the Tonto National Forest is the wide variety of recreation opportunities and experiences that are available; in fact, this is one of the most heavily visited National Forests in the entire United States.

One of the many facets of recreation available to visitors is the system of trails found throughout the Tonto National Forest. At the present time over 800 miles of trail are within that system. They vary from easy loop-hikes just outside Apache Junction to trails only an experienced backcountry hiker can follow in the vast Mazatzal Wilderness.

Trails, however, that can't be found are of little value. As the Forest Service continues to emphasize both maintenance and reconstruction of these trails, we welcome trail guide-books such as this one that are carefully researched and fully coordinated with the managing agency, thereby providing a much-needed service to the public. We hope you enjoy your visit to the trails in and around Phoenix.

W. G. "Pete" Weinel, Assistant Recreation/Wilderness Staff
Forest Service, Southwest Region, U.S. Department of Agriculture

Tonto National Forest

Lower Salt River Nature Trail
and
Coon Bluff

Maps. *Our map 23.* The USGS 1:24,000 topo Stewart Mountain (1964) shows none of the trails.

Access. From the end of the Superstition Freeway (State Route 360, Power Road Exit), drive north on Bush Highway passing Granite Reef Dam. (You can also take McKellips Road east from Scottsdale and intersect Bush Highway.) You enter the Tonto National Forest on Forest Highway #204.

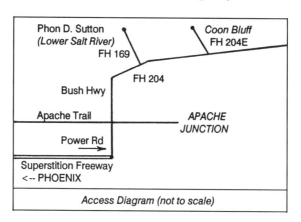

Access Diagram (not to scale)

Lower Salt River Nature Trail

General Description. This short loop trail (total 2.28 miles) was built by the Student Chapter of the Arizona Wildlife Society in 1985. (It is not shown on the revised Tonto National Forest map.) Its main attraction is the transition between the river-bottom (flood-plain or "riparian") environment and the Lower Sonoran desert, made more meaningful by many in-depth interpretive signs. Near the start there is a good view of "Red Mountain" across the river, but beyond this point there are no distant views. There is no significant ascent as the trail runs for a short way along the river bank, then through the flood-plain with its varied forest and desert. After a little more than a mile the trail turns south and east to rejoin itself at the river bank. The elevation is approximately 1,340'. This trail is designed for sequential, one-way use.

Access. Turn left from Forest Highway #204 onto Forest Highway #169 at the intersection to the Phon D. Sutton Recreation Site. The trail leaves from the northwestern corner of the parking lot behind the outhouses, at a sign.

[Previous page: "Red Mountain" from Salt River]

Cautions. Although this is an excellent short hike during the mild winter months, it can be very hot in summer. Note that there are many minor washes and vehicle travelways (now closed to traffic) which can be very confusing away from the river. Be sure to follow the lines of white-topped posts.

Read Down	Detailed Trail Description	Read Up
0.00	From outhouses at S end of parking area (sign) trail descends into a wash and crosses it. Follow white-topped posts.	2.28
0.09	Views of Salt River start.	2.19
0.13	Sign: "The River."	2.15
0.16	Approach edge of river bank. Filtration plant across river near junction of Verde and Salt Rivers.	2.12
0.17	Sign: "Fishes." *(NOTE: Near here trail returns, forming a loop).*	2.11
0.21	Sign: "Bald Eagle."	2.07
0.32	**Junction:** go straight where vehicle travelway bears L. From here trail heads inland away from river.	1.96
0.41	**Junction:** trail turns R onto vehicle travelway.	1.87
0.48	**Junction:** turn sharp R (SW), leaving vehicle travelway at post with arrow.	1.80
0.50	Sign: "Mistletoe."	1.78
0.52	**Junction:** vehicle travelway on L; bear R, heading generally SW, then S.	1.76
0.67	Cross vehicle travelway into woods.	1.61
0.69	Sign: "Salt Cedar."	1.59
0.75	Trail briefly narrows through a rocky, treed area.	1.53
0.80	Sign: "Cottonwood and Willow Forest."	1.48
0.82	Sign: "The Old Giants."	1.46
0.84	Turn L; vehicle travelway (now closed) on R.	1.44
0.99	Sign: "Mesquite Woodland."	1.29
1.04	Sign: "Mesquite: Food for Wildlife."	1.24
1.06	Sign: "Food for Riparian Plants."	1.22
1.14	Trail turns toward E (half-way point).	1.14
1.19	Sign: "The Transition."	1.09
1.24	Turn L (L arrow post).	1.04
1.46	Turn L.	0.82
1.54	Cross vehicle travelway.	0.74
1.59	Sign: "Desert Plant Adaptations."	0.69
1.65	Cross vehicle travelway.	0.63
1.82	Sign: "Seedlings and Nurse Plants."	0.46
1.97	Cross vehicle travelway.	0.31
2.06	Turn L on vehicle travelway.	0.22
2.11	**Junction:** trail rejoins original section near "Fishes" sign (0.17 mi). Turn R here to return to parking lot.	0.17
2.28	Parking lot.	0.00

Coon Bluff

General Description. From Coon Bluff Recreation Site an unofficial trail leads up the Bluff, connecting with other trails and old vehicle travelways and giving good views over the valley and toward distant mountains. This particular route is 0.52 mile long and ascends 260'.

Access. Pass Forest Highway #169 and take the next road left (Forest Highway #204E, about 1.6 miles) to Coon Bluff Recreation Site. There are two paved parking areas, one after the other. Park near the far end of the first area. The trail leaves near the "reserved" parking sign and is not very obvious at its start, but it can be seen ascending the side of a small ridge.

Read Down	Detailed Trail Description	Read Up
0.00	Leave first parking area (1,340') Cross small wash, head up slope, cross barbed wire fence in 100'.	0.52
0.04	Old concrete foundations on L. Ascend.	0.48
0.21	**Junction:** track descends sharp R. Ascend more steadily.	0.94
0.27	**Junction:** on flat area on summit (1,600'), one can head SE along ridge (see below). Excellent VP here of Goldfield Mountains, 4 Peaks, "Red Mountain." Descend NW on old vehicle travelway along crest.	0.32
0.28	**Junction:** trail L descends into valley.	0.27
0.34	**Junction:** poor (revegetated) track descends on R.	0.06
0.37	**Junction:** vehicle travelway on R. Ascend gradually.	0.05
0.40	**Junction:** on crest, poor trail descends on R. Go up and down along crest.	0.03
0.52	Trail ends at last peak (1,593'). Good VP over junction of Salt and Verde Rivers.	0.00

Alternate Route

For the trail to the southeast from 0.27 mile, continue past two junctions at 325' and 435'. Ascend to summit (1,600') at 0.24 mile. Bear left here along crest, leaving the last rise at 0.29 mile, descending a rough vehicle travelway. At 0.38 mile drop left, off the ridge onto a subsidiary ridge, reaching a sag at 0.52 mile and a hump at 120' further. From here, descend steeply to 0.58 mile, where it is necessary to follow the barbed wire fence to the left (west) for 175' to return to the start at 0.71 mile.

Map Legend

NOTE:

(1) All local streets are not shown.

(2) On some maps in the City of Phoenix where there is a crowding of many trails, rough roads and trails may not be distinguished from each other and are then both shown as trails.

	Described	*Not described*	
Paved road	———	●———┓	cul-de-sac parking area
Unpaved, driveable	– – – –	– – – –	
Unpaved, 4-wheel drive only	– – – –	– – – –	
Main or major trail (with designation)	– – – – ⊡	– – – –	
--- Charles M. Christiansen Trail*	–•–•–•·–•		
--- Perl Charles Trail*	–+–+–+–+		
--- Both coinciding*	–•–+–•–+		
Minor or secondary trail	- - - - - -		

Boundaries	— · · — · · —		
Water features (wash; canal; river; lake)	—···— ——	▬▬▬ ▬	
Water tank	● WT		
Building	▪		
Gate	—•—		
Ramada (where shown)	□		
Spot elevation	1785 ●		
Summit of importance	2394 △		
Contour lines	—2000—		

*Phoenix Mountains Preserve

Map 1

(see pages 21 - 26)

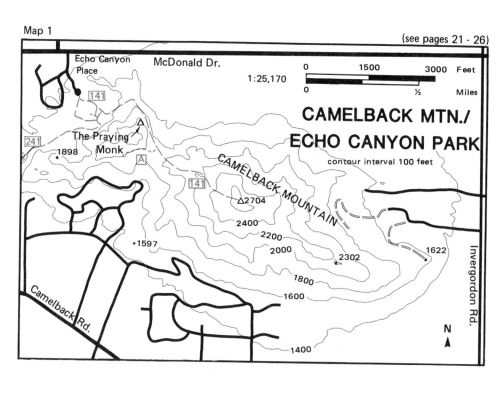

Echo Canyon Place

McDonald Dr.

1:25,170

0   1500   3000   Feet

0   ½   Miles

141

241

The Praying Monk

1898

△

A

141

CAMELBACK MTN./

ECHO CANYON PARK

contour interval 100 feet

CAMELBACK MOUNTAIN

△2704

2400

•1597

2200

2000

•2302

1622

1800

1600

Camelback Rd.

Invergordon Rd.

1400

N
▲

Map 2

Barnes Butte
(Military Reservation)

McDowell Road

Scottsdale →

← Phoenix

Amphitheater

A

1663

A

1500

← 52nd St.

1350

1400

Eliot
Memorial

B

1300

Central Butte

B

1300

Desert Botanical Garden

B

1250

F

Arizona Canal

Golf Course

1250

1300

1350

● 1318

Hole-in-the-Rock

Parkway

C

bikeway

Galvin

1250

1250

← Phoenix

(bus only)

Gov. Hunt's Tomb

1350

Van Buren St.

1413 ●

ZOO

PAPAGO PARK

Phoenix

1200

Tempe

N

1:12,585

| 0 | 1000 | 2000 | 3000 Feet |

0   ½   Miles

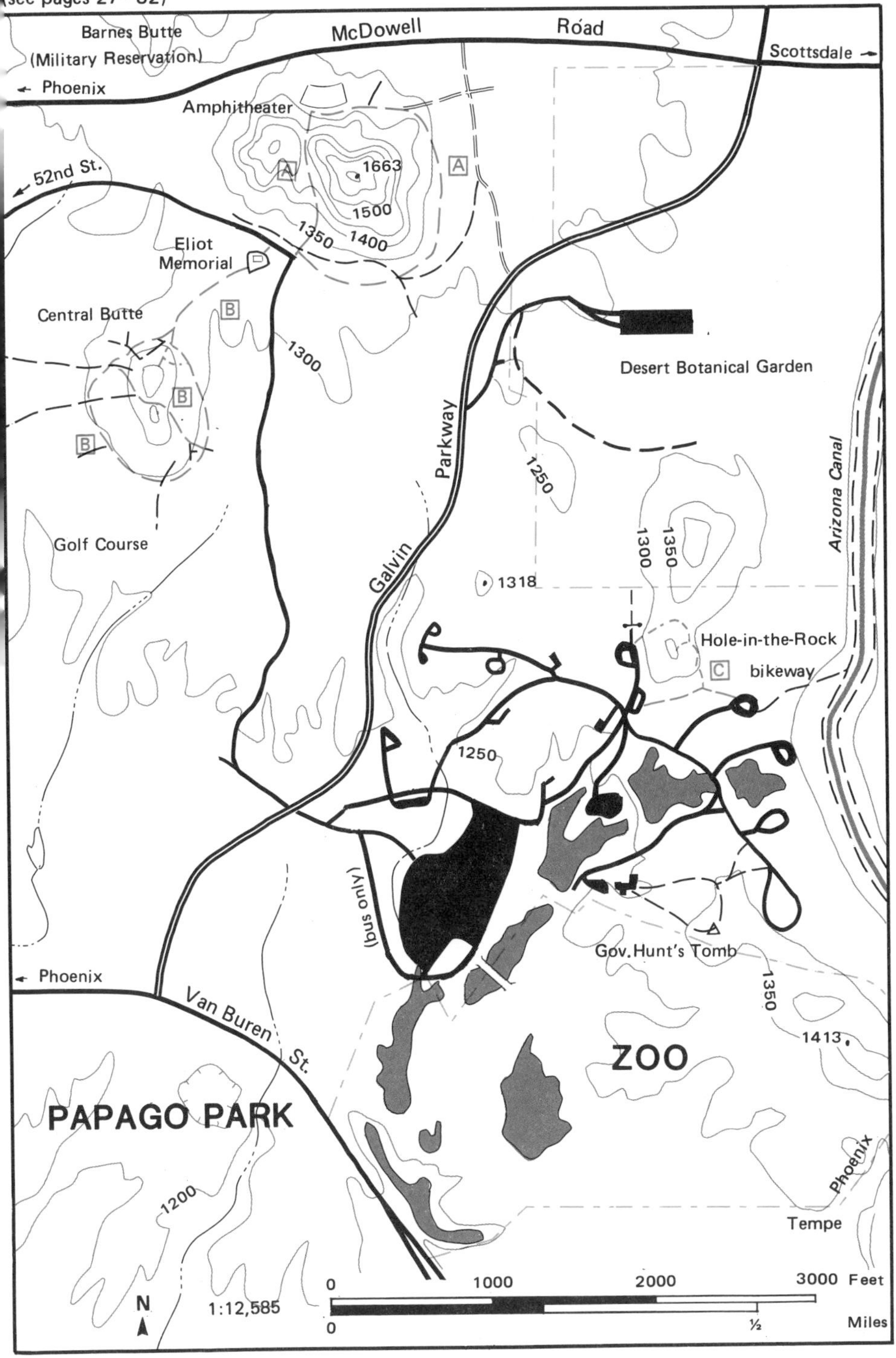

Map 3   (see pages 33 - 41)

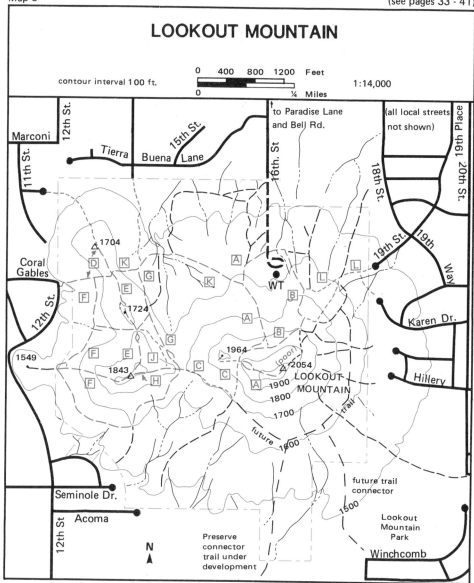

LOOKOUT MOUNTAIN

contour interval 100 ft.

| 0 | 400 | 800 | 1200 | Feet |

0   ¼ Miles

1:14,000

Map 4

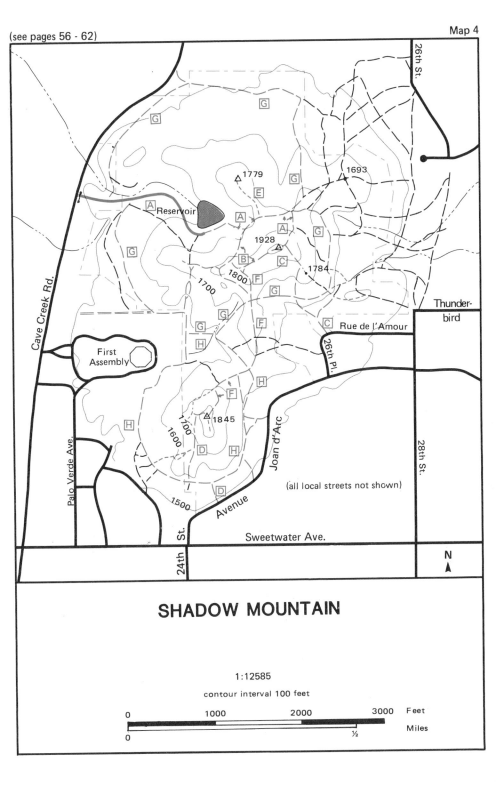

SHADOW MOUNTAIN

1:12585

contour interval 100 feet

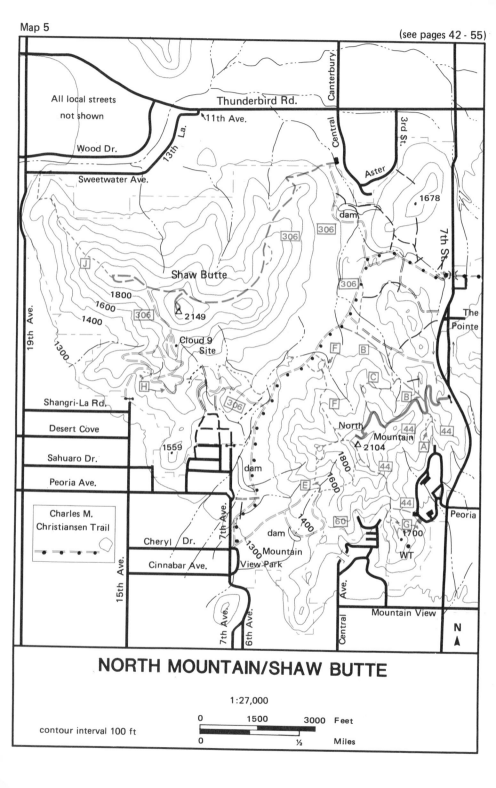

Map 5

(see pages 42 - 55)

NORTH MOUNTAIN/SHAW BUTTE

1:27,000

contour interval 100 ft

Map 6

1:25,170

| 0 | 1500 | 3000 | Feet |
| 0 | | ½ | Miles |

future public access
to Lookout Mtn.

tunnel

Thunderbird Rd.

STONY/ECHO
MOUNTAIN AREA

1565

R

R

1680

Cactus   Rd.

23rd St.

R

Poinsettia

T

1500

Q

M

24th St.

T

R

S

S

1833

U

S

The Pointe at
Tapatio Cliffs

1600

Sunnyside

1400

Cortez

J

M

Cholla

K

1871

L

WT

1700

L

G

M

K

G

E

Desert
Cove

Desert Cove Ave.

Rd.

dam

H

H

1600

F

Christy

Sahuaro

Creek

Peoria

Peoria

D

Shea Blvd.

C

Cave

Charles M.
Christiansen Trail

Cheryl

N

Cinnabar

Gold Dust

STONY

17th St.

Mountain

View Rd.

all local streets
not shown

1400

1500

1600

1800

B

2016

Mtn. View

7th St.

Hatcher Rd.

WT

rough

1300

14th St.

Dunlap

1500

Hatcher

A

1845

approx.
new
location

1922

12th St.

O

Echo Mtn.

1596

Squaw Peak Parkway

dam

Alice Ave.

1721

A

P

1677

Dreamy Draw
Rec. Area

N

Orchid La.

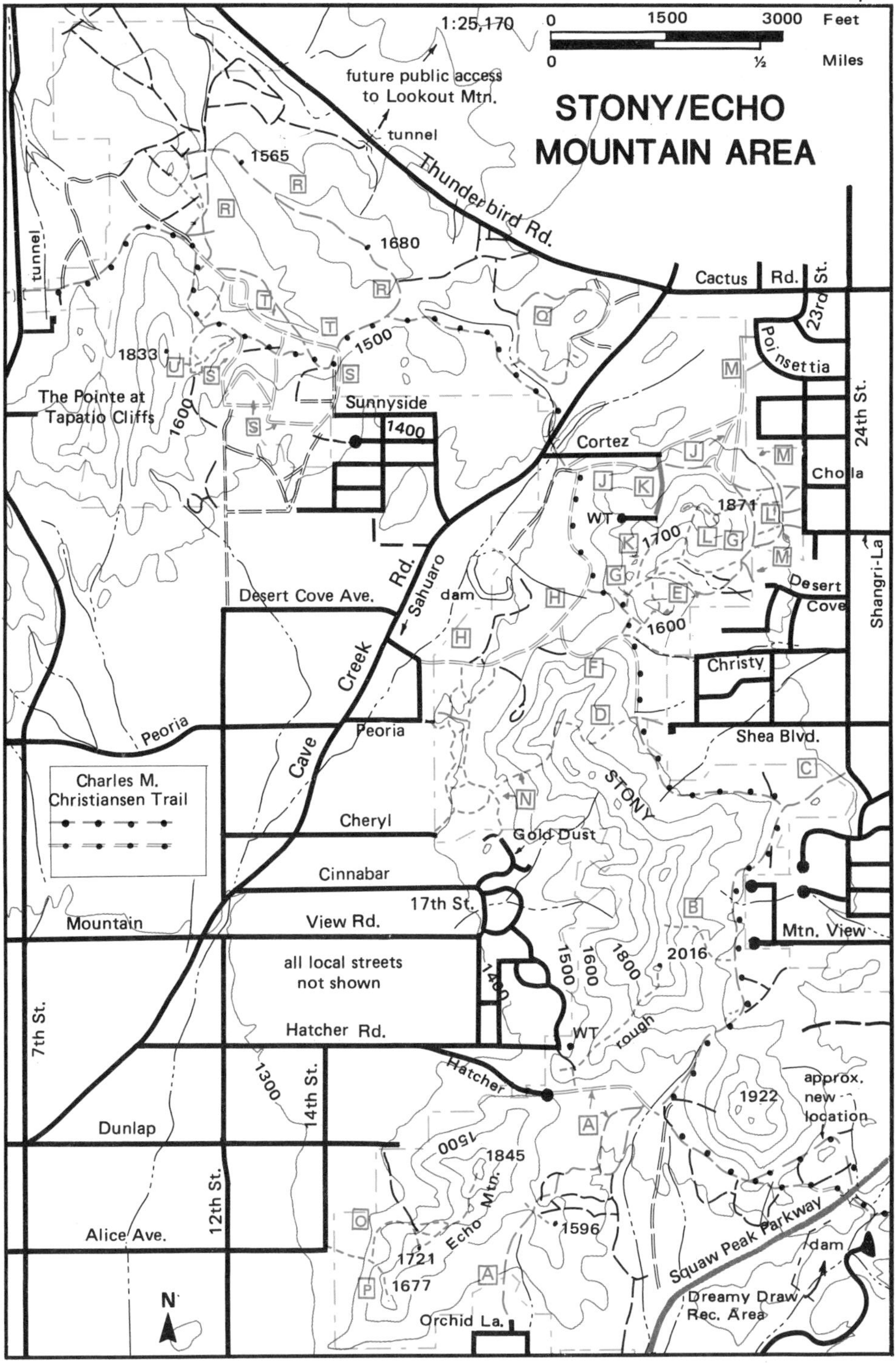

Map 7

(see pages 63 - 97)

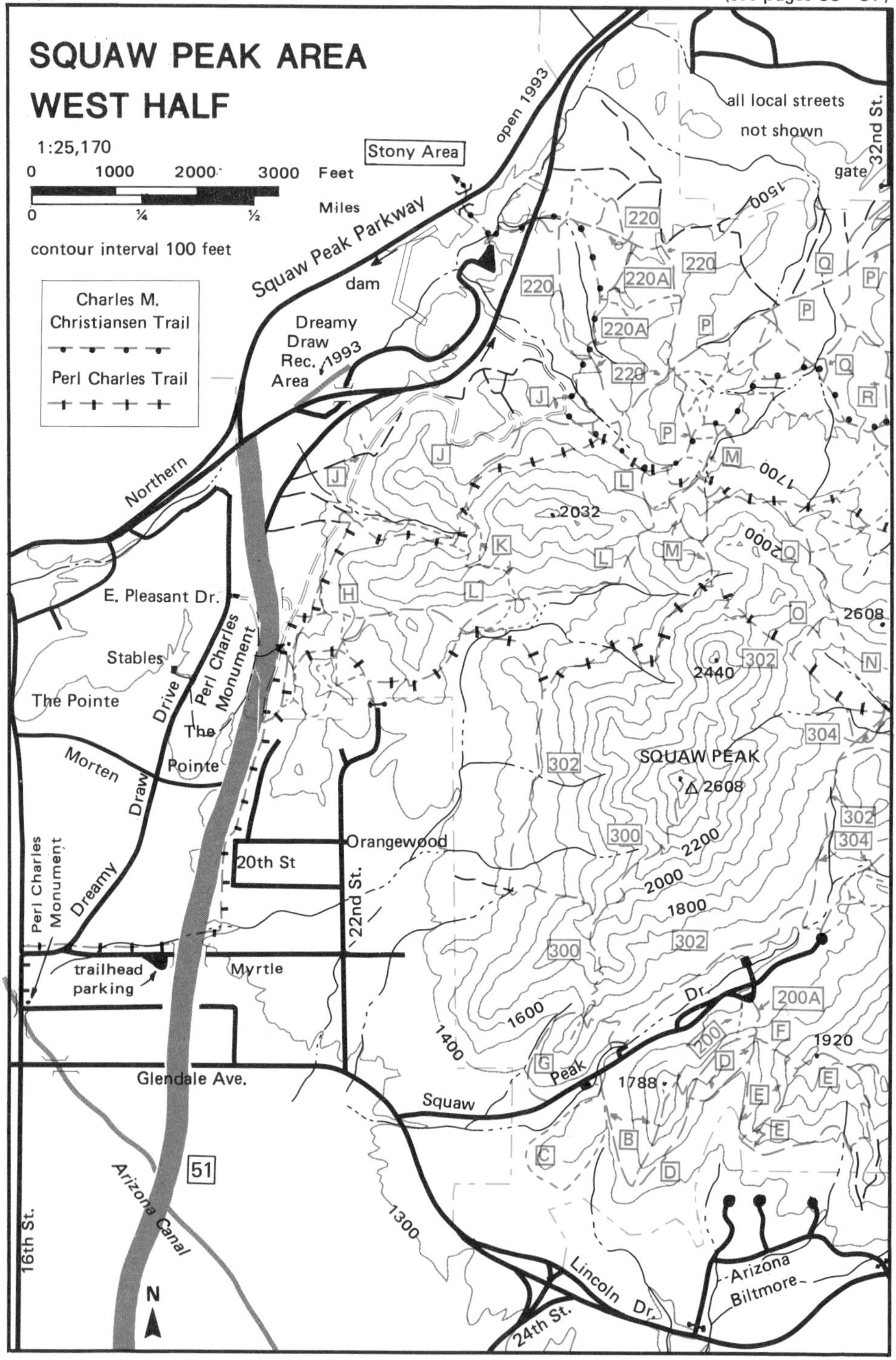

SQUAW PEAK AREA
WEST HALF

1:25,170

Stony Area

Squaw Peak Parkway

dam

Dreamy Draw Rec. Area 1993

open 1993

all local streets
not shown

gate

32nd St.

1500

220
220A
220A
220

220

J

P

P

P

Q

P

Q

R

Charles M. Christiansen Trail

Perl Charles Trail

contour interval 100 feet

0   1000   2000   3000 Feet

0   ¼   ½   Miles

Northern

E. Pleasant Dr.

Stables

The Pointe

Morten Draw

Dreamy

Perl Charles Monument

Drive

Perl Charles Monument

The Pointe

20th St

22nd St.

Orangewood

trailhead parking

Myrtle

Glendale Ave.

Arizona Canal

16th St.

51

N

J

J

H

K

L

L

.2032

L

M

M

L

1700

2000

2000

O

N

2608

302

2440

304

SQUAW PEAK

△ 2608

302

300

302

2200

2000

1800

302
304

302

200A

F

D

E

E

E

1920

Dr.

200

G   Peak

1788 .

B

C

D

1600

1400

1300

1500

Squaw

Peak

Lincoln Dr.

24th St.

Arizona Biltmore

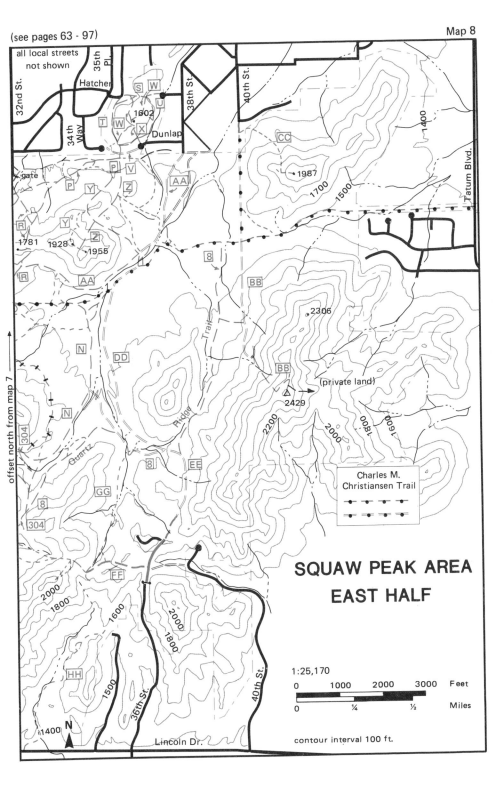

Map 8

all local streets
not shown

32nd St.

35th Pl.

34th Way

Hatcher

S W
U
T W
X

1602

38th St.

40th St.

Dunlap

CC

1987

1700

1500

1400

Tatum Blvd.

gate

P V
P Y Z

AA

R
1781 1928
Y
Z
1955

R

AA

8

BB

N

DD

Trail

Ridge

2306

BB

(private land)

2429

2200

2000

1800
1600
1600

304

N

Quartz

8
EE

Charles M.
Christiansen Trail

GG

8
304

FF

2000
1800

1600

2000
1800

SQUAW PEAK AREA
EAST HALF

1:25,170

| 0 | 1000 | 2000 | 3000 | Feet |

0   ¼   ½   Miles

HH

1500

36th St.

40th St.

1400

N

Lincoln Dr.

contour interval 100 ft.

offset north from map 7

Map 9 (see pages 116 - 132)

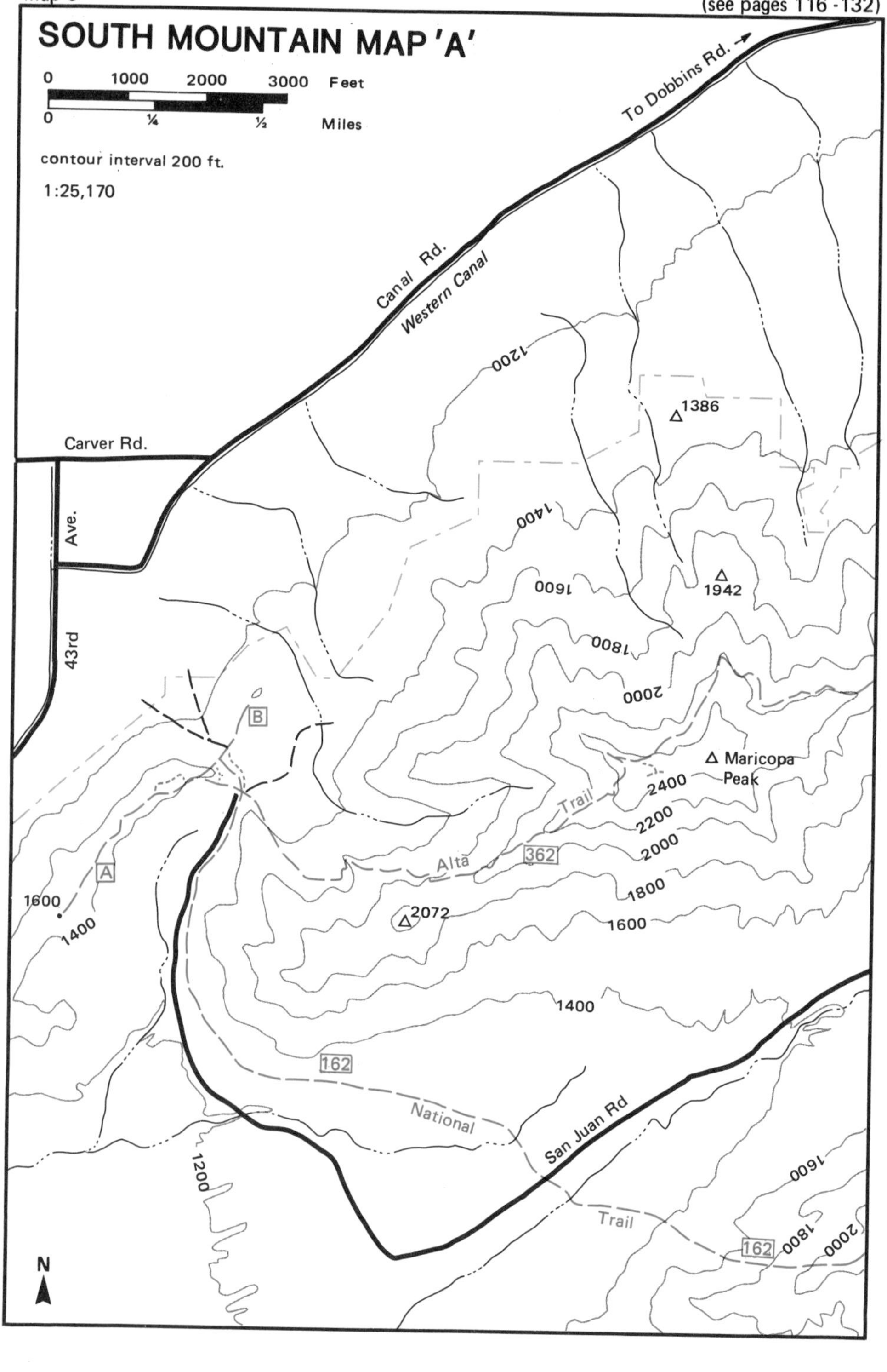

SOUTH MOUNTAIN MAP 'A'

0   1000   2000   3000   Feet

0   ¼   ½   Miles

contour interval 200 ft.

1:25,170

To Dobbins Rd.

Canal Rd.

Western Canal

Carver Rd.

Ave.

43rd

△1386

△1942

1200

1400

1600

1800

2000

B

A

1600

1400

△ Maricopa Peak

Trail

2400

2200

2000

Alta

362

1800

△2072

1600

1400

162

National

San Juan Rd

Trail

162

1800

1600

2000

1200

N

Map 10

Joins 'A'

Joins 'C'

SOUTH MOUNTAIN 'B'

0 1000 2000 3000 Feet

0   ¼   ½   Miles

1:25,170
contour interval 200 ft.

19th Ave.

Phoenix
Police Academy
Rifle Ranges

Park
Administration
Bldg.

Las
Ramadas

1400

1600

2323 △

2359 △

2394 △

Alta Trail

362

2200

2000

1800

1600

San   Juan   Rd.

Ranger Trail

C

Summit Rd

1800

2000

2200

C

162

2526 △
Goat Hill

△ 2504

162

National   Trail

2484 △

2200

2000

1800

D

△ 2241

◄(to private land)

1600

2231
△

N

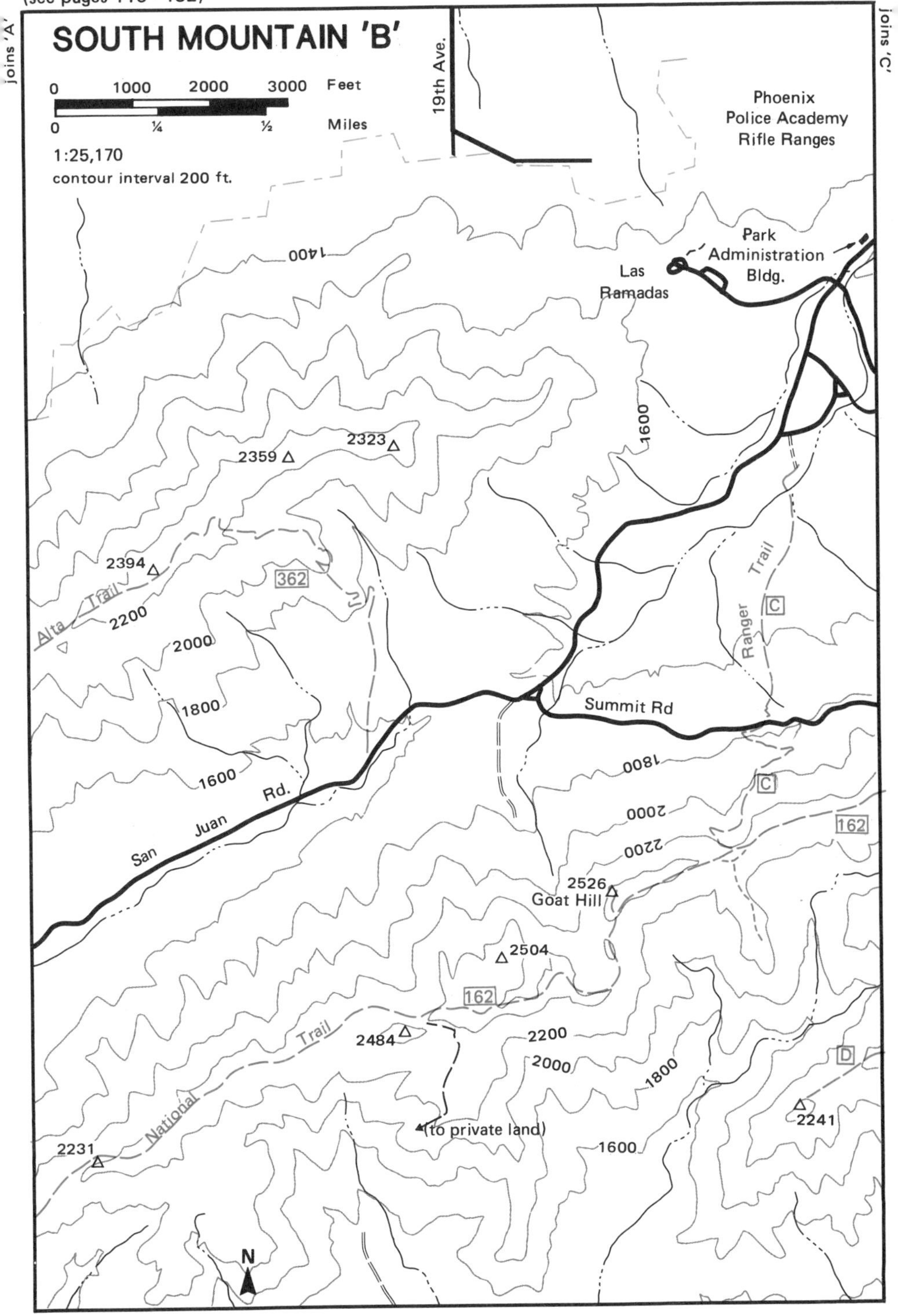

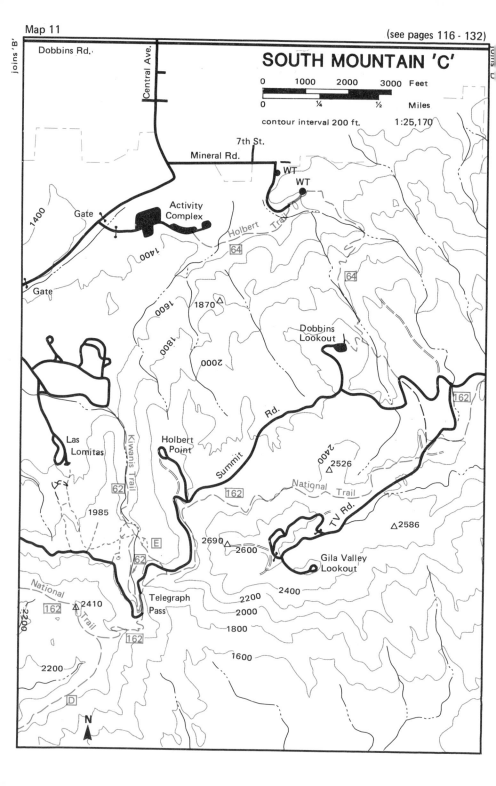

Map 11

(see pages 116 - 132)

SOUTH MOUNTAIN 'C'

joins 'B'

Dobbins Rd.

Central Ave.

0   1000   2000   3000   Feet

0   ¼   ½   Miles

contour interval 200 ft.   1:25,170

joins D

7th St.

Mineral Rd.

WT

WT

1400

Gate

Activity Complex

Holbert Trail

64

1400

Gate

1600

1870

1800

2000

Dobbins Lookout

64

162

Las Lomitas

Kiwanis Trail

Holbert Point

Summit Rd.

2400

2526

National Trail

1985

62

162

TV Rd.

2586

E

2690

2600

Gila Valley Lookout

National

162

2410

Trail

62

Telegraph Pass

162

2200

2000

1800

2400

2200

1600

2200

D

N

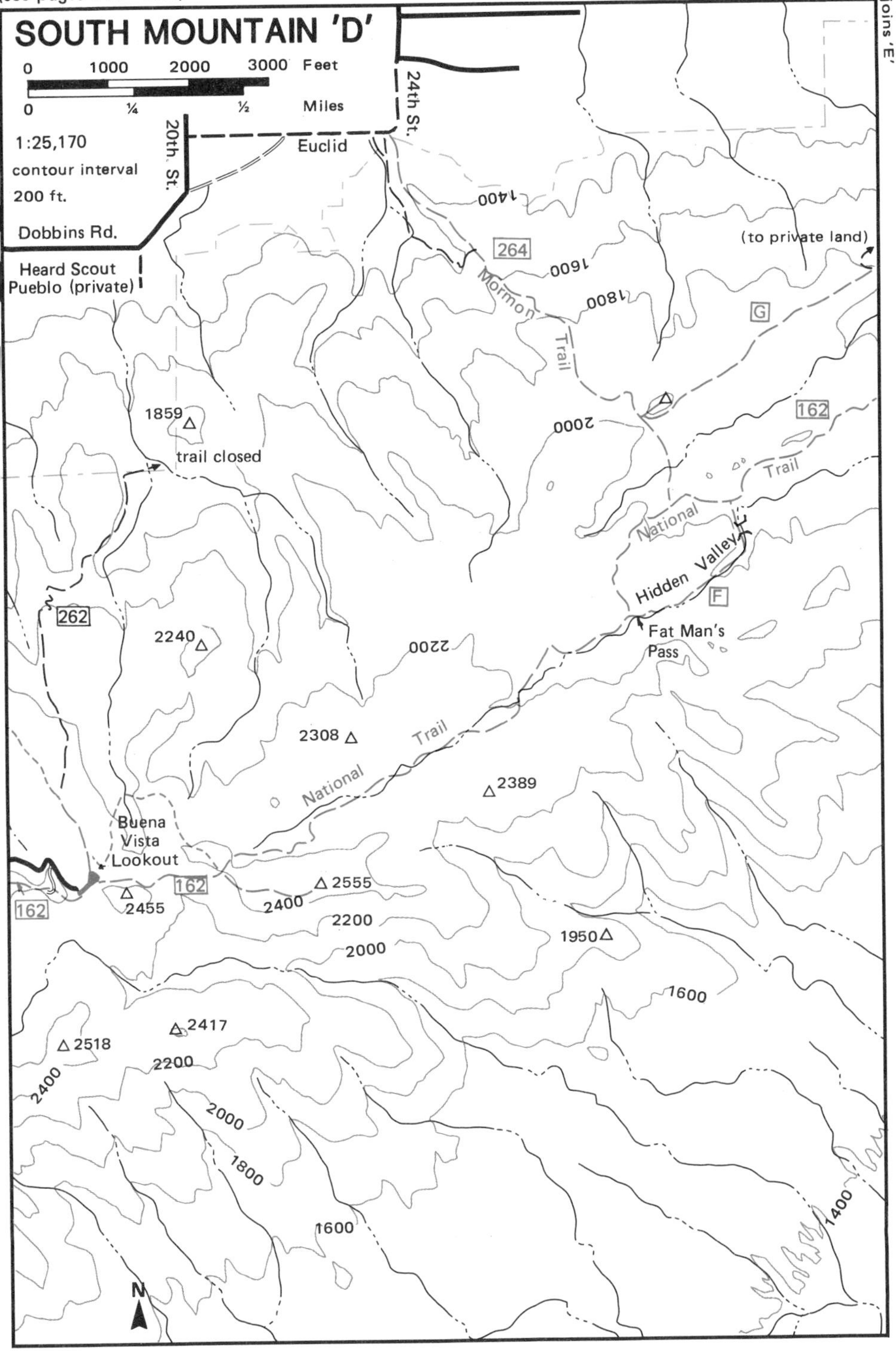

joins 'E'

SOUTH MOUNTAIN 'D'

0   1000   2000   3000 Feet

0   ¼   ½   Miles

1:25,170

contour interval
200 ft.

Dobbins Rd.

Heard Scout
Pueblo (private)

20th. St.

24th St.

Euclid

1400

264

1600

1800

(to private land)

G

1859

trail closed

2000

162

National   Trail

262

2240

2200

Mormon   Trail

Hidden Valley

F

Fat Man's
Pass

2308

National   Trail

2389

Buena
Vista
Lookout

162

2455

2400   2555

2200

2000

1950

1600

2417

2518

2400

2200

2000

1800

1600

1400

N

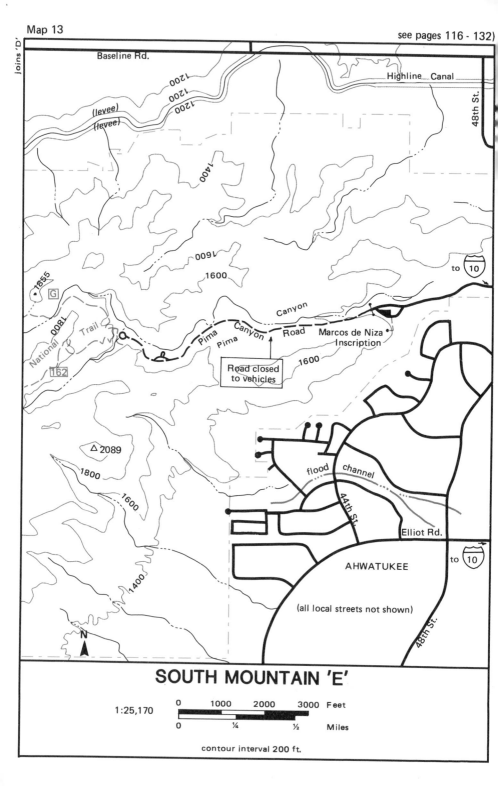

Map 13

see pages 116 - 132)

joins 'D'

Baseline Rd.

1200
1200
1200

Highline   Canal

48th St.

(levee)
(levee)

1400

1600
1600

to 10

1855

G

1800

National   Trail

162

Canyon

Pima   Canyon   Road

Pima

Road closed
to vehicles

Marcos de Niza
Inscription

1600

△ 2089

1800

1600

flood   channel

44th St.

Elliot Rd.

to 10

AHWATUKEE

(all local streets not shown)

48th St.

1400

N

SOUTH MOUNTAIN 'E'

1:25,170

0   1000   2000   3000   Feet

0   ¼   ½   Miles

contour interval 200 ft.

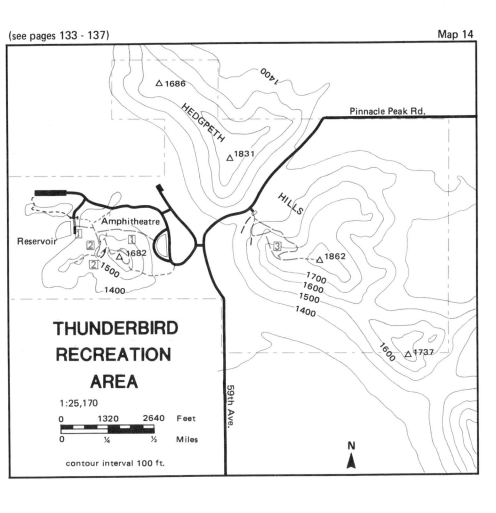

△ 1686

HEDGPETH

1400

△ 1831

Pinnacle Peak Rd.

HILLS

Amphitheatre

Reservoir

2   1

△ 1682

3

△ 1862

2 1500

1400

1700
1600
1500
1400

1600 △ 1737

THUNDERBIRD
RECREATION
AREA

1:25,170

| 0 | 1320 | 2640 | Feet |

| 0 | ¼ | ½ | Miles |

contour interval 100 ft.

59th Ave.

N

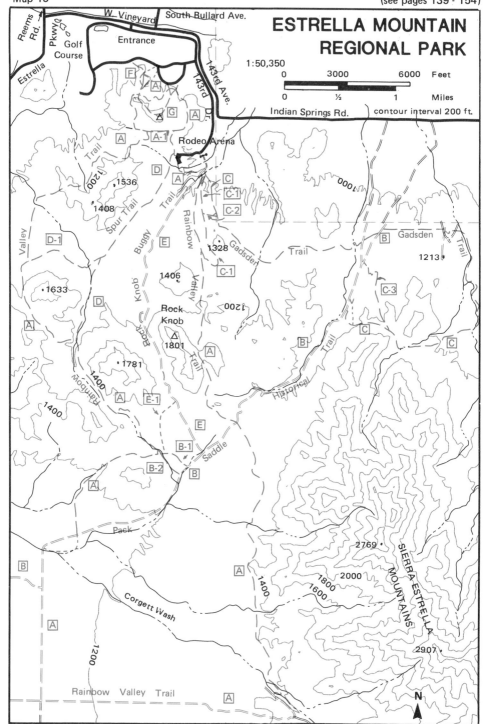

Map 15

(see pages 139 - 154)

ESTRELLA MOUNTAIN REGIONAL PARK

1:50,350

0   3000   6000   Feet

0   ½   1   Miles

contour interval 200 ft.

W. Vineyard

South Bullard Ave.

Reems Rd.

Pkwy

Golf Course

Entrance

Estrella

143rd Ave.

143rd Dr.

Indian Springs Rd.

F

A

G

A

A-1

Rodeo Arena

D

A

C

C-1

C-2

1536

1408

Spur Trail

Buggy Trail

Rainbow Trail

E

1328

Gadsden Trail

B

Gadsden Trail

1213

C-3

C-1

D-1

Valley

1633

1406

Rock Knob

Rock Knob Trail

1200

B

Historical Trail

C

C

1801

A

1781

Rainbow

1400

A

E-1

1400

E

B-1

Saddle

B-2

B

A

Pack

2769

B

Sierra Estrella Mountains

2000

1800

1600

A

1400

A

Corgett Wash

1200

2907

Rainbow Valley Trail

A

N

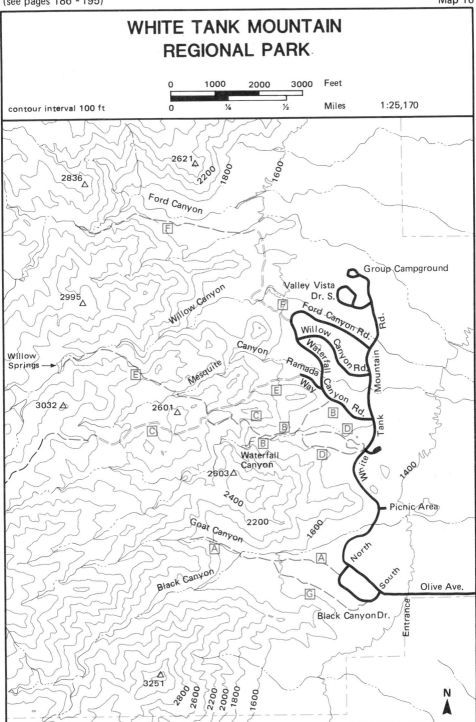

WHITE TANK MOUNTAIN
REGIONAL PARK

contour interval 100 ft

| 0 | 1000 | 2000 | 3000 | Feet |

| 0 | ¼ | ½ | Miles | 1:25,170 |

2621 △

2836 △

Ford Canyon

F

Group Campground

Valley Vista Dr. S.

2995 △

Willow Canyon

Ford Canyon Rd.

F

Willow Canyon Rd.

Canyon

Waterfall Canyon Rd.

Willow Springs →

Mesquite

E

Ramada Way

E

Tank Mountain Rd.

3032 △

2601 △

C

B

White Tank

C

B

D

B

Waterfall Canyon

D

2603 △

1400

2400

Picnic Area

2200

Goat Canyon

1600

North

A

A

South

Black Canyon

G

Olive Ave.

Black Canyon Dr.

Entrance

△
3251

2800 2600 2200 2000 1800 1600

N

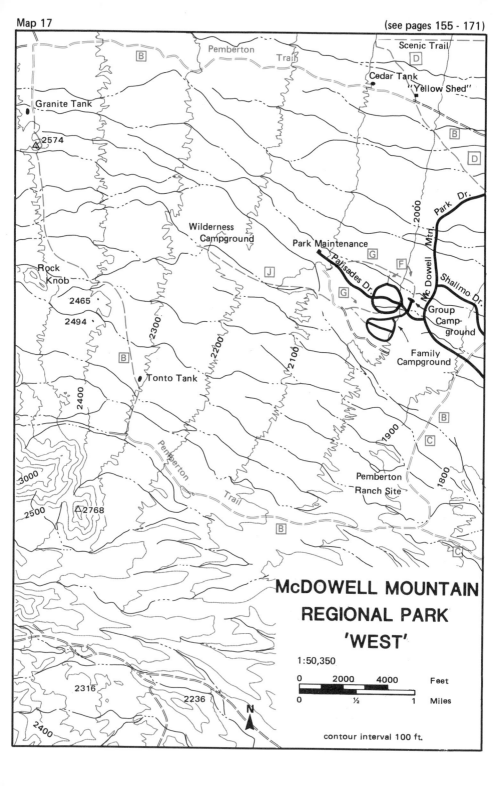

Map 17

(see pages 155 - 171)

Pemberton Trail

Scenic Trail

B

D

Cedar Tank
"Yellow Shed"

Granite Tank

B

△2574

D

2000

Park Dr.

Mc Dowell Mtn.

Wilderness
Campground

Park Maintenance

G

F

J

Palisades Dr.

Shallmo Dr.

Rock
Knob

G

Group
Camp-
ground

2465

2494

2300

B

2200

Family
Campground

Tonto Tank

2100

2400

B

1900

C

Pemberton

3000

1800

Trail

Pemberton
Ranch Site

2500

△2768

B

C

McDOWELL MOUNTAIN

REGIONAL PARK

'WEST'

1:50,350

0	2000	4000	Feet
0	½		1 Miles

2316

2236

N

2400

contour interval 100 ft.

(see pages 155 - 171)

Map 18

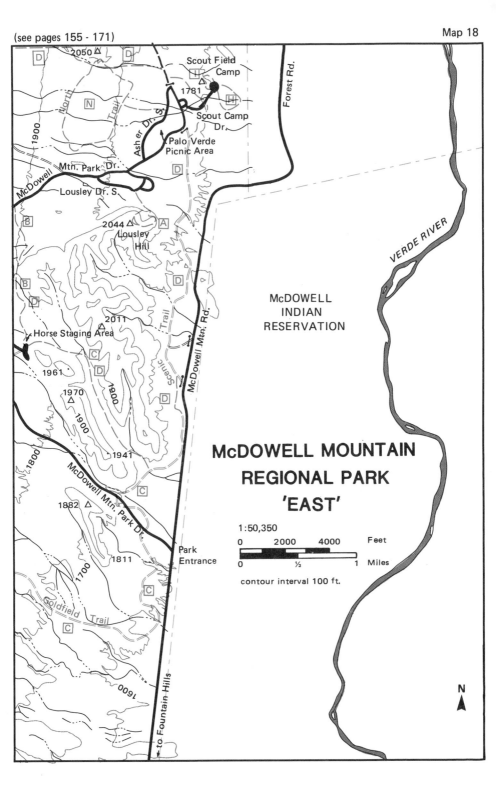

Scout Field Camp

Forest Rd.

1781

North Trail

Scout Camp Dr.

Asher Dr. S.

Palo Verde Picnic Area

1900

Mtn. Park Dr.

McDowell

Lousley Dr. S.

VERDE RIVER

2044 △ Lousley Hill

McDOWELL INDIAN RESERVATION

2011

Scenic Trail

McDowell Mtn. Rd.

Horse Staging Area

1961

1970 △

1900

1900

1941

McDOWELL MOUNTAIN REGIONAL PARK 'EAST'

McDowell Mtn. Park Dr.

1800

1882 △

1:50,350

0   2000   4000   Feet

0   ½   1   Miles

1811

Park Entrance

contour interval 100 ft.

1700

Goldfield Trail

1600

to Fountain Hills

N ▲

Map 19　　　　　　　　　　　　　　　　　　　　　　　(see pages 172 - 185)

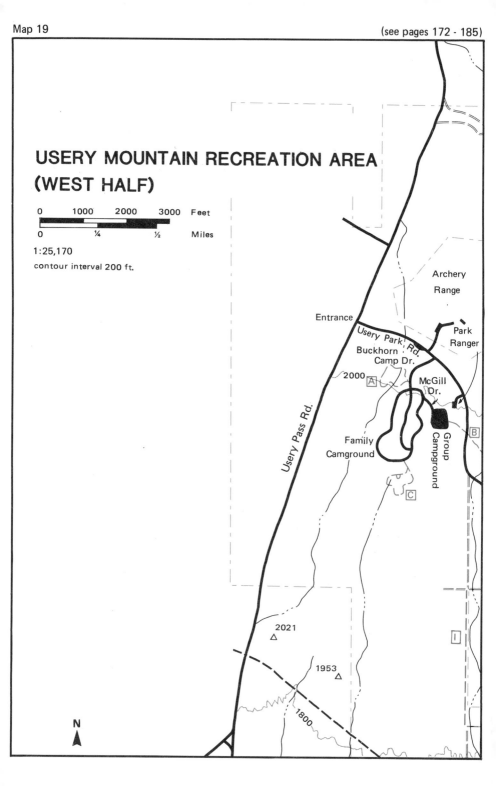

USERY MOUNTAIN RECREATION AREA (WEST HALF)

1:25,170

contour interval 200 ft.

USERY MOUNTAIN RECREATION AREA
(EAST HALF)

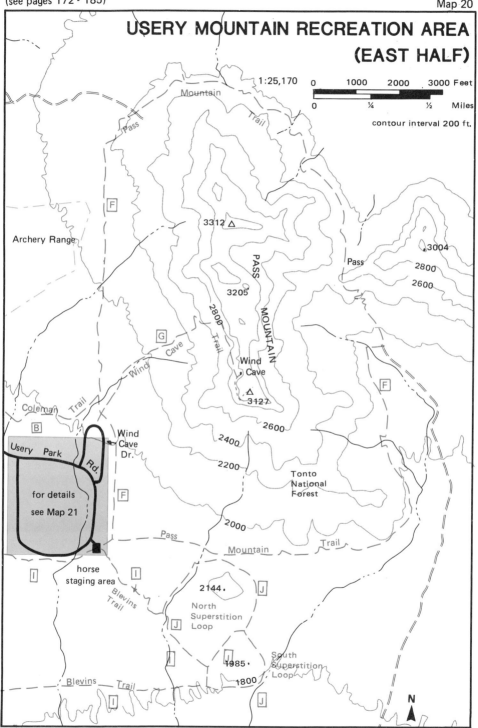

1:25,170

0   1000   2000   3000 Feet

0   ¼   ½   Miles

contour interval 200 ft.

Mountain

Trail

Pass

F

Archery Range

3312 △

PASS

3004

Pass

2800

2600

3205

2800

Trail

MOUNTAIN

Wind
Cave

G

Cave

Wind

△
3127

Trail

Coleman

2600

F

B

2400

Wind
Cave
Dr.

Usery   Park

Rd.

2200

for details
see Map 21

Tonto
National
Forest

F

2000

Pass

Mountain   Trail

I

horse
staging area

I

2144 ·

J

Blevins

North
Superstition
Loop

Trail

J

I

J

1985 ·

South
Superstition
Loop

Blevins   Trail

1800

I

J

N
▲

Map 21

(see pages 177 - 179)

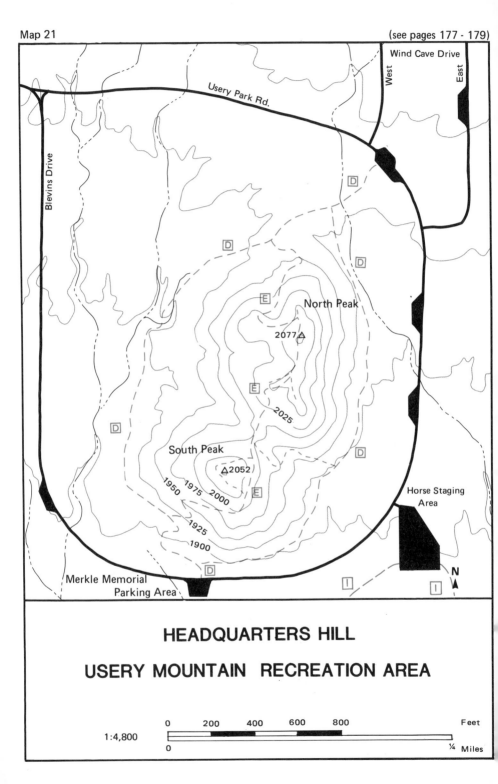

Wind Cave Drive

West

East

Usery Park Rd.

Blevins Drive

D

D

D

E

North Peak

2077 △

E

2025

D

South Peak

△2052

1950 1975 2000

E

1925

D

1900

Horse Staging Area

Merkle Memorial Parking Area

D

I

I

N

HEADQUARTERS HILL

USERY MOUNTAIN RECREATION AREA

1:4,800

0   200   400   600   800   Feet

0   ¼ Miles

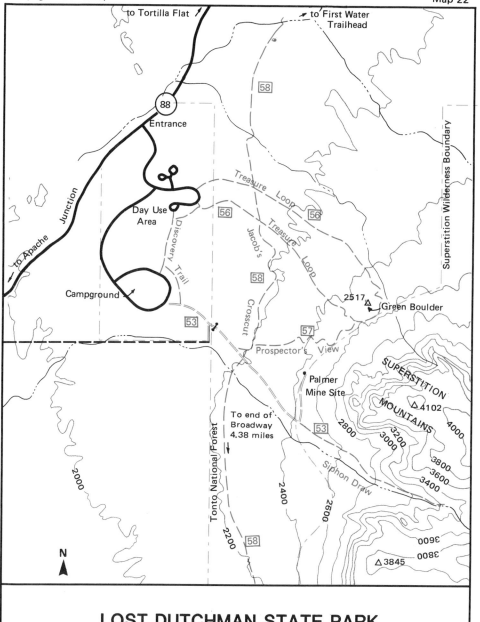

to Tortilla Flat

to First Water
Trailhead

58

88

Entrance

to Apache
Junction

Treasure Loop

Day Use
Area

56

56

Discovery
Trail

Jacob's

58

Campground

Crosscut

Treasure Loop

2517
Green Boulder

53

57

Prospector's View

Palmer
Mine Site

SUPERSTITION

4102

MOUNTAINS

4000

To end of
Broadway
4.38 miles

53

2800

3200

3000

3800

3600

Tonto National Forest

2400

Siphon Draw

3400

2000

2200

2600

Superstition Wilderness Boundary

3600

N

58

3800

3845

LOST DUTCHMAN STATE PARK

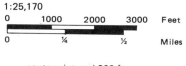

1:25,170

0   1000   2000   3000   Feet

0   ¼   ½   Miles

contour interval 200 ft.

Map 23 (see pages 205 - 208)

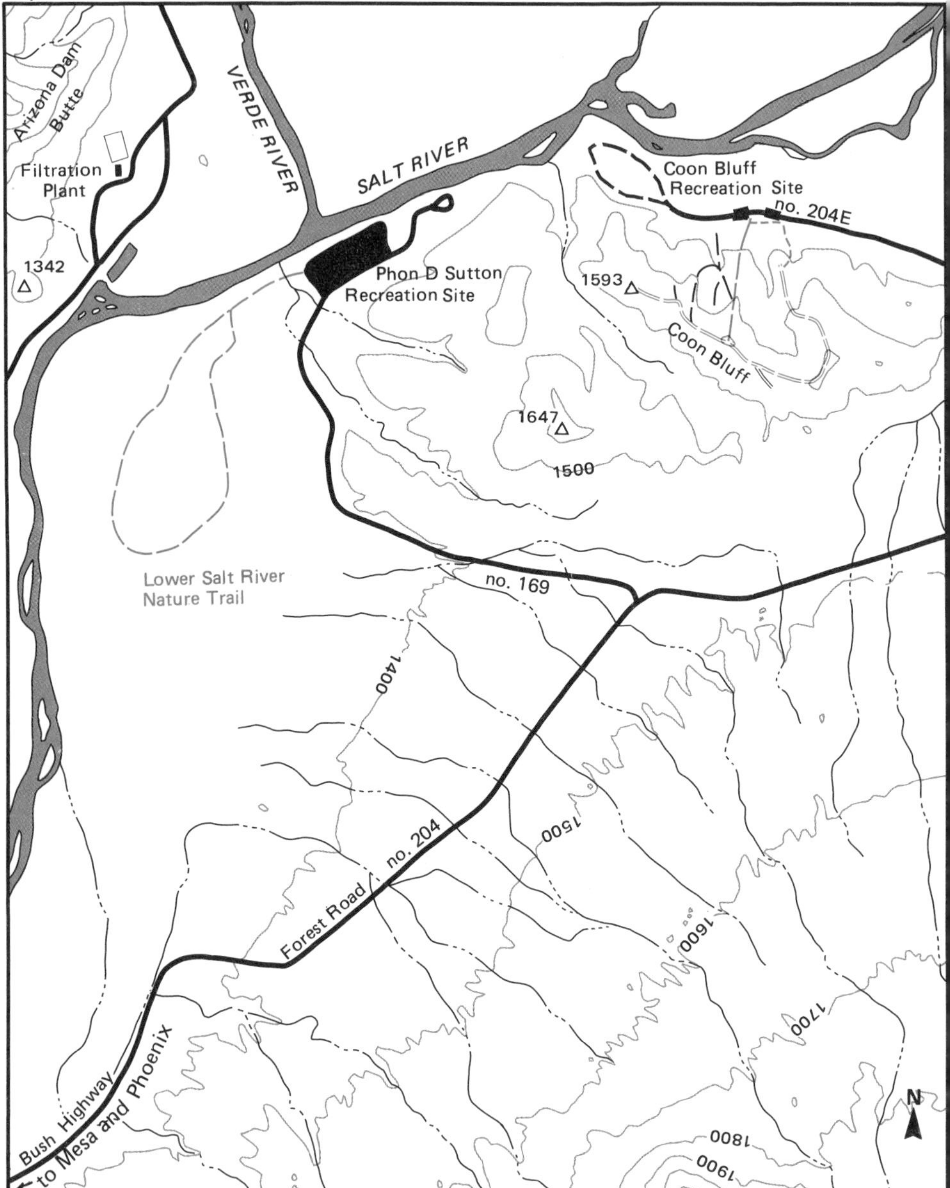

Arizona Dam Butte

VERDE RIVER

SALT RIVER

Coon Bluff
Recreation Site
no. 204E

Filtration
Plant

Phon D Sutton
Recreation Site

1593 △

Coon Bluff

1342
△

1647 △

1500

Lower Salt River
Nature Trail

no. 169

1400

1500

Forest Road / no. 204

1600

1700

Bush Highway

← to Mesa and Phoenix

N ▲

1800

1900

TONTO NATIONAL FOREST
LOWER SALT RIVER NATURE TRAIL
AND
COON BLUFF

0   1000   2000   Feet

contour interval 100 ft

0   ¼   ½   Miles

1:25,170

Appendix A. Glossary

Arroyo. A dry, steep-walled canyon [Spanish].

Cairn. A pile of stones used to mark a trail or trail junction.

Draw. A small valley that narrows as it rises.

Jog. To jog left or right on a trail or road means to join it briefly and then diverge from it.

Ramada. A man-made shelter from sun and rain, usually for picnicking.

Sag. A minor depression, less dramatic than a pass or canyon.

Side-hill. As a verb, means to angle along a hill-side without going straight up.

Switchback. A sudden reversal of direction, like a "hairpin bend" on a road.

Tank. A depression (natural or artificial) that holds water for stock.

Tinaja. Another word [Spanish] for tank.

Track. A broad way, not as narrow as an ordinary trail. It may previously have been a constructed or unofficial road.

Trail-head. Where the trail starts, usually at a road or ramada.

Trail of use. A minor or obscure trail developed by irregular usage, not constructed or designated. It often peters out or serves as a short-cut. In parts of the desert minimal use can create such a trail.

Traverse. A long segment of switchbacking trail that leads across a hill-side.

Vehicle travelway. A term used by some agencies for a way created by unplanned vehicular use.

Wash. An eroded channel that is ordinarily dry except after prolonged or intense rain.

Appendix B. Resources

Governmental Organizations

Arizona State Parks
#415 - 800 West Washington Street, Phoenix 85007
(Phone: 602-542-1996)

> Lost Dutchman State Park
> 6109 North Apache Trail, Apache Junction 85219
> (Phone: 602-982-4485)

Bureau of Land Management, Phoenix District Office
2015 West Deer Valley Road, Phoenix 85027
(Phone: 602-863-4464)

Forest Service, USDA, Southwest Region
2324 East McDowell Road, Phoenix 85010
(Phone: 602-225-5237)

Glendale, City of, Leisure Services
5850 West Glendale Avenue, Glendale 85301
(Phone: 602-435-4100)

Maricopa County Parks & Recreation Department
3475 West Durango Street, Phoenix 85009
(Phone: 602-272-8871)
All parks can be reached through the central office above.

Phoenix Parks, Recreation & Library Department
2333 North Central Avenue, Phoenix 85004
(Phone: 602-262-6861)

> East District Office [Camelback, Papago]
> 1001 North 52nd Street, Phoenix 85008
> (Phone: 602-256-3220)

> Northeast District [Lookout, Shadow, North Mountain/Shaw Butte, Stony, Squaw]
> 17642 North 40th Street, Phoenix 85032
> (Phone: 602-262-6696)

> South District [South Mountain]
> 10919 South Central Avenue, Phoenix 85040
> (Phone: 602-495-0222)

Non-Governmental Organizations

Mountaineers, Incorporated was organized in 1985 to physically restore and protect the Phoenix Mountains Preserve. The all-volunteer membership accomplish their goals by a strategy they call the "CREST," an acronym standing for Cleanup, Revegetation, Education, Security and Trails. In their short history they have removed over 900 tons of trash and debris from the Preserve, planted over 500 native plants and maintained miles of desert trails. They are organized into chapters which are roughly divided between the different mountains and peaks within the Preserve system.

Membership information can be obtained by writing to the group at P.O. Box 9279, Phoenix, Arizona 85068-9279, or by calling (602) 978-8779.

The Phoenix Mountains Preservation Council, Inc. (or _PMPC_ as it has become known) was founded in August 1970 with the objective of saving "the Phoenix Mountains as a unique wilderness park." It organized a series of horseback rides (and later, hikes) to acquaint Phoenix officials and citizens with the unspoiled nature of the area and to enlist their support in acquiring and preserving the mountains.

PMPC members were among those appointed by former Mayor John Driggs to recommend a financial plan for acquiring the Phoenix Mountains range and the north slopes of South Mountain. They provided grassroots support for that plan and their enthusiastic backing has helped persuade voters to approve four successful bond issues for land acquisition.

Concerned that Preserve land was being whittled away by development, the PMPC led successful drives for two amendments to the Phoenix City Charter. As a result the Phoenix and South Mountain Preserves now have permanent boundaries which can only be changed by a favorable vote of the people. PMPC members continue to serve on boards and advisory committees concerned with the future of the Mountain Preserves.

For further information, or for a history of the preservation efforts, please write P.O. Box 26121, Phoenix, Arizona 85068-6121, or telephone (602) 265-8397.

The Sierra Club was founded in 1892 by John Muir. The original goal of the Sierra Club was to protect national scenic resources, especially mountain areas. Today, the Club's goals include maintaining a livable environment, protecting coasts and rivers, and developing park, forest, seashore, and wilderness areas.

Ten years after the Club was formed the outings program was established in the belief that first-hand exposure to the wilderness was the best way for people to learn about and appreciate the value of nature. The Sierra Club outings program has expanded to every corner of the world and to individual chapters and groups throughout the United States.

Information about local outings and membership can be obtained by calling (602) 267-1649 or 277-8079 or write Sierra Club, 730 Polk Street, San Francisco, CA 94109.

The Arizona Mountaineering Club [AMC] was started in the early 1960s to promote safe rock climbing and other mountain-related activities. Membership is now about 300. Phoenix is unique in that it has rock climbing areas within the city limits. There are many excellent climbing areas in the Phoenix Valley. Classes for beginners are taught in April and October. In January 1988 the AMC adopted the Camelback Mountain Trail and is currently re-building it. For more info write AMC, P.O. Box 1695, Phoenix, Arizona 85001 or call (602) 256-0052.

Appendix C. Bibliography

Annerino, J. 1987. *Outdoors in Arizona: A Guide to Hiking and Backpacking.* Phoenix: Arizona Highways (Arizona Department of Transportation).

Arnberger, L.P. 1982. *Flowers of the Southwestern Mountains.* Tucson: Southwest Parks and Monuments Association.

Christensen, A.D., Lambert, L.Q. & Sikes, D.O. 1986. *Phoenix: A Guide to Phoenix, Scottsdale and the Valley (6th ed.).* Phoenix: Valley Publishing Company (distributed by Gem Guides, Pico Rivera, CA).

Chronic, H. 1983. *Roadside Geology of Arizona.* Missoula, Montana: Mountain Press Publishing Company.

Davis, B. 1986. *Birds of the Southwest, Vol. I. Guide to Birds of the Desert and Grasslands.* Tucson: Treasure Chest Publications.

Dodge, N.N. 1985. *Flowers of the Southwestern Deserts.* Tucson: Southwest Parks and Monuments Association.

Ganci, D. 1987. *Desert Hiking (2nd ed.).* Berkeley, California: Wilderness Press.

Holbert, H. 1979. *South Mountain Park: The Time and the Man.* Privately published by Harry Holbert, printed by Hearne's Bookcrafts of Riverside , 3669 Sixth St., Riverside, California 92501.

Larson, P. & Larson L. 1977. *A Sierra Club Naturalist's Guide to the Deserts of the Southwest.* San Francisco: Sierra Club Books.

Lehman, C.A. 1988. *Desert Survival Handbook.* Phoenix: Primer Publishers.

Lowe, C.H., Schwalbe, C.R., & Johnson, T.B. 1986. *The Venomous Reptiles of Arizona.* Phoenix: Arizona Game and Fish Department.

MacMahon, J.A. 1985. *Deserts (Audubon Society Nature Guides).* New York: Alfred A. Knopf.

Nations D. & Stump E. 1981. *Geology of Arizona.* Dubuque, Iowa: Kendall/Hunt Publishing Company.

Niehaus, T.F. 1984. *Peterson Field Guide: Southwestern and Texas Wildflowers.* Boston: Houghton Mifflin.

Olin, G. 1982. *Mammals of the Southwest Deserts.* San Diego: Southwest Parks and Monuments Association.

Spellenberg, R. 1986. *Familiar Flowers: Western Region (Audubon Society Pocket Guides).* New York: Alfred A. Knopf.

Van Cleve, P.W. 1973. *An Open Space Plan for the Phoenix Mountains.* Phoenix: City Government.